The Subjectivity Effect in Western Literary Tradition

OCTOBER Books
Joan Copjec, Rosalind Krauss, and Annette Michelson, editors

The Lacanian conception of the otherness of desire—desire of an other and for an other—is a core principle in much of Fineman's subsequent work. The implications of the principle for psychoanalytic theory are explored in "Psychoanalysis, Bisexuality, and the Difference before the Sexes." Here Fineman grants the force of recent criticisms of Freud's conception of gender difference but argues that at the center of "Freud's outmoded, seemingly dessicated sexual dialectic" is a novel and powerful vision in which "the difference between the sexes precedes the appearance of the sexes themselves." This paradox emerges from Freud's derivation of gender out of frustration, or more precisely "out of an unfolding process in which brute need is transformed by frustration into psychological desire, whereupon desire— increasingly specific in terms of its objects, but in itself neutral, valueless, blank—is transformed by increasingly focused frustrations into the particular wishes, strategies and fantasies of consummated subjectivity." In this Lacanian reading of Freud, it is not only gender that arises out of negation but subjectivity itself: the human subject derives frustration and estrangement from an "original difference." It is possible, indeed necessary, in Fineman's account, to lose before you have anything to lose, for it is this loss that gives you something to lose.

In "Gnosis and the Piety of Metaphor: The Gospel of Truth," this psychoanalytic argument finds its theological equivalent in a reading of an aphorism by the Gnostic Valentinian: "The Name of the Father is the Son." Fineman explicates this formula (or, more accurately perhaps, makes it an allegory for contemporary theory) by way of the Lacanian definition of metaphor as "the substitution of a new signifier for an original signifier which, as a result or condition of the metaphoric process, drops to the level of a signified." This disappearance of the original signifier, a signifier that can be conceived only as having already disappeared, has been elaborated by Jean Laplanche as the representative "of the formation of the Freudian unconscious through primal repression" and serves for Fineman as the key to the meaning of the riddling Gnostic text: "the propriety of the Name, its adequacy to its reference, is revealed only in the dispossession of the Name from its denomination, i.e., in its being given to the Son. . . . On the one hand, the Name is a principle of authority prior to its author. On the other hand, the Name is the devolution of truth as its own displacement." This is "negative theology" with a vengeance, and so conceived it is virtually identical to Lacan's theory not only of the origin of metaphor but of the origin of language: "The infant," Fineman writes, "loses an imaginary plenitude of being, his ego, for the sake of the symbolic meaning he becomes by being positioned through the discourse of the Other as subject in the cultural order." And in just this way, he argues, the sacred in Gnostic theology arises from the father's loss of his name to the son.

I spoke of Fineman's reading of Valentinian as an allegory of theory, but it might be more accurate to call it an allegory of literary criticism. Theology leads back through psychoanalysis to the literary, the enabling link being the Gnostic proposition that "Truth did not come into the world naked, but it came in types and images." This textualization and metaphorization of the cosmos commit Gnosticism, like criticism, to the endless proliferation of allegories of allegories. It became important for Fineman then to give an account of allegory, and he attempted to do so in one of his most ambitious essays, "The Structure of Allegorical Desire." Here too the concern is with a lost origin, the inherent nostalgia of a literary mode that "makes up for the distance, or heals the gap, between the present and a disappearing past which, without interpretation, would be otherwise irretrievable and foreclosed." Allegory then "emerges out of recuperative originology" and defines for itself a middle position: neither a "literalism pure and simple" nor "an exegesis of the free-floating signifier." The latter qualification is revealing, because it signals the distance between Fineman's literary vision and that of a more thoroughgoing deconstruction. Fineman in effect tries to occupy the middle position he claims for allegory, between literalism and the free-floating signifier, and his work frequently expresses a sense that a critical theory founded on an original absence runs the risk of missing the specific uses, literary and psychological, of this absence.

Fineman's exploration in "The Structure of Allegorical Desire" of these uses suggests just how literally he took "literalism pure and simple." I refer to his attempt to show, by a mingling of Jakobson and Chaucer, that since desire is a function of language, desire is for that which is by definition unreal, and hence that origin is loss and loss origin. These paradoxical propositions may be verified, he claims, by phonological analysis: the primal unpronounced and unpronounceable *pa* must be "murdered" in order to generate the nasal *ma* and the labial *pa* on whose generativity and hence on whose desire all of culture depends. Fineman then finds this oedipal phonemic drama reiterated in the insemination of *Ma*rch by the paternal *A*pril in the General Prologue to the *Canterbury Tales*.

The zaniness of these arguments is wonderfully appealing, but I find in this essay, with its universal claims, a certain claustrophobia, for it is itself quite self-consciously and schematically based on a totalizing originology such as it locates in allegory, a fantasy that everything can be explained if only we locate the Primal Scene. This fantasy seems to me belied both by the enormous range, diversity, and cultural specificity of languages and by the richness, complexity, and cultural specificity of Chaucer's poem.

This embrace of the literal was one to which Fineman willingly submitted virtually all of his work; but in his subsequent essays he repeatedly found ways to demonstrate that the little room made of letters in which he felt we were locked was full of infinite riches. Thus in "The Significance of Literature: *The Importance of Being Earnest*" (an essay that is, if anything, still more fantastically literal, schematic, and totalizing than "The Structure of Allegorical Desire"), Fineman managed to yoke a characteristically provocative, universalizing vision—"the fundamental desire of the reader of literature is the desire of the homosexual for the heterosexual, or rather, substituting the appropriate figurative embodiments of these abstractions, the desire of the man to be sodomized by the woman"—with a wonderfully nuanced, elegantly convincing explication of the "brittle yet mandarin tenor and texture" of Wilde's farce. Specifically, he tries to explain why the farce has at its heart a play on names, why this play in turn implies a specific thematics of homosexual and heterosexual desire, and why this desire in turn is implicated in at least one conception of the "self in literature." That self, argues Fineman, is constituted neither by a philosophical language that dreams of being a perfect imitation of its object nor by a literary language that dreams, in a formalism to which Fineman himself largely subscribed, of turning all of its apparent imitations into absolute self-reference. Rather, the "self who is committed to language" must be located "in the slippage between its immediate presence to itself and its mediated representation of itself in a symbolic system."

The riddling formulations of Fineman's Wilde essay are not a display of theoretical bravado; they are the condensed articulation of a carefully mediated literary vision that received its fullest elaboration in his book *Shakespeare's Perjured Eye: The Invention of Poetic Subjectivity in the Sonnets* (University of California Press, 1985). For it is in Shakespeare's sonnets, Fineman sought to demonstrate, that the literary formation of the self in the slippage from presence to representation finds definitive expression, and it is in the sonnets too that the desire of the homosexual for the heterosexual finds its most powerful and poignant voice. For Fineman the sonnets to the young man reiterate the tradition of the poetry of praise, or epideictic poetics, while the sonnets to the dark lady at once replicate this poetics and render it paradoxical. Homosexual desire in the young man sonnets is visual and visionary desire, based upon an idealized homology between signifier and signified, the exhibition of praise and the perfect object of that praise. Heterosexual desire in the dark lady sonnets is, by contrast, self-consciously and explicitly verbal; it represents a fall into language that conceals as much as it shows, that has as its object a beloved characterized by her inadequacy and deceptiveness. This desire, writes Fineman, is a "desire *of* language," that is, both a craving for words and a craving generated by words.

Shakespeare's Perjured Eye originated as the introductory chapter to a study of literary subjectivity in Shakespeare's entire canon; that introductory chapter grew into a book, while the book on the canon—which Fineman intended to call *Shakespeare's Will*—never got written. What did get written, in the very short time between the publication of the book on the sonnets and Fineman's death, were three remarkably dense, original, and disturbing essays that were fragments of the larger study: "Shakespeare's *Will*: The Temporality of Rape," "The Turn of the Shrew," and "The Sound of *O* in *Othello*." Of the three essays, "Shakespeare's *Will*" is most directly and obviously a development of the argument of the sonnet book. The theoretical narrative of that book—the fall from praise to praise paradox, from man to woman, from vision to language—functions now as a kind of nightmarish machine, a trap into which characters stumble simply by virtue of speaking at all: "when Collatine, at the end of the poem, at what I have called its climax, 'pronounces "Tarquin" plain,' he exemplifies what happens to a person when he 'begins to talk,' something the poem amplifies as an inaugural moment of constitutive, subjectifying transition in which the truth and clarity of vision is supplanted and belied by verbal speech."

It would follow that Shakespeare himself cannot remain safely outside of this nightmare: the same erotic and temporal structure is invoked by Fineman to characterize "Will" (understood as authorial signature, as half-realized literary character, and as quasi-allegorical attribute to male identity): "he is the subject of an unprecedentedly heterosexual, and therefore misogynist, desire for an object that is not admired." "Heterosexual, and therefore misogynist." What is the force of the provocative "and therefore"? Were I to try to answer that question, I suppose I would look in the theological and medical contexts of Renaissance literature, in discourses that offer ample evidence that men for the most part believed that women for the most part were morally and physically inferior to men. Hence heterosexual love, if understood to mean the love of men for women (and not the reverse), would be the love of superior for inferior, perfect for defective. (It is in this spirit that Spenser's EK tells us that "pederastike" is preferable to "gynerastike.") And hence heterosexual love in the Renaissance has an almost inevitable current of misogyny.

But this would by Fineman's standards be a weak and inadequate answer, mired in "for the most part" and "almost." For Fineman characteristically locates causality not in cultural circumstances or historical contingencies but in linguistic structures. His "and therefore" derives from language, specifically Shakespearean language, a set of recurrent, willed rhetorical features that have strong discursive consequences: the establishment of a powerful representation of male subjectivity, the generation of heterosexual desire, the fashioning of that desire as rape. Fineman is able to get from rhetoric to rape by means of a fantastically intricate close reading. Typically he takes what goes without saying, what seems merely conventional, and makes it seem at once intolerably strange and intolerably exigent. Here as always in his baroque prose there is less narcissistic self-indulgence than meets the eye; that prose is an astonishing instrument, a tool to draw out into critical discourse what has gone without saying because it seemed impossible to say. Thus, for example, the dedicatory inscription—"The loue I dedicate to your Lordship is without end; whereof this Pamphlet without beginning is but a superfluous Moity"—is made to disclose a phenomenology of male desire that motivates the rape and hence reveals the presence of Shakespeare's Will within the poem. Tarquin the rapist is not set off against Shakespeare the poet; on the contrary, Fineman argues, "the end of Tarquin's desire (the rape), and the motivation of Tarquin's desire ('that name of "chaste"'), and also the movement of Tarquin towards the satisfaction of his desire (Tarquin's 'posting'), are all located in the same expulsive *in extremis* in-betweenness as is the Dedication's 'superfluous moity': they are all intrinsically excessive to the boundaries that chiastically enclose them, boundaries folded over on each other in a way that leads what lies between them into an open-ended *cul-de-sac*." Here, if I understand the argument, writing (or at least Shakespeare's characteristic mode of writing in "The Rape of Lucrece") and rape are twinned.

This twinning allows Fineman to answer a question that hovered behind *Shakespeare's Perjured Eye*. Granting for the moment the narrative of the fall into language, how is that fall effected? How does one get from idealization to loss and deception? In "The Rape of Lucrece," Collatine's praise of the chastity of his wife arouses Tarquin's lust: we have passed from an idealizing naming to a violation. The question is how one gets from one to the other—how does naming chastity arouse desire? Fineman argues that the act of naming is itself exciting—exciting because it establishes a "let," a blockage, that male desire longs to break through. That is, male desire battens on obstacles—without resistance, there can be no desire. It is in this sense that Fineman can claim disturbingly that "Tarquin and Lucrece are inverse versions of each other" and still more disturbingly that Lucrece is the rapist's "rhetorically willing victim." "Rhetorically willing" because for the rapist resistance is itself erotically exciting and because that resistance is crucially figured in rhetoric: above all, in the cross-coupling figure of chiasmus. But rhetoric is not the zero degree of linguistic resistance; the primal "let" is revealed to be the letter itself: the originary erotic obstacle is writing. "Writing in 'The Rape of Lucrece'," Fineman writes, "is what leads its subject into speech. . . . As something intermediate, writing introduces differences into what ideally is the same." And once again, writing understood in this way is not something that is only thematized in the poem (in Lucrece's letter and, metaphorically, in the uses of the words "let" and "post"); it is very obviously enacted *by* the poem, so that Shakespeare is himself entirely implicated in the process.

With a fantastic ingenuity and recklessness, Fineman works in his essay to make that implication total by discovering an occulted Shakespearean signature—in a punningly literal sense, the *characteristically* Shakespearean—throughout the poem. Shakespeare's "Will," he writes, "is graphically inscribed at the criss-cross of *MW*." Fineman's writing in these pages takes on the air of seventeenth-century commentaries on the book of Daniel or the Apocalypse and awakens in me, I confess, a snorting resistance. Would Shakespeare's work, I ask myself, be substantially different if his first name had been Fred? Still, I am forced to admit that in the sonnets at least Shakespeare undeniably plays with his name, and that this kind of play is to be found in other authors of the period as well. Moreover, the punning and twisting and signing is not idle, for names are charged with a special intensity in Shakespeare and more generally in Renaissance discourse, and Fineman's weirdly literal insistence upon the materiality of the letter may actually correspond to something, as it were, out there, to an historical conjuncture of linguistic structure and pure contingency in a demystified culture still paradoxically clinging to the shreds of a residual Cratylism. The notion that the name is itself the sign of a loss, that the letters mark a longing for what is absent, that literary subjectivity is realized in empty marks on a page has a power that resonates well beyond the scope of "The Rape of Lucrece."

Acknowledging this resonance, however, leads me to record a final resistance to this brilliant essay on the erotics of resistance. Part of the force of "Shakespeare's *Will*" lies in its suggestion that what Fineman is discovering in the poem applies to Shakespeare's work as a whole and even functions "as general model for the motivating and consummating *friction* of heterosexual desire *per se*." Now I am persuaded that much of what Fineman discovers actually is there in "The Rape of Lucrece," and I am willing to grant that there are powerful echoes of this linking of the letter, erotic friction, and rape elsewhere in Shakespeare's writings. But I am emphatically not willing to concede that this violent, compulsive misogyny is the sole model for heterosexual desire either in Shakespeare or in the western literary tradition. As in his sonnets book, Fineman seems to me too easily drawn to a jauntily despairing theory of linguistic inexorability—as if there had been in that tradition no swerving from, no alternative to, the structure he so subtly decodes, as if human agency were entirely collapsed into the law of the letter.

On Fineman's behalf one could cite a large number of passages like the following, from an early seventeenth-century legal compendium called *The Lawes Resolutions of Womens Rights*: "If the rampier of Lawes were not betwixt women and their harmes, I verily thinke none of them, being above twelue yeares of age and under an hundred, being either faire or rich, should be able to escape ravishing." Still, the "rampier of Lawes" and other constraints on sexual violence must at least raise the question of how far Fineman's claims can legitimately be extended beyond the bounds of the literary.

This is the question that is implicit in "The Turn of the Shrew," an essay concerned with the incorporation of a woman's skeptical resistance into a master narrative and (like the conference paper "'The Pas de Calais': Freud, the Transference and the Sense of Woman's Humor") with the relation between Lacan and Derrida. Fineman suggests that "the words and actions of *The Taming of the Shrew* rehearse a familiar antagonism, not simply the battle between the sexes but, more specifically, though still rather generally, the battle between the determinate, literal language traditionally spoken by man and the figurative, indeterminate language traditionally spoken by woman." Fineman observes that the play "self-consciously associates this thematically subversive discourse of woman with its own literariness and theatricality." Why then, he asks, is the result "a play that speaks neither for the language of woman nor against the authority of man"? Why does Petruchio tame his shrew? And, more generally, "Is it possible to voice a language, whether of man or of woman, that does not speak, sooner or later, self-consciously or unconsciously, for the order and authority of man?"

To this last, general question Fineman appears to answer both yes and no. If by the phrase "voice a language" one means participate in "the logic of the literary word in the west," then the master narrative of patriarchal discourse will always eventually triumph. Fineman argues, that is, that this logic is essentially male, constantly marking out a difference that makes speech and desire possible and as constantly asserting mastery over that difference. Fineman explores this process by means of a subtle reading of Shakespeare's play and an astonishing analysis of two illustrations from the work of the Jacobean hermetic philosopher Robert Fludd. Thus, as Fineman observes in one of these illustrations, "Man is figured by the sun which is always the same as itself, whereas woman is figured by a waxing-waning moon which is always other than itself, because its mimic light of likeness is what illuminates its difference from the sameness of the sun. Perhaps this constitutes a paradox, this lunar light which folds up likeness into difference. But if so, it is a paradox that stands in service of an orthodox erotics for which woman is the other to man, the *hetero-* to *Homo*, precisely because her essence is *to be* this lunatic difference between sameness and difference." In this logic, there is no escape from male authority that is constituted precisely upon difference and subversion. But Fineman does not quite embrace the grim claustrophobic implication of this analysis. The quarrel between Lacan and Derrida, he suggests, even as it recapitulates both the opposition between Petruchio and Kate and the structural misogyny of Robert Fludd, also marks out the limits of the literary word and opens up "the possibility of an extraliterary reading of literature." "The Turn of the Shrew" ends with a gesture toward such a reading—"the relation to literature is not itself a literary relation, and there is no compelling reason, therefore, especially with the examples of Lacan and Derrida before them, why readers or critics of master literary texts should in their theory or their practice act out what they read."

This remark implies the availability of an escape from the literary, an escape that Fineman, it seems to me, never fully articulated and never perhaps completely believed in. For in his work the "examples of Lacan and Derrida" are not themselves instances of such an escape; on the contrary, they are the powerful contemporary articulations, the end points, of a literary logic and a form of expressive, self-conscious subjectivity initiated by Shakespeare. They function not as independent theoretical illuminations of the Shakespearean text but as consequences of that text. Hence, to glance at the last of Fineman's Shakespeare essays, "The Sound of O in *Othello*: The Real of the Tragedy of Desire," Lacan and Shakespeare function in effect as twins, mutually disclosing the "necessary lack, gap, absence, disjunction, hole, determined for the subject by the very registration or denomination of the all, the complete, the total, the one, the whole, in which the subject finds himself, and therefore finds himself as lost."

The fragments of *Shakespeare's Will* that were written suggest that it would have been a book not about escape from the literary but about its inescapability: the "thematic homologies between Lacan's theorization of subjectivity and the characteristically Shakespearean," the discovery of identity in absence, the founding of the subject in a dialectical relation to a generalized Other. If there is something tormented and tormenting about this inescapability, there is also something exhilarating: the pleasure of inexhaustibly inventive literary criticism, provoked by the Shakespearean hero's "substantialized emptiness." For that emptiness—the sound of O in Othello—was in Fineman's work less a tragic revelation of futility than a comic incitement of interpretive intelligence in the face of contingency. In this sense, the O was an emblem of opening and hence a tiny version of what, in his last essay, Fineman would call the anecdote. The thesis of "The History of the Anecdote: Fiction and Fiction" is that "the anecdote is the literary form that uniquely *lets history happen* by virtue of the way it introduces an opening into the teleological, and therefore timeless, narration of beginning, middle, and end." Fineman finds this opening exemplified in Thucydides whose anecdotes, at once modeled upon and swerving from Hippocratic medical case histories, produce "the effect of the real, the occurrence of contingency." The moments of openness are soon closed, but there is always the possibility, the promise, of other anecdotal openings, or of further histories in which the closed narratives, now reframed through a kind of theoretical *Aufhebung*, themselves serve as anecdotes.

Joel wrote "The History of the Anecdote" when, as we say, the handwriting was on the wall, when the teleological master narrative of his life and early death was ineradicably inscribed in the tissues of his body. "Never trust the body," he said on his deathbed. I replied that the idea of standing so far away from the body as to be able to trust it was itself an odd one. "I know," he said, "I'll never do it again." He must have felt in the end that his body had violated the dream of his writing, the dream that there is nothing *but* writing. And yet perhaps that is only *my* projection, *my* sense of violation and loss; he behaved through it all as if his body, even in its excruciating self-betrayal and vanishing, were somehow fulfilling the dream. Sitting by his bed, I said, in the feeble attempt at consolation to which one is driven in such circumstances, that he was just going a little before the rest of us. "O worthy pioneer," he replied with a smile, wittily playing half-adoring, half-mocking Hamlet to his own grave-digging Ghost. He told me something else. He couldn't eat any longer—that part of his bodily life was already over—for he couldn't swallow. But he said that he was getting incredible pleasure from taking sips of New York Seltzer and letting the bubbles burst on his lips and tongue.

Stephen Greenblatt

I   The Subjectivity Effect

The Structure of Allegorical Desire

Μῆνιν ἄειδε, Θεά, Πῃ

I mean my title to be read backwards and forwards, its "of" taken as objective and subjective genitive. On the one hand, I am concerned with the ways allegories begin and with the ends towards which they tend. In general, this is the problem of allegorical narrative, primarily a temporal issue regarding the way allegories linearly unfold, but also, as has often been pointed out, a symbolic progress that lends itself to spatial projection, as when the Temple translates the Labyrinth, or the music of the spheres sounds the order of the stars. On the other hand, I am concerned with a specifically allegorical desire, a desire *for* allegory, that is implicit in the idea of structure itself and explicit in criticism that directs itself towards the structurality of literature. This is to say not only that the notion of structure, especially of literary structure, presupposes the same system of multiply articulated levels as does that of allegory, but also that the possibility of such coherently polysemic significance originates out of the same intention—what I call desire—as does allegorical narrative.

I speak of desire in deference to the thematics of allegory and to describe the self-propelling, digressive impulse of allegorical movement: for example, the way the meandering *Canterbury Tales* begins by setting the scene and establishing the atmosphere in which folk properly "longen" to go on pilgrimages, that longing being motivation for each pilgrim's journey to Canterbury but also the way the tales themselves set off towards the equally sacred center of their own allegorical space. I therefore psychoanalytically assume that the movement of allegory, like the dreamwork, enacts a wish that determines its progress—and, of course, the dream-vision is a characteristic framing and opening device of allegory, a way of situating allegory in the *mise en abyme* opened up by the variety of cognate accusatives that dream a dream, or see a sight, or tell a tale. On the other hand, with this reference to psychoanalysis, I mean also to suggest that analysis itself, the critical response to allegory, rehearses the same wish and therefore embarks upon the same pilgrimage, so that psychoanalysis, especially structural psychoanalysis, by which today we are obliged to mean Lacan, is not simply the analysis of, but the extension and conclusion of, the classic allegorical tradition from which it derives—which is why psycho-analysis so readily assimilates the great archetypes of allegorical imagery into its dis-course: the labyrinths, the depths, the navels, the psychomachian hydraulics.

I want to argue that there is, for literary criticism, an historical importance in the fact that psychoanalysis founds its scientificity on the hermeneutic circle traced by its own desire to know, as in the dream that begins psychoanalysis, Freud's dream of Irma's injection, whose wish is that its own interpretation be correct.[1] To the extent that psychoanalysis is the prevailing paradigm for critical inquiry today, it is precisely because *The Interpretation of Dreams* in this way develops itself as the dream, and therefore as the desire, of interpretation itself. In thus basing itself on its own critical reflection, however, desire becomes in psychoanalysis, as in allegory, both a theme and a structuring principle, and its psychology, its theory of the human, thus becomes, in the words of another and famously ambiguous genitive, the allegory of love, whereas its metapsychology, its theory of itself, becomes the allegory of alle-gory. I am concerned with the logic, presumably the psycho-logic—etymologically, the logos of the soul—that in our literary tradition links allegory, interpretation, and desire each to each, and with what happens to interpretation when its desire is no longer controllable by a figure.

That there should be formal reciprocity between allegory and its criticism is not surprising. Theoretical discussions of allegory regularly begin by lamenting the breadth of the term and relating its compass to the habit of mind that, as it is irri-tatedly put, sees allegory everywhere. Thus generalized, allegory rapidly acquires the status of trope of tropes, representative of the figurality of all language, of the distance between signifier and signified, and, correlatively, the response to allegory becomes representative of critical activity *per se*. As Frye says, "it is not often realized that all commentary is allegorical interpretation, an attaching of ideas to the structure of poetic imagery"—as, indeed, Frye's comment demonstrates, in its presumption of global, archetypal structure, which is already allegoricization, whatever purely lit-erary claims he may make for it.[2] Often, allegory will internalize this critical mood that it evokes, and this is what gives it its characteristically didactic and sententious tone, as in Spenser's emblematic stanzas, or the way Chaucer's pilgrims, however ironic the context, draw the exemplary morals of their own and each other's tales, or the relation of the second half of the *Roman de la Rose* to the first, or, even more patently, the way EK's appendixes to *The Shepheardes Calender* or Eliot's pedantic footnotes to *The Waste Land* seem integral parts of the poems rather than gloss. This tendency on the part of allegory to read itself, for its theme to dominate its narrative, or, as Frye says, to prescribe the direction of its commentary, suggests the formal or phenomenological affinities of the genre with criticism.[3]

More historically, we can note that allegory seems regularly to surface in critical or polemical atmospheres, when for political or metaphysical reasons there is something that cannot be said. Plutarch is generally instanced as the first to substitute ἀλληγορία for the more usual ὑπόνοια, and he does so in the double context of defending poetry and demythologizing the gods.[4] In this he picks up the protoallegorical tradition of euhemerism which goes back to the third century BC, or to Plato, or beyond that to the Pythagoreans, and whose importance for literary theory is not so much its dismantling of the pagan pantheon as, rather, the defensively recuperative intention it displays towards authoritative texts whose literalism has failed.[5] The dignity of Apollo is deflated, but the prestige of Homer preserved, when the licentious intrigues of the gods are reinterpreted as philosophic, naturalistic, or scientific parables.

This deployment of allegory in the service of established literary tradition, a way of reviving prior literary authorities by making them new through critical revision—for example, *Ovid moralisée*—forms the basis of Edwin Honig's theory of allegorical conception,[6] which has itself been forcefully revived and redeveloped in Harold Bloom's more psychoanalytical (allegorical?) *Anxiety of Influence*.[7] In this context, and relating more directly to the historical development of our own exegetical tradition, it is significant that Philo, who was the first to employ an extensively allegorical mode of scriptural criticism, was also the first to introduce the terms of negative theology into theological discourse.[8] Here there is a kind of euhemerism in reverse, with a God whose ineffability and incomprehensibility—knowable as existent but not in essence—answers His embarrassingly anthropomorphic involvement in history, just as His essentially mysterious divinity explains the necessity for a revelation expressed through figural extravagance. Again, with Philo we note a self-conscious and sacralizing nostalgia in response to authoritative but in some sense faded origins, whether they be historical (the disturbingly unphilosophical account of the creation of the universe presented in Scripture) or textual (the way Philo's commentary works at one inspired and translated remove from its original source).[9] It is as though allegory were precisely that mode that makes up for the distance, or heals the gap, between the present and a disappearing past, which, without interpretation, would be otherwise irretrievable and foreclosed, as, for example, the pseudohieroglyphology of Horapollo, whose magic, hermetic graphesis is developed just at that moment when the legibility of hieroglyphs is lost.[10]

With the Patristics (leaving aside the exact proportion of Philonic and Stoic influence) these allegoricizing perspectives and purposes turn into the dogma that lies at the base of all medieval and renaissance critical theory. Again allegory is directed to critical and polemical ends, and again the motive to allegoricize emerges out of recuperative originology. The Old Testament is revived when interpreted as typologically predictive of the New Testament, and the Gospels themselves receive the benefit of spiritualizing exegesis when the apocalypse they prophesy is indefinitely deferred. Here, allegory acquires what will be in our tradition its primarily intermediate position between interpretative extremes: more figural than Montanist literalism, for which the arrival of the Paraclete is already officially announced by Scripture, and less recursively allusive than doceticizing Gnosticism, for which history, Christ, and Truth itself are but discrete moments in an infinite series of suggestively unstable images of images.[11] This is the major strain of allegoricizing sensibility in our tradition: the second and third century legacy on which the four- or three-fold medieval schemes will depend. Between a literalism pure and simple and what today might be called an exegesis of the free-floating signifier, allegory becomes, for literature as for theology, a vivifying archaeology of occulted origins and a promissory eschatology of postponed ends—all this in the service of an essentially pietistic cosmology devoted to the corroboration of divinely ordered space and time, precisely the two matrices against which, as Auerbach showed, the connotative nuances of "figure," formal and chronic, develop.[12]

That allegory should organize itself with reference to these spatial and temporal axes, that, as it were, it should embody *figura,* follows directly from the linguistic structure attributed to the figure by classic rhetorical theory. The standard formulation, of course, is Quintilian's, which characterizes allegory as what happens when a single metaphor is introduced in continuous series.[13] For grave Quintilian this is more often than not a defect, an excess of metaphor likely to lead to enigma, but whether avoided as a vice of style or assiduously "invented" for the sake of decorous amplification, allegory will be defined up through the Renaissance as the temporal extension of trope (Thomas Wilson: "An Allegorie is none other thing, but a Metaphore used throughout a whole sentence or oration").[14] As such, the procedure of allegory, and the relations that obtain between its spatial and temporal projections, are strictly circumscribed. Metaphor is the initial equivocating insight into the system of doubly articulated correspondences and proportions upon which depends the analogizing logic of any troping proposition. As the shepherd to his flock, so the pilot to his boat, the king to his realm, the priest to his congregation, the husband to his wife, the stomach to the body—metaphor will select from such a system of hierarchically arranged ratios (*logoi*) the particular similarity that, as Aristotle puts it, it chooses to see in differences.[15] Developed at length, in narrative succession, the continued metaphor will maintain the rigor of the original conceit by appealing to the overall structure that governs each term in the series, with the result that narrative logic directs itself towards introducing the fox, the tempest, the cuckold, or the canker as specifically structural, predetermined consequences of the first metaphorization (Abraham Fraunce: "The excellencie of tropes is then most apparent, when either manie be fitlie included in one word, or one so continued in manie, as that with what thing it begin, with the same it also end: and then it is called an Allegorie or Inversion").[16]

Thus there are allegories that are primarily perpendicular, concerned more with structure than with temporal extension, as, say, illustrations of Fortune's wheel, or Fludd's famous diagram of the great chain of being, or the emblem as a general literary genre, or pastorals like *The Shepheardes Calender,* which make only the slightest gestures towards full-scale narrative progress. And, on the other hand, there is allegory that is primarily horizontal, such as picaresque or quest narrative, where figurative structure is only casually and allusively appended to the circuit of adventures through time. Finally, of course, there are allegories that blend both axes together in relatively equal proportions, as in *The Canterbury Tales,* where each figurative tale advances the story of the pilgrimage as a whole. Whatever the prevailing orientation of any particular allegory, however, up and down through the declensions of structure, or laterally developed through narrative time, the allegory will be successful as allegory only to the extent that it can suggest the authenticity with which the two coordinating poles bespeak each other, with structure plausibly unfolded in time, and narrative persuasively upholding the distinctions and equivalences described by structure. In Roman Jakobson's linguistic formula, which here simply picks up classic rhetorical theory (along with the awkward metaphoricity of the definition of metaphor itself), allegory would be the poetical projection of the metaphoric axis onto the metonymic, where metaphor is understood as the synchronic system of differences which constitutes the order of language (*langue*), and metonymy as the diachronic principle of combination and connection by means of which structure is actualized in time in speech (*parole;* cf. Taleus: "continued *metonymia* is also allegory").[17] And while Jakobson goes on to associate metaphor with verse and romanticism, as opposed to metonymy, which he identifies with realism and prose, allegory would cut across and subtend all such stylistic categorizations, being equally possible in either verse or prose, and quite capable of transforming the most objective naturalism into the most subjective expressionism, or the most determined realism into the most surrealistically ornamental baroque.[18]

Thus defined, allegory fully deserves the generalization that renders it representative of language employed for literary ends, and at the same time we can see why, for contemporary structuralism, allegory would be the figure of speech *par excellence.* No other figure so readily lays itself out on the grid constructed out of the hypothesized intersection of paradigmatic synchrony and syntagmatic diachrony, which is to say that no other figure so immediately instances the definition of linguistic structure which was developed by Jakobson out of Saussure and the Russian Formalists, and that has since been applied to all the so-called "sciences of man," from anthropology (Lévi-Strauss) to semiotics (Barthes) to psychoanalysis (Lacan).

Several paradoxes, however, or apparent paradoxes, follow from this curiously pure structurality possessed by allegory, though taken singly none is at odds with our basic literary intuitions. On the one hand, as does structuralism itself, allegory begins with structure, thinks itself through it, regardless of whether its literary realizations orient themselves perpendicularly or horizontally, that is, as primarily metaphoric or primarily metonymic. At each point of its progress, allegory will select its signifying elements from the system of binary oppositions that is provided by what Jakobson would call the metaphoric code, that is, the structure, and, as a result, allegory will inevitably reinforce the structurality of that structure regardless of how it manipulates the elements themselves. For Jakobson and for allegory, "The poetic function projects the principle of equivalence from the axis of selection onto the axis of combination,"[19] and so it is always the structure of metaphor that is projected onto the sequence of metonymy, not the other way around, which is why allegory is always a hierarchicizing mode, indicative of timeless order, however subversively intended its contents might be. This is why allegory is "the courtly figure," as Puttenham called it, an inherently political and therefore religious trope, not because it flatters tactfully, but because in deferring to structure it insinuates the power of structure, giving off what we can call the structural effect.[20] So too, this is what leads a theoretician such as Angus Fletcher to analogize the rhythm of allegory to that of obsessional neurosis: it is a formal rather than a thematic aspect of the figure, deriving directly from the structure that in-forms its movement.[21]

On the other hand, if allegorical themes are in a sense emptied of their content by the structure that governs them, if the particular signifiers of allegory become vehicles of a larger structural story that they carry but in which they play no part, they

are at the same time ostentatiously foregrounded by the very structurality that becomes immanent in them. There is no clearer example of this than that of rhyme, which is precisely the poetic feature with which Jakobson illustrated his definition of the poetical as the superimposition of structural similarity on syntagmatic continuity. With rhyme we do indeed have "equivalence in sound, projected into the sequence," such that the principle of equivalent selection does indeed govern syntax;[22] and the resulting literary effect is exactly that we hear the sound of the sound rather than the meaning of the meaning. The same holds for the other metrical and intonational means of marking poetic periods as isochronic, all of which render "the time of the speech flow experienced."[23] Thus, if before we saw signifiers lose their content when they were subsumed in a metaphoric structure to which they only obliquely referred, we here see them lose that content once again when they stagily embody that structure in sequential movement. We hear the sounds but not the sense when the signifiers, graded as similarity superinduced on continuity, point to themselves as signifiers rather than to what they signify: poetic sense is exchanged for poetic sensuousness when the palpability and texture of the *signans* take precedence over, and even, as in doggerel, occlude the *signatum* altogether. With regard to Jakobson's famous typology of the six communicative functions—the referential, which stresses the context; the emotive, which stresses the addresser; the conative, which stresses the addressee; the phatic, which stresses the contact between addresser and addressee; the metalinguistic, which stresses the code in which the message is couched—allegory would be exemplary of Jakobson's purely poetic function, namely, the message that, charged with reflexive poeticality, stresses itself as merely message.[24] This leaves us, however, with the paradox that allegory, which we normally think of as the most didactic and abstractly moral-mongering of poetic figures, is at the same time the most empty and concrete: on the one hand, a structure of differential oppositions abstracted from its constituent units; on the other, a clamor of signifiers signifying nothing but themselves. Remembering the sententiousness of allegory, we are entitled to ask whether with such a structuralist description the thematic has not been "structured" out of court.

The paradox is, of course, only an apparent one, but I draw it out in this way so as to point to a real difficulty in structuralist poetics: namely, that in order to maintain any thematic meaning at all, structuralism, like allegory, must assume a meaningful connection between metaphoric and metonymic poles. That meaning is either what permits the two to join or it is the consequence of their juncture. What this means in practice is that Jakobson will pick up the tradition of Pope and of Hopkins, or, for that matter, of Wimsatt, and argue that sound is echo to sense. Of course, Jakobson does not intend the naïve claim that there are different phonemes for different qualities—the notorious murmuring of innumerable bees—though he does accept studies that support Mallarmé's discriminations of dark and light vowels. Rather, Jakobson wants to say that the structure of poetic sounds functions in relation to the structure of its poetic signifieds as a kind of Peircean index, a *little* like that to which it points, or, in negatively contrapuntal fashion, conspicuously, but equally indicatively, unlike.[25] In pointing to themselves, therefore, as in rhyme, the sounds thus also point beyond themselves to the structure of their signifieds, and the same goes for the signifieds themselves, which at a semantic and thematic level are again a structure of signifiers pointing both to themselves and to a structure of signifiers beyond themselves, all of them, alone or together, eventually pointing to the structure of language itself. This is the essentially Hegelian assumption that lies behind Jakobson's claim that "The history of a system is in turn also a system," that is, that historical diachrony, the evolution of a language, reacts structurally upon the synchronic linguistic code.[26] Once the signifier's relation to the signified, that is, the sign as a whole, is in this way understood to be relatively motivated, rather than utterly arbitrary as in Saussure, it is possible to make the sign itself into an index pointing to the structure it embodies and supports, and thus all the levels of allegory, up through and including the thematic, will display themselves and each other with resoundingly poetic and emphatically structural effect.[27]

But this harmonious, now Leibnitzian structure, depending as it does on an utter idealization of the structure of the sign, occurs at a significant cost. Out of the romantic and organicizing formalism of its axiological assumptions, the affinity of structuralism with the old New Criticism comes as naturally as leaves to either Keats's or Yeats's tree, and so too does the same fetishization of irony as a poetic feature. "The supremacy of poetic function over referential function does not obliterate the reference but makes it ambiguous."[28] What this typically unbending aphorism means is that, in a structuralist poem, every signifier will be simultaneously metaphor and metonymy. Jakobson's example is the girl in the Russian folk tale who comes to be symbolized by the willow under which she walks: ever after in the poem, girl and tree are metaphors, each of the other, by virtue of their metonymic intersection, just as the sequential movement of the poem is conditioned by their metaphoric equivalence.[29] In classical rhetoric, we would call this a synecdoche: the girl is represented by the tree or it by her, in that one daemonically possesses the other. In Jakobson's terms, however, what we have is a metaphoric metonymy and a metonymic metaphor, and the result, not surprisingly, is allegory:

> Similarity superimposed on contiguity imparts to poetry its thorough-going symbolic, multiplex, polysemantic essence which is beautifully suggested by Goethe's *"Alles Vergängliche ist nur ein Gleichnis"* (Any-thing transient is but a likeness). Said more technically, anything sequent is a simile. In poetry where similarity is superinduced upon contiguity, any metonymy is slightly metaphorical and any metaphor has a meto-nymic tint.[30]

Undoubtedly, poems, and allegories in particular, work this way: think of Spenser's forests that metaphorize his heroes while they wander through them, or the play of light imagery in *The Faerie Queene*. The question is, How can structuralism work this way? What does it mean for a metonymy to be slightly metaphorical, and what is this "tint" that makes a metaphor a little metonymic? If structuralism is the diacritical sci-ence because it begins with the difference around which binary oppositions assem-ble, what happens to its scientific status when its own most fundamental opposites, metaphor and metonymy, are from the very beginning already implicated one in the other, the difference between them collapsed for the sake of hierarchicized, struc-tured, "symbolic, multiplex," allegorical meaning? If these seem merely abstract and theoretical issues, we can reformulate them again in terms of our original literary problem: How does time get into structure and structure into time, how does alle-gory begin and why does it continue?

For reasons that will become clearer later, I want to illustrate the problem with the opening of *The Canterbury Tales,* which is an instance of the poetical whose structurality has never yet been questioned, and where the allegorical relationship of space and time is a straightforwardly thematic as well as a formal issue. This is the case in several ways, but, for our purposes, most importantly so with regard to the opening description of the months and seasons, which is the stylized convention by means of which the Prologue places itself squarely in a tradition of allegorical begin-ning. In part, of course, such a description is a convention of courtly romance, one that Chaucer employs several times elsewhere (*The Legend of Good Women, The Book of the Duchess, Troilus and Criseyde*), and whose force he would know from the *Roman de la Rose,* which he had already translated, and where the description of May is preface to the allegorical dream-vision itself. But so too, and equally alle-gorical, the description of months and seasons is a long-established convention immediately evocative of, and convenient to, cosmological and metaphysical inven-tion, a way of alluding through allegorical structure to the mysterious order of the cosmos and the position of God as unmoved mover within it; here the Prologue can rely on a tradition that goes back to Lucretius, Ovid, and Vergilian eclogue, and that is thoroughly alive and popular throughout the Middle Ages, whether in manuscript decoration, cathedral ornament, or various scientifically and philosophically inclined compendia. The details and history of this convention, which have been magisterially summarized for us by Rosemond Tuve,[31] need not concern us now, save to the extent that they allow us to refer with some certainty to the explicitly allegorical intentions of *The Canterbury Tales* and to remark that here, as with any deployment of a convention within a literary tradition, we have precisely the joining of paradigm and syntagm by means of which a literary text will position itself within the structurality of literature as a whole (with the text presenting itself as either like or unlike others in the conventional paradigm—for Jakobson this would be the literary code, a structure of generic oppositions—at the same time as it actualizes the paradigm in the temporality of literary history, though whether Chaucer's *parole* is here intended ironically remains an open question).

In any event, it is with reference to this complex tradition of allegorical literature and to the burden of cosmological, theological, and scientific speculation that it carries, that we enter the poem. And it is also within this context that we discover in the Prologue's first two lines, with the piercing of March by April, the metaphoric metonymy that for Jakobson constitutes the specifically poetic effect. That is, when April with its sweet showers pierces the drought of March, we have the code of the months, or, more precisely, the system of oppositions which makes up the code, translated directly into consecutive sequence, such that the binary oppositions between the months—rainy April versus dry March, but, of course, within the tradition there are other oppositions at stake besides the merely meteorological—are projected systematically onto the continuous progress of the months through the year—after March, then April—in a progression that completes and corroborates itself only when the entirety of the monthly paradigm unfolds itself through the temporal totality, or what properly we should here call the syntagm, of the year. Inevitably—and for the author of a treatise on the astrolabe, tautologically—this is picked up by the surrounding or encapsulating astrological references, which tell us again that we are in the first month, April, because the Ram has run through half his course and therefore, as with April and March, that the paradigmatic zodiacal opposition of Aries and Taurus is directly translatable onto or as the sequence of metonymy unrolled by celestial rotation.

All this is a rather complicated way of saying what for a competent reader should presumably go without saying, but, for the sake of argument, let us assume

that the initial structural disposition of these first few images is then repeated with utter systematicity in the pattern of images which the poem develops throughout its opening few lines, so that the series of oppositions, which we might summarize as wet and dry, up and down, sky and earth, male and female, fecundity and sterility, pagan as opposed to Christian divinities, inside and outside, near and far, health and illness—all function structurally in relation to each other and to themselves as kinds of mirror images, indexes, of the first metaphorico-metonymic structuration intro-duced by the intersection of March and April, each of them graded as structure on sequence. Let us even assume that the same thing happens metrically, so that the ictus on the unstressed position that we get in April is structurally related to the stress on the stressed position that we get with March, and that this in turn sets up a stress struc-ture of rhythmical and intonational patterning which the poem will reserve for spe-cifically metaphorico-metonymic emphasis; for example, "... with his shóurĕs soote/Thĕ droúghte. . ." Let us also assume, again only for the sake of argument and in pursuit of the ideal structural analysis, that the themes introduced by our now hypothetically structuralized Prologue imagery are in turn developed in the tales themselves, and that this enlargement proceeds with the same structural determi-nations that are sketched out in the first few lines, so that the implicit hierarchy pre-sumed in the order of months is what finally lies behind the social hierarchy into which the pilgrims fit, from the Knight on down to the Miller (as well as the dictional hierarchy that governs the manner in which each tale is decorously related), and that the primacy of male April to female March is the structural source not only of the patriarchal orientation of the marriage tales, but also of presumptively analogous arrangements of cosmological and literary order which the tales regularly, allegor-ically ally with this—as, say, in The Wife of Bath's prologue and tale, where familial, sexual, theological, and literary "authorities" are all developed in terms of the hier-archicized sexuality already built into the piercing of March by the potent, engen-dering liquidity of April. Finally, so as to complete this imaginary, exhaustively structural analysis, let us assume that the relation of April to March, developed as structure superinduced on sequence, also describes the most general literary fea-tures of *The Canterbury Tales* as a whole, so that, in the same way that Jakobson's metaphorized metonymies point both to themselves as signifiers and to the structure of signifiers from which they derive, so too do we have in little with April-March a prototypical enactment of the procedure by means of which Chaucer characteris-tically manages to distance his text from its own textuality—whether in the way the tales comment upon each other by reference to their common frame, or the way they point to themselves by stepping out of themselves, as with the Pardoner's claims for his own rhetoric, or, in that culminating instance of self-reflection so dear to dialectical Chaucerians, the way the narrator's tale of Sir Thopas lapses into the allegorical prose of the *Tale of Melibee,* accomplishing thereby an instance of mirroring self-mockery surpassed only by the absolute duplicity of the Retraction itself, where Chaucer either turns Pardoner or steps out of literature altogether, but in either case piously and conventionally defers to the only moral imperatives that his allegorical system allows him in the first place.

Having now assumed so much—and I realize that to suggest either the possibility or the shape of a completely successful, all-encompassing structural analysis of *The Canterbury Tales* is to assume a great deal—we are now entitled to ask in what way this structure accounts for the poeticality of the text. In what sense can our hypothesized structure explain either the pleasure or the meaning taken from, or generated by, a text organized by the projection of metaphoric equivalence onto metonymic succession. The poem tells us that when the sweet showers of April pierce the drought of March to the root, when Zephyrus inspires the crops in every woodland with his sweet breath, when small birds begin to make melody, "*thanne* longen folk to goon on pilgrimages." How does the structurality of the first few lines which we have now assumed manage to generate this longing, or to justify it, or to explain it? How does such structurality entice a reader further into the poem, leading him on through and into its sequentiality? How is structure extended, "longed," into time?

We might conceivably answer by referring ourselves directly to the immediate referents of the text. Here it would be a simple positivist matter of fact that when spring comes, and the Ram runs through half his course, and small birds begin to sing, *then,* by nature, people desire to go on pilgrimages, with professional pilgrims rushing off to foreign shrines, while ordinary folk who happen to live in England instead typically wend their way to Canterbury. This would be an unsatisfing solution, I take it, not only because we can assume other urges to be commonly operative in the spring but also because such a realist's account ignores the spectrum of allegorical reference which we respond to in the text, at the same time as it fails to recognize the specifically literary, conventional dimension of the opening. Alternatively, then, we might forgo the natural referents of the text entirely and answer the question formally rather than realistically by saying instead that the text presents us with a self-contained structure of relations, in which elements are manipulated as in a game, and that therefore there is neither need nor reason to adduce any extraliterary explanation or justification at all for the particular arrangements that the structurality of the text allows us to observe. The most that we might hazard as explanation for the pleasure that we take in such a text as we continue through it would be the kind of vibratory sympathy between its organization and the structure of our thought which Lévi-Strauss suggests in the overture to *The Raw and the Cooked,* where he takes up the issue of the anthropologist's response to the phenomena with which he is engaged.[32] I take it that this too is also unsatisfying, not only because it rather sentimentalizes the reading experience, but, again, more importantly, because it too ignores the manifestly allegorical intention of a text that explicitly directs its structure, such as it is or as we have idealized it, to correspond to other structures of experience—psychological, physical, metaphysical, and literary—from which the text derives its own authority and indeed much of its literary interest. How then, if neither philistine realism nor naïve structuralism—what we have been taught sternly to call "mere formalism"—is adequate, might we account for the "longing" of *The Canterbury Tales*? If the piercing of March by April is the primal structural scene to which the text repeatedly recurs, how does that first image, with its astrological, calendaric eroticism, control the structural unfolding of so massive and perfected an allegory as *The Canterbury Tales* is generally pleasurably and meaningfully taken to be? In the terms of my title, how does the structure of the poem yield its allegorical desire?

For an answer, I turn to another famous essay by Jakobson in which he applies the procedures of structural analysis to phonemic patterning, and where he develops the theory of distinctive phonetic features which remains the greatest achievement of structural linguistics, recognized as such even by linguists with entirely different theoretical perspectives.[33] I should say in advance that it is because of Jakobson's theoretical success with the conceptualization of phonemes, which reduces the infinity of humanly producible sounds to a few significant phonological oppositions, that structural linguistics has become the prestigious model for disciplines that are only marginally, or at least not obviously, related to language per se. All of them readily pay the price of analogizing their subject matter to language in exchange for the rigorous structurality that Jakobson's method provides.

In principle, then—and my account will be perfunctory paraphrase—Jakobson begins with Saussurean diacriticality, the thesis that we perceive positivities as systems of differences rather than as simple existents whose being immediately imposes itself upon our senses. We hear the structured differences between phonemes rather than the phonemes themselves, as we know from the fact that what is a significant sound to a speaker of one language may not even be heard by the speaker of another. For each language, then, Jakobson proposes that a system of binary phonological oppositions may be constructed whose systematicity can account for all the potentially significant sounds producible within the language.

This will be the phonological code of the *langue* which is actualized in metonymic *parole*. These systems naturally vary from language to language, depending on the phonological structure of each, but what concerns us now are features that, because of the structure of the human mouth, are universal phonological facts. Here, then, like a Ramist proposing his initial dichotomization, Jakobson applies structuralist methodology and searches out what would be the maximum binary opposition of which the mouth is capable, which he discovers in the first syllable, contrast of consonant and vowel, transcribed as /pa/. The constituents of this utterance, vocalic /a/ and the voiceless labial stop /p/, represent absolute phonological difference in the mouth: namely, with /p/ the buccal tract is closed at the front, whereas in /a/ the tract is opened at the end as wide as possible. As a labial stop, /p/ exists for but a moment and requires a minimum of energy for its articulation; in contrast, /a/ is a continual voicing of sound and requires maximum energy. Whereas /p/ is the stopping of sound, /a/ is pure vocality. For all these diacritical reasons, /pa/ is plausibly identified as the largest binary opposition the mouth can articulate and, as such, from a structuralist perspective, is conceptually the first syllable. This theoretical claim is, in turn, supported by studies in language acquisition and aphasia which report that /pa/ is both the first utterance children learn and the last that aphasics lose, striking empirical corroboration of Jakobson's structuralist claim that language begins and ends with the combination of vocalic /a/ with voiceless labial stop /p/ in the primal utterance, /pa/.

The hypothesis is clearly ingenious, and if we assimilate voiceless /p/ to its twin labial stop, voiced /b/, sound and sense begin in Jakobson's sense structurally to cohere, as, for example, when we call the infant incapable of speech a *baby,* or when the Greeks call foreigners whose speech is strange *barbaroi* because they *babble,* as at the Tower of *Babel,* or when we begin our alpha-bets by joining *A* to *B.*[34] But /pa/ is only the beginning of a system. In order to build a structure, at least two sets of oppositions are required so as to construct a series of proportions and *logoi* that can be actualized in speech. Thus Jakobson and the infant must identify a second binary opposition, structurally opposable to the first, so as to specify a paradigmatic code, and this they do by introducing the nasal consonant /m/. With the acquisition of /m/, the pure differentiality that was first presented by /pa/ is, as it were, plugged up, recuperated. As a nasal consonant, a continuant sound, /m/ combines the vocality of /a/ with the positionality of /p/ at the front of the mouth. As a little of one and a little of the other, /m/ is a kind of average or collapse or juncture of the original opposition, just as metaphor and metonymy seemed to collapse in Jakobson's theory. At this point, once /m/ is articulated as a distinctive feature in its own right, we have the diacritical material with which to establish a structure of phonological sound: /p/ and /m/ being both opposed to /a/, whereas /p/ and /m/ are also opposed to each other. As Jakobson puts it: "Before there appeared the consonantal opposition nasal/oral, consonant was distinguished from vowel as closed tract from open tract. Once the nasal consonant has been opposed to the oral as presence to absence of the open tract, the contrast consonant/vowel is revalued as presence vs. absence of a closed tract."[35]

Again, there is striking cross-cultural empirical support for Jakobson's claim. In nearly every natural language that has been observed, some variation of "Papa" and "Mama," or their reversal, as in "Abba" and "Ema," are the familiar terms for father and mother.[36] What I am concerned with right now, however, quite apart from whatever empirical power Jakobson's insight might possess, is how the first two terms of this series, /pa/ and /ma/, develop themselves as a structure. We remember that it is only with the introduction of the second opposition adduced by /ma/ that we can say we have a system. At that point, each term in the series can be seen as diacritically significant with respect to its opposition to another term in the structure. Until then, however, /pa/, insofar as it signifies anything, signifies only the sheer diacriticality through which the system as a whole is thought. But this original differential determination is thereupon lost, retroactively effaced, when the introduction of /ma/ "revalues" the first *valueless* contrast consonant/vowel, or silence/sound, that is, /pa/, as "presence vs. absence of a closed tract." In other words, /pa/ loses its original status as mark of pure diacriticality when it is promoted to the level of significant signifier within the system as a whole. This new significant /pa/ is utterly unrelated to the first simply diacritical /pa/ that it replaces, or, as Derrida would say, that it places under erasure. And it is precisely this occultation of the original /pa/, now structurally unspeakable because revalued as something else entirely, which allows the system to function as a structure in the first place. In short, the structure of significant sounds must erase the original marking of diacriticality upon which it depends, and from which it emerges, in order to signify anything at all. In a formulation whose resonance with contemporary literary criticism will be embarrassingly obvious, there is buried in the structurality of any structure the ghostly origin of that structure, because the origin will be structurally determined as a ghost, a palpably absent origin, by virtue of the very structurality it fathers. Every structure must begin with such an effacing, retroactive revaluation of its beginning, with such a murder of its diacritical source, just as Freud said when he identified the origin of human culture in the murder of the father, the primal /pa/, who lives on only in and as the guilty memory responsible for the structure of society.[37]

Turning back to the opening of *The Canterbury Tales*—which it will now be clear was selected precisely because there in the intersection of *April* and *March* we have also the juncture of /pa/ and /ma/—we can answer the question of how an allegory begins and why it continues. What we can say is that with its poeticality defined as structure superinduced upon metonymy, allegory initiates and continually revivifies its own desire, a desire born of its own structurality. Every metaphor is always a little metonymic because in order to have a metaphor there must be a structure, and where there is a structure there is already piety and nostalgia for the lost origin through which the structure is thought. Every metaphor is a metonymy of its own origin, its structure thrust into time by its very structurality. With the piercing of March by April, then, the allegorical structure thus enunciated has already lost its center and thereby discovered a project: to re-cover the loss dis-covered by the structure of language and of literature. In thematic terms, this journey back to a foreclosed origin writes itself out as a pilgrimage to the sacred founding shrine, made such by murder, that is the motive of its movement.[38] In terms of literary response, the structurality of the text holds out the promise of a meaning that it will also perpetually defer, an image of hermeneutic totality martyred and sacralized by and as the poetical. This is the formal destiny of every allegory insofar as allegory is definable as continued metaphor. Distanced at the beginning from its source, allegory will set out on an increasingly futile search for a signifier with which to recuperate the fracture of and at its source, and with each successive signifier the fracture and the search begin again: a structure of continual yearning, the insatiable desire of allegory.[39]

Perhaps this is one reason why, as Angus Fletcher has remarked, allegory seems by its nature to be incompletable, never quite fulfilling its grand design.[40] So too, this explains the formal affinity of allegory with obsessional neurosis, which, as Freud develops it in the case of the Wolfman, derives precisely from such a search for lost origins, epitomized in the consequences of the primal scene, which answers the child's question of where he came from with a diacritical solution that he cannot accept and that his neurosis thereupon represses and denies. But this would in turn suggest the affinity of psychoanalysis not only with obsessionality but also with allegory.[41] For the theoretical concern of the Wolfman case, argued out in the context of a polemic with Jung, is precisely to determine whether the scene of parental intercourse, the piercing of /ma/ by /pa/, observed by the Wolfman was indeed a primal scene or instead a primal fantasy. And when Freud, relying on a hypothesis of universal, cross-cultural phylogenetic inheritance, tells us that it is a matter of indifference whether we choose to regard it as either, we may well wonder whether the theory of the primal scene, which is in some sense at the center of every psychoanalysis, is not itself the theoretical primal fantasy of psychoanalysis, a theoretical origin that the theoretical structure of Freud's thought obliged him to displace to the recesses of mythic history.[42] The question becomes perhaps more urgent when we recall the theoretical status of what for Freudian metapsychology is its own maximum binary opposition, namely, the instinct theory, with its dualism of Eros and Death. For to the extent that these two instincts are different, it is only insofar as the recuperative, unifying impulses of Eros are provoked as response to the differentiating impulses of death, a /ma/ to the thanatotic /pa/. And even before this, death is already conceived by Freud as itself such a dualism, already extended into time as the compulsive, obsessive repetition of its own diacriticality, that is, the repetition compulsion, which is the vicious Freudian metonym of the metaphoricity of death. Is it any wonder, then, that for evidence of all of this Freud can but point in *Beyond the Pleasure Principle* to another piece of allegorical literature, to Plato's story of Aristophanes' story of divinely diacriticalized hermaphrodites, yet another case where desire originates in and as the loss of structure.[43] And it is by no means accidental that Freud develops these same Aristophanic themes elsewhere, as in the allegory of his gender theory, with its unending quest by both hetero-sexes for the castrated phallus, powerful only in the division it teaches in its loss.[44] And so too with psychoanalytic interpretation, which completes itself only when it points mutely to that

> passage in even the most thoroughly interpreted dream which has to be left obscure . . . a tangle of dream-thoughts which cannot be unravelled and which moreover adds nothing to our knowledge of the content of the dream. This is the dream's navel, the spot where it reaches down into the unknown. The dream-thoughts to which we are led by interpretation cannot from the nature of things, have any definite endings; they are bound to branch out in every direction into the intricate network of our world of thought. It is at some point where this meshwork is particularly close that the dream-wish grows up, like a mushroom out of its mycelium.[45]

Does this mean, then, that psychoanalysis as à science is "mere" allegory? Does the fact that the exposition of Freud's theory of the psyche acts out its own theorization mean that psychoanalysis is but a symptomatic instance of its own thwarted desire to know: a neurotic epistemophilia at the end of a bankrupt tradition of philosophy? It is thanks to the genius of Lacan that we can see in this theoretical self-reflection of psychoanalysis, mirror of Freud's original analysis of himself, both the historical necessity and the scientific validity of psychoanalytic allegoricization. For when Lacan makes the subject an effect of the signifier, when he defines the unconscious as the "discourse of the Other" (let us note, a direct translation of the etymology of allegory: ἀλλος, other; ἀγορεύω, to speak), he establishes psychoanalysis as precisely that science whose concern is the split in the subject occasioned by the subject's accession to language. If psychoanalysis has discovered anything, it is precisely this loss of the self to the self which we vaguely refer to when we speak of the function of the unconscious. And what Lacan has taught us, in a series of blindingly lucid formulations still defensively resisted by the psychoanalytic establishment, is that in the same way that *The Canterbury Tales* is divided and directed when it enters language, so too is the psyche when it learns to speak.[46] This famous Lacanian barring of the subject—the loss of being that comes from re-presenting oneself in language as a meaning, correlative with the formation of the unconscious and the onset of desire, the Oedipeanization of the subject, and the acquisition of a place in the cultural order through the recognition of the Name of the Father—is what makes the psyche a critical allegory of itself and is what justifies psychoanalysis as the allegory of that allegory. For it is in search of the meaning of this division of the subject through the dialectics of desire, brought on by the structurality of the logos, that psychoanalysis finds its own epistemological project and its own initiatory desire.

If, then, the structure of Freud's thought, as it develops, becomes immanent as theme, if Freud's theory repeatedly valorizes those very images of loss which make his conceptual representations possible in the first place, this is to say no more than that Freud's hermeneutics are at one with the object of their inquiry. This is not the internalist fallacy; rather, it is the way psychoanalysis realizes itself as practice—by determining its object under a concept (Hegel's definition of science). For psychoanalysis is no empty theory but is instead the operative science of the unconscious, and the unconscious is precisely that part of the self lost to the self by its articulation, just as Freud's theory embodies itself only through its endless, questing theoretical self-deconstruction; or so the heroic, allegorical example of Freud and the rigorously figurative style of Lacan persuasively suggest.

This is to see in psychoanalytic structure and in psychoanalytic structuralism the conclusion of a search for wisdom that has motivated Western philosophy from the very beginning. In the declension of theoretical speculation about the order of order that begins as ontology, cosmology, theology, and that, starting with the Renaissance, is internalized in the sciences of man as anthropology, sociology, psychology, there occurs a completing or a breaking of the hermeneutic circle when psychology, defining the psyche as an effect of the logos, is itself transformed, in Kenneth Burke's phrase, into logology.[47] This is the Heideggerean theme straightforwardly developed in Lacan's thought. And, of course, it is against just this appeal to the order of order and the meaning of meaning that Derrida has directed his critique of Lacan, seeing in such a psychoanalysis nothing but the inherited after-effects of Western logocentric metaphysics, where the phallus is the castrating, fascistic, transcendental signified that condemns man's desire to a forever unsatisfying nostalgia for the lost origin of a chimerical Golden Age.[48] As an alternative, as we now all know, Derrida proposes instead a metaphysics and a psychoanalysis of difference itself, *"la différance"* of both structure and time, to be comprehended by a philosophy *avant la lettre,* before structure, before logos; in short, a philosophy of the effacing and trace of prelinguistic, diacritical /pa/.

But as Derrida is well aware, and as he repeatedly reminds the most enthusiastic *Derridistes,* this return to structuralist first principles can occur only *after* the structural fact, for it is only *in* structure that the origin and its loss emerges. The sign is always thought through difference, but it is always eventually thought out to the signifying conclusion that erases the difference upon which it depends, which is why "difference cannot be thought without the trace."[49] Thus, if Lacan is logocentric, as Derrida says, it is because Lacan characterizes the first logocentric lapse through which *"différance"* itself will be thematized and conceived, so that any criticism of Lacan, including Derrida's, will already have committed the Lacanian lapse. This accounts for the positivist illusion that there are things before differences, but it also explains the intrinsic belatedness of every deconstruction.[50]

For this reason, too, we cannot accept any of the so-called post-structuralist critiques of structuralism, again including Derrida's, as being themselves anything more than the aftereffects of structuralism. They are already defined, by the criticism implicit in their "post" and in their hyphen, as the allegorical response to a metaphor of structure and a structure of metaphor in which they are already implicated and by which they are already implied. Whether the origin is perpetually displaced by Derridean *"différance,"* or whether it is historically located and crystallized by the Girardian catastrophe of "no-difference" whatsoever, the thematic valorization of origin as loss survives.[51] And post-structuralism therefore gains its prestige only insofar as it thus pro-longs itself as the critical metonymy of the structuralist metaphor.[52]

But this is also why we must stress again in what sense the scientific thematization of structure which we find in psychoanalysis spells an end to the tradition of literary allegory as we have known it since first century Alexandria. For when psychoanalysis itself turns into allegory, criticism for the first time in our tradition must admit to the irrecuperable distance between itself and its object. Having consciously formulated the allegory of its own desire, criticism must wake up from its dream of interpretation to a daylight where desire is but the memory of the night's desire. We have laid it down as a law of literary form that the diacriticality effaced by literary structure emerges as theme in the register of loss. Our example has been the way pilgrimage is thematized in *The Canterbury Tales,* but we might have illustrated the point with any of a wide variety of texts. We may lay it down as a second law that profoundly self-conscious texts eventually realize their responsibility for the loss upon which their literariness depends, and that, when this happens, this responsibility is itself thematized as sin. From silence, to difference, to loss, to sin—and sometimes, in texts whose literary integrity is absolute, through sin back to silence once again, as in the Retraction with which *The Canterbury Tales* concludes, where the allegory, as Derrida again would say, re-marks what is its most distinctive mark, re-tracts its constituting trait. These laws of literary form apply also to the structure of literary history, whether we consider the development of an individual author or the evolution of a literary genre.

But this leaves open a way for poetry and for the history of poetry to remain literary even in their silence, whereas criticism ceases to be criticism when it turns mute. Because the things of poetry are words, poetry can, in a way that criticism cannot, conclude itself when it cannot continue. When poetry can find no new words with which to maintain the meaning of its longing, it can lapse into significant literary silence, thereby pro-longing its desire ad infinitum, as when *The Shepheardes Calender* concludes by promising yet more poetry beyond its end, or the way *The Faerie Queene* concludes by breaking off before its end with the vision of Colin Clout making melody to the Muses and the image of his own desire.[53] But criticism, whose things are not words but the meanings of words, meanings forever foreclosed by words, will find in silence only the impetus for further speech and further longing, which it will thereupon thematize as its own responsibility for the loss of meaning. Whereas a poem can be closed poetically even by a gesture of self-abandon, criticism, discovering the futility of its pro-ject, can only go on and on, frustratingly repeating its own frustration, increasingly obsessed with its own sense of sin—unless, of course, in the psychoanalytic sense, it projects its own critical unhappiness onto literature whose self-deconstructions would then be understood as criticism.[54]

Thus it is that when the tradition of English pastoral which begins with Chaucer's Prologue finds its own conclusion, it remains literary even in its self-disgust. And Eliot, drawing the thematic structure of the genre to its absurdly melancholic, ultimate reduction, can still articulate a meaning pre-dicative of yet more poetic desire:

> April is the cruelest month, breeding
> Lilacs out of the dead land, mixing
> Memory and desire, stirring
> Dull roots with spring rain.

With his habit of making a beginning out of ends, Eliot can imagine that the gap in landscape poetry, which his poem proleptically prepares, will become a significant silence in a perpetually meaningful literary tradition that will forever feed meaning back into his *Waste Land.* In contrast, Freud, whose Judaic thematizations of guilt and sin, as in *Civilization and Its Discontents,* are at least as forceful and serious as any of Eliot's Anglican regrets, can do no more than continue to repeat his themes with increasingly phlegmatic and precisely nuanced resignation, as in the fragment with which his corpus movingly concludes, prophetically and self-reflectively entitled "The Splitting of the Ego in the Process of Defence."[55] This is the insight into self-division and sin which psychoanalysis—*interminable* analysis—leaves as legacy to contemporary critical thought, which continues to repeat Freud's themes, though perhaps without the rigor of Freud's resignation. Here I refer to that note of eschatological salvation which sounds so strangely in current literary discourse, as when Girard looks forwards to a revivification of difference through sacralizing violence, or when Derrida, telling us it is not a question of choosing, includes himself amongst those who "turn their eyes away in the face of the as yet unnameable which is proclaiming itself and which can do so, as is necessary whenever a birth is in the offing, only under the species of the non-species, in the formless, mute, infant, and terrifying form of monstrosity."[56] It would seem, by the rules of the endgame Beckett wrote in *Waiting for Godot,* that contemporary thought here turns pastoral nostalgia for a golden age into the brute expectations of a sentimental apocalypticism. But we will wait forever for the rough beast to slouch its way to Bethlehem; so too, for a philosophy or a literary criticism of what the thunder said: DA.[57]

Notes

Reprinted from *Allegory and Representation,* ed. Stephen J. Greenblatt (Baltimore and London: Johns Hopkins University Press, 1981), 26–60.

1.   Sigmund Freud, *The Interpretation of Dreams (1900;* 1959) in *The Standard Edition of the*

Complete Psychological Works of Sigmund Freud (hereafter cited as SE), ed. James Strachey et al., 24 vols. (London: Hogarth Press, 1953–74), 4, ch. 2, "The Method of Interpreting Dreams: An Analysis of a Specimen Dream," 105–21. The date in italic is the original publication date; the date in roman is that of publication in the SE.

2.   Northrop Frye, *Anatomy of Criticism: Four Essays* (Princeton: Princeton University Press, 1971), 89.

3.   Ibid., 90.

4.   See Jean Pépin, *Mythe et allégorie: Les origines Grecques et les contestations Judéo-Chrétiennes* (Paris: Aubier, 1958), 87–88. Plutarch is ambivalent about such figurative readings. On the one hand, "by forcibly distorting these (Homeric) stories through what used to be termed 'deeper meanings' (ὑπονίας), but are nowadays called 'allegorical interpretations' (ἀλληγορίαις) some people say that the Sun is represented as giving information about Aphrodite in the arms of Ares, because the conjunction of the planet Mars with Venus portends births conceived in adultery, and when the Sun returns in his course and discovers these, they cannot be kept secret" ("How the Young Man Should Study Poetry," *Moralia,* 19E, The Loeb Classical Library, vol. 1 [Cambridge: Harvard University Press, 1949], 100–101). On the other hand, "Such, then, are the possible interpretations which these facts suggest. But now let us begin over again, and consider first the most perspicuous of those who have a reputation for expounding matters more philosophically. These men are like the Greeks who say that Cronus is but a figurative name for Chronus (time) . . . (ὥσπερ Ἕλληνες Κρόνον ἀλληγοροῦσι τὸν χρόνον . . .)" ("Isis and Osiris," *Moralia,* 363D, vol. 5, 76–77).

5.   See John D. Cooke, "Euhemerism: A Medieval Interpretation of Classical Paganism," *Speculum* 2, no. 4 (1927): 396–410. Cooke's survey of the medieval tradition concludes by noting that "Chaucer nowhere subscribes to the euhemeristic interpretation" (p. 409). For the Patristics, euhemerism is a strategy of antipagan polemic, but one can also argue, like Cicero, that certain heroes did indeed become gods, just as the myths detailing divine transmogrification report. Euhemerism is allied with etymologization, the search for the truth in and of words; see, for a famous example, Plato, in the *Cratylus.* As such, it is the beginning of a tradition that treats words as substantialized philosophical essences, a tradition that leads directly to Heidegger.

6.   Edwin Honig, *Dark Conceit: The Making of Allegory* (Evanston, Ill.: Northwestern University Press, 1959).

7.   Harold Bloom, *The Anxiety of Influence: A Theory of Poetry* (New York: Oxford University Press, 1973).

8.   On Philo and the unknowability of God, see Harry Wolfson, *Philo: Foundations of Religious Philosophy in Judaism, Christianity, and Islam* (Cambridge: Harvard University Press, 1962), 2, ch. 11, esp. 110–14. Wolfson says that nowhere in Greek philosophy before Philo is there "a conception of God as a being unknowable in essence and unnamable and ineffable" (2:115). Philo is not the first allegorizer, not even the first allegoricizing Alexandrian Jew; see R. M. Grant, *The Letter and the Spirit* (London: Butler & Tanner, 1957), 31–33. What is important is that, drawing on Stoic and Jewish predecessors, Philo formulates the theological necessity for philosophical, allegorical exegesis in the face of divine ineffability; see Wolfson, *Philo,* 2:128–30. On Philo's exegetical method, see Wolfson, *Philo,* 1:87–138; also see Jean Daniélou, *Philon d'Alexandrie* (Paris: Arthème Fayard, 1957), ch. 4.

9.   On the historical uncertainty of the literal history of Genesis and the allegorical consequences thereof for Philo's reading of scripture, see H. A. Wolfson, "The Veracity of Scripture from Philo to Spinoza," in *Religious Philosophy: A Group of Essays,* ed. H. A. Wolfson (Cambridge: Harvard University Press, 1961); see also Wolfson, *Philo,* 1:120–22. As for Philo's distance from his text, it is by no means clear that Philo knew Hebrew, but in any event he would have been working in a tradition that understood the *Septuagint* translation as authoritative because divinely inspired (Wolfson, *Philo,* 1:88). Philo assumes that prophecy, translation, and his own exegetical insights are secured by divine inspiration (Grant, *Letter and Spirit,* p. 34; Wolfson, *Philo,* 2:54).

10.   Sir Alan Gardiner, *Egyptian Grammar; Being an Introduction to the Study of Hieroglyphs,* 3d ed. (London: Oxford University Press, 1957), 10–11. Along with bestiaries and the tradition of dream symbolism that goes back to Artemidorus, the Renaissance rediscovery of the Horapollo manuscript sparks the vogue for emblems (Ficino, Alciati, Ripa); see George Boas's introduction to his translation of *The Hieroglyphics of Horapollo* (New York: Bollingen Foundation, Pantheon Books, 1950); Rosemary Freeman, *English Emblem Books* (New York: Octagon Books, 1970). Ong connects this to the transition from a writing to a print culture, along with the rise of Ramist logic: Walter J. Ong, "From Allegory to Diagram in the Renaissance Mind: A Study in the Significance of the Allegorical Tableau," *The Journal of Aesthetics and Art Criticism* 17, no. 4 (June 1959): 423–40. The hieroglyph remains a topos for allegorical speculation up through Pound's and Fenellosa's sense of the ideogram, of which Derrida speaks approvingly when he takes up the hieroglyph as an instance of "irreducibly graphic poetics"; Jacques Derrida, *Of Grammatology,* trans. Gayatri Chakravorty Spivak (Baltimore: Johns Hopkins University Press, 1974), 92–93, 334–335. The metaphorics of picture *versus* word, sensible *versus* intelligible, are picked up by Freud when he distinguishes conscious word-representations (*Wortvorstellungen*) from unconscious thing-representations (*Sachvorstellungen*); "The Unconscious" (*1915*; 1957), SE, 14:201–4; see also appendix C, 209–15, for relevant portions of Freud's 1891 monograph *On Aphasia*. Similarly, as has lately been more and more stressed, Freud is regularly biased against the pictorial female (body) as opposed to the legible male (soul); so too, psychoanalytic therapeutics consists of translating a traumatic visible "scene" into intelligible words—"the talking cure." On the relation between Freudian madness and Freudian misogyny, see Shoshana Felman's excellent "Women and Madness: The Critical Phallacy," *Diacritics* 5, no. 4 (Winter 1975): 2–10. There is, however, a tension in all of Freud's developments of these issues, so that psychoanalysis in effect repeats within itself the Inigo Jones–Ben Jonson argument about *ut pictura poesis* and emblematic theatrical representation. See D. J. Gordon, "Poet and Architect: The Intellectual Setting of the Quarrel between Ben Jonson and Inigo Jones," *Journal of the Warburg and Courtauld Institutes* 12 (1949): 152–78. This is the same tension we can note in the Mosaic Freud's ambivalent obsession with things Egyptian—"Moses an Egyptian." Freud refers directly to Artemidorus's *Oneirocriticon* at the beginning of *The Interpretation of Dreams*; and bases his analysis of Leonardo on a reference to Horapollo, "Leonardo Da Vinci and a Memory of His Childhood" (*1910*; 1955), SE, 11:88–89. The argument about picture *versus* words is repeated once again, in the controversy between Lacan and Laplanche, as to whether the unconscious is the condition of language (Laplanche) or language is the condition of the unconscious (Lacan): see Jean Laplanche and Serge Leclaire, "The Unconscious: A Psychoanalytic Study," *French Freud: Structural Studies in Psychoanalysis,* Yale French Studies, no. 48 (1972):118–78; originally in *L'Inconscient,* VIᵉ Colloque de Bonneval (Paris: Desclée de Brouwer, 1966); see Lacan's introduction to Anika Lemaire, *Jacques Lacan,* trans. David Macey (London: Routledge & Kegan Paul, 1977). This argument will lead to two kinds of psychoanalytic aesthetics: compare and contrast with Lacan's theory of the gaze, the philosophical Kleinianism of Richard Wollheim, *On Art and the Mind* (Cambridge: Harvard University Press, 1974), esp. "The Mind and the Mind's Image of Itself," 31–51. Wollheim's would be the strongest alternative to a Lacanian hermeneutics.

11.   Grant, *Letter and Spirit,* esp. 62–63; for a summary of the development of orthodox exegesis, see R. P. C. Hanson, *Allegory and Event: A Study of the Sources and Significance of Origen's Interpretation of Scripture* (London: SCM Press, 1959). For the orthodox horror of Gnostic infinite exegesis, see Irenaeus *Adversus Haereses* 2.19.1; see also J. Fineman, "Gnosis and the Piety of Metaphor: The Gospel of Truth," *The Rediscovery of Gnosticism: Studies in the History of Religion,* ed. B. Layton (Leiden: Brill, 1980). Not all Gnostics are docetic, including the Valentinians; see E. Pagels, "Gnostic and Orthodox Views of Christ's Passion: Paradigms for the Christian's Response to Persecution?", also in *The Rediscovery of Gnosticism.*

12.   Erich Auerbach, "Figura," in *Scenes from the Drama of European Literature,* trans. R. Manheim (New York: Meridian, 1959), 11–76 (originally published in *Neue Dantestudien* [Istanbul, 1944], 11–71).

13.   Quintilian *Institutio Oratoria* 8.6.14–15; cf. Cicero: *Orator* 94; *De Orat.* 3.166.

14.   Thomas Wilson, *The Arte of Rhetorique* (1553) (Gainesville, Fla.: Scholars' Facsimiles & Reprints, 1962), 198.

15.   "But the greatest thing by far is to be a master of metaphor. It is the one thing that cannot be learned from others; and it is also a sign of genius, since a good metaphor implies an intuitive perception of the similarity in dissimilars," *Poetics*, 1459A 5–6, in *The Basic Works of Aristotle*, ed. R. McKeon (New York: Random House, 1941), 1479. For Aristotle on metaphor and proportional analogy, see *Poetics*, 1457B 6–33.

16.   Abraham Fraunce, *The Arcadian Rhetorike* (1588), ed. Ethel Seaton (Oxford: Basil Blackwell, 1950), 3–4.

17.   Roman Jakobson, "Linguistics and Poetics," in *The Structuralists: From Marx to Lévi-Strauss*, ed. R. and F. DeGeorge (New York: Anchor, 1972), 95. Hereafter cited as LP. Originally published in *Style and Language*, ed. Thomas A. Sebeok (Cambridge: MIT Press, 1960). Talaeus, *Rhetorica* (1548), cited in Lee A. Sonnino, *A Handbook to Sixteenth Century Rhetoric* (New York: Barnes & Noble, 1968), 121.

18.   Roman Jakobson and Morris Halle, eds., "The Metaphoric and Metonymic Poles," in *Fundamentals of Language* (The Hague: Mouton, 1971), 90–96. Angus Fletcher, *Allegory: The Theory of a Symbolic Mode* (Ithaca: Cornell University Press, 1964), 1–23; see also Graham Hough, *A Preface to the "Faerie Queene"* (London: Gerald Duckworth, 1962), 106ff.

19.   LP, 95.

20.   George Puttenham, *The Arte of English Poesie* (1589), facsimile reproduction (Kent, Ohio: Kent State University Press, 1970), 196.

21.   Fletcher, *Allegory*, 279–303.

22.   LP, 109.

23.   LP, 96.

24.   LP, 89–95.

25.   LP; see also Roman Jakobson, "Quest for the Essence of Language," *Diogenes*, 5, no. 51 (1965): 21–37.

26.   Jurii Tynianov and Roman Jakobson, "Problems in the Study of Language and Literature," in DeGeorge and DeGeorge, *The Structuralists*, 82.

27.   Similarly, because messages about the code are selected from the code, Lacan denies the possibility of a radical concept of metalanguage: "There is the relation here of the system to its own constitution as a signifier, which would seem to be relevant to the question of metalanguage and which, in my opinion, will demonstrate the impropriety of that notion if it is intended to define differentiated elements in language." Jacques Lacan, "On a Question Preliminary to any Possible Treatment of Psychosis," in *Ecrits*, trans. Alan Sheridan (New York: W. W. Norton, 1977), 185.

28.   LP, 112.

29.   LP, 111.

30.   LP, 111.

31.   Rosemond Tuve, *Seasons and Months: Studies in a Tradition of Middle English Poetry* (Paris: Librairie Universitaire, 1933).

32.   Claude Lévi-Strauss, *The Raw and the Cooked: Introduction to a Science of Mythology*, trans. John and Doreen Weightman (New York: Harper & Row, 1970). Originally published as *Le Cru et le cuit* (Paris: Librairie Plon, 1964).

33.   Roman Jakobson, "Phonemic Patterning," in Jakobson and Halle, eds., *Fundamentals of Language*, 50–66.

34.   We are justified in thus assimilating /p/ with /b/ because at this stage the distinction between voiced and voiceless has not yet been made. "As the distinction voiced/voiceless has not yet been made, the first consonant may be shifting and sometimes indistinct, varying between types of /b/ and types of /p/, but still within a distinct family of sounds." R. M. Jones, *System in Child Language*

(Cardiff: University of Wales Press, 1970), 2:85. Our alphabet reflects this "family" orthographically, writing "p" as upside-down "b."

35.   Jakobson, "Phonemic Patterning," 51.

36.   Roman Jakobson, "Why 'Mamma' and 'Papa,'" *Selected Writings* (The Hague: Mouton, 1962), 1:538–45.

37.   Freud, *Totem and Taboo,* SE, 13:1–161, esp. 141–46.

38.   Thus *The Canterbury Tales* begins with a beginning already past the beginning, with the Ram already having run half his course. In liturgical iconography, this is the *first* period of "erring, or wandering from the way": "The whole of this fugitive life is divided into four periods: the period of erring, or wandering from the way; the period of renewal, or returning to the right way; the period of reconciliation; and the period of pilgrimage. The period of erring began with Adam and lasted until Moses, for it was Adam who first turned from God's way. And this first period is represented, in the Church, by the part of the year which runs from Septuagesima to Easter. During this part of the year the Book of Genesis is recited, this being the book which contains the account of the sin of our first parents." Jacobus de Voraigne, *The Golden Legend,* trans. Granger Ryan and Helmut Ripperger (New York: Longmans, Green, 1941), 1–2; cited in Robert P. Miller, *Chaucer: Sources and Backgrounds* (New York: Oxford University Press, 1977), 14. Adam's fall (which brings death into this world) is an affective projection of this origin-displaced-from-itself—a decisive example in our tradition of the way literature thematizes its own enabling displacement as sin. Woman, namely Eve, is the characteristic occasion of this disjunction, which is why in literature she is /ma/, not /pa/. From this Lacan develops a theory of desire.

39.   I am concerned here with the way literary structures are thought and so feel no obligation to restrict my argument to cases that explicitly instance Jakobson's phonological thesis; nevertheless, in the course of writing this essay, I have enjoyed collecting concrete examples, as in the first line of the *Iliad* from which I take my epigraph, where the wrathful Μῆ is joined to the stress on Πη in the first syllable of Lacan's and Achilles' Name of the Father. With regard to the pastoral tradition that I focus on in the essay, from Chaucer's Prologue through Spenser to Eliot, we should think of Marvell's "The Garden," which opens with another Pa-Ma:

> How vainly men themselves amaze
> To win the palm, the oak, or bays.

and tells another story of Eden lost through diacriticality:

> Two paradises 'twere in one
> To live in paradise alone.

There are also examples from the novel; for example, *Mansfield Park* or *The Charterhouse of Parma* (Parme), or "Stately plump *Buck Mu*lligan," or, my favorite, because its three syllables sum up Lacan's theory of the acquisition of language through the castration of the paternal metaphor: *Moby Dick* (the female version of which, of course, is *Madame Bovary*).

40.   Fletcher, *Allegory,* 174–80.

41.   The issue of Freud's and psychoanalysis' obsessionality is a subject for another essay. It takes the hermeneutic form of attempting to plug up what are thematized as gaps. The culminating moment of Freud's analysis of the obsessional Ratman comes, for example, when Freud's interpretation *participates* in the Ratman's deepest homosexual fantasies:

> Was he perhaps thinking of impalement? "No, not that; . . . the criminal was tied up . . ."—he expressed himself so indistinctly that I could not immediately guess in what position—" . . . a pot was turned upside down on his buttocks . . . some rats were put into it . . . and they . . ."—he had again got up, and was showing every sign of horror and resistance—"bored their way in . . ."—Into his anus, I helped him out.

"Notes upon a Case of Obsessional Neurosis" (*1909*; 1955), SE, 10:166. Murray Schwartz suggested this reading of the Ratman to me. I would say that we can follow out the same language and desire, not only in Freud's biography, but in psychoanalytic theory and metatheory—a hermeneutic sodomy. This anal thematic also follows from the structure of "Pa/Ma." I develop this point briefly in terms of the difference between a philosophical and a literary name in "The Significance of Literature: *The Importance of Being Earnest*," in *October* 15 (1981) [reprinted in this volume].

42.   "From the History of an Infantile Neurosis" (*1914*; 1955), SE, 17: "I should myself be glad to know whether the primal scene in my present patient's case was a phantasy or a real experience; but taking other similar cases into account, I must admit that the answer to this question is not in fact a matter of very great importance" (97).

43.   "Beyond the Pleasure Principle" (*1920*; 1955), SE, 18.

44.   SE, 19; 1961. "The Dissolution of the Oedipus Complex" (*1924*; 1961); "The Infantile Genital Organization" (*1923*; 1961); "Some Psychical Consequences of the Anatomical Distinction between the Sexes" (*1925*; 1961). Freud's psychoanalytic theory develops as a whole in exact imitation of the little boy whose sexual development the gender theory describes, with the theory itself passing through oral, anal, and phallic stages as it strives to develop a grown-up theory of desire. In the course of this canonical development, a moment of castration disavowal occurs in the essay "On Narcissism" (*1915*; 1961), in which Freud denies the importance of castration. The bad faith of this theoretical disavowal effects Freud's subsequent rethinking of psychoanalytic metapsychology, which is why his theory never fully resolves its Oedipus Complex and therefore never fully justifies, or even attains, the coherent theoretical genitality to which it aspires.

45.   "Interpretation of Dreams" (*1900*; 1953), SE, 5:525; see also SE, 4:111n.

46.   These themes run through all of Lacan's work. In *Ecrits,* see "The Mirror Stage as Formative of the Function of the I," "The Function and Field of Speech and Language in Psychoanalysis," "On a Question Preliminary to any Possible Treatment of Psychosis," "The Signification of the Phallus," and "The Subversion of the Subject and the Dialectic of Desire in the Freudian Unconscious." With regard to the subjective occultation induced by metaphor, see especially Lacan's formulas for metaphor and metonymy in "The Agency of the Letter in the Unconscious or Reason since Freud." See also J. Fineman, "Gnosis and the Piety of Metaphor."

47.   Kenneth Burke, *The Rhetoric of Religion: Studies in Logology* (Berkeley and Los Angeles: University of California Press, 1961); idem, "Terministic Screens," in *Language as Symbolic Action* (Berkeley and Los Angeles: University of California Press, 1966), 47.

48.   The "Pa/Ma" model phonologically instantiates what Heidegger describes more generally in terms of the history of metaphysics: "In the service of thought we are trying precisely to penetrate the source from which the essence of thinking is determined, namely *alētheia* and *physis,* being as unconcealment, the very thing that has been lost by 'logic.'" *An Introduction to Metaphysics,* trans. R. Manheim (New York: Anchor Books, 1961), 102. For Derrida's criticism of Lacan, see "Le Facteur de la vérité," in *La Carte postale: de Socrate à Freud et au-delà* (Paris: Flammarion, 1980); an early version of this in *Poétique/* 21 (1975); and a version of this in *Graphesis: Perspectives in Literature and Philosophy,* Yale French Studies, no. 52 (1975). For Derrida's criticism of Heidegger, which proceeds by applying Heidegger's critique of Western metaphysics to itself, see "'ὀυσία and γραμμή': A Note to a Footnote in Being and Time," in *Phenomenology in Perspective,* ed. F. J. Smith (The Hague: Martinus Nijhoff, 1970); "The Ends of Man," in *Philosophy and Phenomenological Research* 30, no. 1 (1969); and *Marges de la philosophie* (Paris: Minuit, 1970).

49.   Derrida, *Of Grammatology,* 57.

50.   For this reason, I think it is a mistake to assimilate Derrida and Lacan each to the other, and to see in the critical practice of both an equivalent response to textuality, e.g., Gayatri Spivak, "The Letter as Cutting Edge," *Literature and Psychoanalysis,* Yale French Studies 55/56:208–26; Barbara Johnson, "The Frame of Reference: Poe, Lacan, Derrida," in ibid., 457–505. This is to reduce the historical importance that their confrontation represents both for psychoanalysis and for philosophy. Derrida is very much son to Lacan's father, which is why he attempts the critical parricide of "Le

Facteur de la vérité" or *Positions*. In this sense, Derrida is quite right to characterize the Lacanian enterprise in terms of a passé Hegelian project. On the other hand, in accord with the Freudian paradigm, Derrida's philosophical success only makes the mortified Lacan that much more authoritative.

51. René Girard, *Violence and the Sacred* (Baltimore: Johns Hopkins University Press, 1977); originally published as *La Violence et le sacré* (Paris: Editions Bernard Grasset, 1972).

52. Thus *Of Grammatology* positions itself with an attack on structural linguistics, diacriticalizing difference itself, pt. 1, ch. 2, 27–73.

53. Spenser self-consciously expands Chaucer's description of months and seasons into allegorical eclogue when both he and Colin Clout, poet-hero of *The Shepheardes Calender,* look directly back to Tityrus-Chaucer, "the loadestarre of our language" (EK, quoting Lydgate in the preface), as to an inspiring origin and poetic source that now is lost forever: "The God of shepheards *Tityrus* is dead" (June, 81). In accord with a familiar Renaissance theory of poetic imitation, Spenser dramatizes the situation of the poet whose poetic desire grows out of his foredoomed effort to match an original model, which he lags after, from which he is distanced, and which he therefore adores:

> Goe lyttle Calender, thou hast a free passeporte,
> Goe but a lowly gate emongste the meaner sorte.
> Dare not to match thy pipe with Tityrus his style,
> Nor with the Pilgrim that the Ploughman playde a whyle:
> But followe them farre off, and their high steppes adore.

> (Envoy to December)

Out of the death of Tityrus, then, or the death of Chaucer (the reference to the pilgrim-ploughman is to pseudo-Chaucer, which Spenser would have taken as authentic; see Alice S. Miskimin, *The Renaissance Chaucer* [New Haven: Yale University Press, 1975], 93) comes *The Shepheardes Calender's* allegory of poetic vocation, which concludes only when Colin himself becomes an eclogue ("he proportioneth his life to the foure seasons of the year," Argument, December) and, in the December-winter of his years, forswears poetry the better to look forward to his death. There is play here, surely, as there always is in the poetry of silence, but the play is real-ized very seriously by Spenser when he omits the emblem at the end of December, thereby marking the conclusion of his poem with the very silence about which Colin merely speaks. This missing emblem at the end (corresponding to Chaucer's absent origin at the beginning of the Prologue) is the promise of yet more poetry, a way of concluding, without betraying, the impulse to indefinite extension which is the essence of allegory. This is the only appropriate conclusion to an eclogue, which, according to the hierarchy of genres, is but the poetical beginning of a poet's career—as EK reminds us in the preface to the poem. When Spenser gives up his Shepheardes weeds and Oaten reeds for the sterner trumpets of epic, he concludes the allegory of his own poetic vocation; at the same time, Colin Clout comes home once again, this time to see the image of his desire disappear (*FQ*, VI, 10; all Spenser citations are from *The Poetical Works of Edmund Spenser,* ed. J. C. Smith and E. de Selincourt [Oxford: Oxford University Press, 1912]).

For the infinite intentions of allegory, its intention to enclose its own infinities, see Bunyan's "Apology" for *The Pilgrim's Progress:*

> And thus it was: I, writing of the way
> And race of saints in this our gospel day,
> Fell suddenly into an allegory
> About their journey and the way to glory,
> In more than twenty things, which I set down;
> This done, I twenty more had in my crown,
> And they again began to multiply,
> Like sparks that from the coals of fire do fly.

Nay then, thought I, if that you breed so fast,
I'll put you by yourselves, lest you at last
Should prove *ad infinitum,* and eat out
The book that I already am about.

54.   See, for example, Gayatri Spivak: "Je voudrais suggérer la possibilité d'envisager la poésie dans une perspective exactement contraire [contrary to a common understanding that would see poetic language as that in which sign and sense are identical, as in music], comme ce qui tend à maintenir la distance entre le signe et le sens sémantique. J'aurai recours, pour étayer mon argumentation, à la notion d'allégorie." "Allégorie et histoire de la poésie: Hypothèse de travail," *Poétique* 8 (1971):427–41, 427.

In effect, I am suggesting that we are still entitled to retain the idea of the book, the poem, the artifact, as opposed to the infinite, indefinite, unbounded extension of what is currently called textuality. Thus I also maintain the critical force of the distinction between literature and its criticism, though, in accord with my argument above, this distinction only becomes speakable or operative relatively recently with the conclusion of psychoanalytic hermeneutics. What distinguishes the literary from its criticism is that the logocentric book or poem can effect the closure of representation precisely because it can structure silence, as silence, into its discourse, just as language does with the combination of consonant and vowel. The result is a polysemic, structured literary universe. If contemporary literary criticism can do this, it chooses not to and thus pronounces itself the ongoing voice of the inconclusive textuality it attributes to literature.

I realize that Derrida would characterize the distinction between structure and time which structuralism thus proposes as dependent upon, in Heidegger's phrase, a "vulgar concept of time" (see *Of Grammatology,* p. 72). My concern is, however, with how these concepts have functioned and continue to function as decisively powerful metaphors in the Western literary critical tradition, regardless of how philosophically untenable they may have been for thousands of years, for they have had their historical effect even as phantasms. More precisely, I am assuming here, and drawing the conclusion that follows from, the *necessary* and perennial "recuperation," if that is what it should be called, of *différance* by logocentrism. This is a decisive, repeated, and historical metaphysical occurrence, with its own directionality, one that determines the contours and the contents of both our literary and our philosophical traditions. Thus we will even agree that all literary texts share the same indeterminate meaning, for they can make even their own silence echo itself. But we conclude, therefore, for just this reason, that this predetermined indeterminacy of meaning in turn determines a specific literary significance. Only sentimentally can one deny the necessity or the specificity of this significance, which inexorably generates the (meaningless but significant, phantasmatic but nevertheless effective) distinction between the literary and the philosophico-critical. At the level of generality with which we deal here, this literary significance is, generically, the significance of literature, but, in principle, there is no reason why we cannot characterize this significance more precisely in local cases so as to speak to the thematic particularities of a given text's literariness. For example, if we were at present engaged upon a close literary reading of the opening lines of the Prologue to *The Canterbury Tales*—and it should be clear that we are not now so engaged—we would necessarily take up the way the lines erotically regret the allegorical Pa/Ma structure that they nevertheless refresh. Thus there is something immediately and noticeably disturbing about the way a traditionally female April is made to fecundate a traditionally male March, and this is the case not simply because conventional sexual agency is in this way instantly reversed. By tradition, woman is receptively but not ejaculatively moist, so it is doubly peculiar to introduce April in terms of "his shoures soote." The same thing is true in reverse for "The Droughte of March" (Mars), though in our literature the male is only rarely thematized as actively damp. Similarly, the image of veins, the conduit of liquid, themselves bathed by a liquidity in which they are immersed— "And bathed every veyne in swich licour"—establishes an antistructure of invaginated categoriality whose insides and outsides, contents and forms, introvertedly coalesce. Again, we have preparation in these first few lines for larger thematizations in *The Canterbury Tales* as a whole; for example, the stipulated reversal of sex roles and of the norms of specifically literary, bookish, patriarchal "Auctoritee" in the Prologue and the story of the Wife of Bath. Yet these and other imagined alternatives to the structure of allegorical desire all serve to reinscribe the initial literary authority of Pa/ Ma. Thus the riddle of the Wife of Bath, "What thyng is it that wommen moost desiren" (line 905), has as its answer the desire of women to be men:

> Wommen desiren to have sovereynetee
> As wel over hir housbond as hir love,
> And for to been in maistrie hym above.

(lines 1038–40)

All Chaucer citations are from F. N. Robinson, ed., *The Works of Geoffrey Chaucer* (Boston: Houghton Mifflin, 1957). The enigmatic power of the question of desire, which is the question that constitutes desire, thus survives even its answer, as was the case with Freud: "The great question that has never been answered and which I have not yet been able to answer, despite my thirty years of research into the feminine soul, is 'What does a woman want? (Was will das Weib?)'" Reported by Ernest Jones, *The Life and Work of Sigmund Freud*, ed. L. Trilling, S. Marcus (New York: Basic Books, 1961), 377. This is why Lacan, characteristically faithful to the literary tradition out of which psychoanalysis derives, says: "il n'y a pas de dames." *Le Séminaire de Jacques Lacan: Encore* (Paris: Éditions du Seuil, 1975), 54.

55. "The Splitting of the Ego in the Process of Defence" (*1940*) SE, 23:275–78. The essay takes up the "rift in the ego which never heals but which increases as time goes on," p. 276. Freud's illustrative example is castration disavowal.

56. Girard, *Violence and the Sacred*. See also Jacques Derrida, "Structure, Sign, and Play in the Discourse of the Human Sciences," in *The Languages of Criticism and the Sciences of Man*, ed. R. Macksey and E. Donato (Baltimore: Johns Hopkins Press, 1970), 247–65; also published in Derrida's *L'Écriture et la différence* (Paris: Editions du Seuil, 1967). If Girard is the theoretician of an unthinkable sacred Origin, and Derrida the philosopher of an indefinitely deferred Origin, then Foucault, with his inexplicable transitions between epistemic *frames*, is, despite his disclaimers, the post-structuralist of missing middles. And Foucault shares post-structuralist millenarianism: "In attempting to uncover the deepest strata of Western culture, I am restoring to our silent and apparently immobile soil its rifts, its instability, its flaws; and it is the same ground that is once more stirring under our feet." Michel Foucault, *The Order of Things* (New York: Vintage Books, 1970), xxiv; originally published as *Les Mots et les choses* (Paris: Editions Gallimard, 1966).

57. See Lacan, *Ecrits,* the end of "Function and Field of Speech and Language," esp. 106–7.

The Significance of Literature:
The Importance of Being Earnest

Man, poor, awkward, reliable, necessary man belongs to a sex that has been rational for millions and millions of years. He can't help himself. It is in his race. The History of Women is very different. We have always been picturesque protests against the mere existence of common sense. We saw its dangers from the first.

—A Woman of No Importance

What I am outlining here summarizes portions of a longer essay I have been writing on Oscar Wilde's *The Importance of Being Earnest.* For the most part, I will forego discussion of the play and focus on the way in which Wilde's farce precisely figures the problem of "The Self in Writing."[1] You will perhaps recall that Jack-Ernest, the hero of the play, discovers the unity of his duplicity when he learns that as an infant he was quite literally exchanged for writing in the cloakroom of Victoria Station, his absent-minded governess having substituted for his person the manuscript of a three-volume novel which is described as being "of more than usually repulsive sentimentality." As a result, because Jack-Ernest is in this way so uniquely and definitively committed to literature, with literature thus registered as his alter-ego, he is one of those few selves or subjects whose very existence, as it is given to us, is specifically literary, an ego-ideal of literature, as it were, whose form is so intimately immanent in his content as to collapse the distinction between a name and that which it bespeaks, and whose temporal destiny is so harmoniously organic a whole as to make it a matter of natural fact that his end be in his beginning—for Ernest is indeed, as Lady Bracknell puts it, paraphrasing traditional definitions of allegory, one whose origins are in a terminus.

Yet if Jack-Ernest is thus an ideal image of the relation of the self to writing, he is nevertheless himself a piece of literature, and therefore but a literary representation of the self's relation to literature, a fiction, therefore, if not necessarily a farce, and for this reason not to be trusted. This is the difficulty, I take it, that our forum has been established to address, recognizing that while the self and writing are surely implicated each in the other, perhaps even reciprocally constitutive each *of* the other, they are so in a way that at the same time undermines the integrity and the stability of both. This we can see even in the delicate phrasing of our forum's title, where the vagueness of the preposition, the problematic and diffusive metaphoricity of its innocuous "in"—"The Self *in* Writing"—testifies to the fact that the Self *and* Writing, as literal categories with their own propriety, can only be linked together in a figural discourse, which, even as it is spoken, calls the specificity and the literality of its terms into question. Strictly speaking, of course, "The Self in Writing" is an impossible locution, for in writing we do not find the self but, at best, only its representation, and it is only because *in* literature, in a literary mode, we characteristically, if illegitimately, rush to collate a word both with its sense and with its referent that we are, even momentarily, tempted to forget or to suspend the originary and intrinsic difference between, on the one hand, the self who reads, and, on the other, the literary revision of that self who is read.

This is to insist upon the fact that the self's relation to literature is not itself a literary relation, and that only a sentimental and literary reading will obsessively identify a thing with its word, a signified with its signifier, or the self with its literary image. This is also to avoid simplistic dialectical accounts of the act of reading— either identificatory or implicative—whose mechanical symmetries programmatically reduce the self to its idealization: the so-called "ideal reader" of whom we hear a great deal of late. Instead, this is to recognize that if we are to speak of the relation of the self to the writing in which it finds itself written, or, stylizing this familiar topos, if we are to speak of the relation of the self to the language in which it finds itself bespoken, then we must do so in terms of a critical discourse that registers the disjunction and the discrepancy between being and meaning, thing and word, and which therefore locates the self who is committed to language in its experience of the slippage between its immediate presence to itself and its mediated representation of itself in a symbolic system. Moreover, since Being, to be thought, must be thought as Meaning, even this self-presence of the self to itself will emerge only in retrospect as loss, with the self discovering itself in its own meaningful aftermath, just as Being can only be spoken in its own effacement, as Heidegger—not Derrida—has taught us.[2]

As is well known, it is thanks to the patient, painstaking, and rigorous labors of the tradition of psychoanalysis—a tradition that begins with Freud and which probably concludes with Lacan—that we possess a theoretical vocabulary sufficiently supple to capture this subject born in the split between self-presence and the representation of self. The insights of this tradition, however perfunctorily and schematically I refer to them here, are what enable us to situate the self of "The Self in Writing" in the metaphorical *in* whose very figurality is what allows us to articulate the problem in the first place, which is to say, in the same displacing place that Wilde—whose play will thematize this very problem of the place of the subject—places *Being,* midway between the import of *Importance* and a specifically literary pun on *Earnest*—the importance of *being Earnest*—as though the indeterminacy of meaning in turn determined *Being* as its own rueful double entendre.

What I should like to do here, however, recognizing, with some regret, that both the theory and the vocabulary of this psychoanalytic tradition are for many people both irritating and opaque, is translate its discourse into the more accessible and familiar terms of what today we will parochially call the Anglo-American speculative tradition. To that end, in an effort to sketch out the necessary contours of any psychoanalysis of what we can now identify as the "subject of literature," I would like to rehearse a rather well-known paradox of logical reference, first formulated in 1908 by Kurt Grelling, but of interest to philosophy from Russell at least through Quine.

The paradox itself is relatively straightforward. Let us say, says the paradox, that there is a set of words that describe themselves. For example, *polysyllabic,* the word, is itself polysyllabic, *short* is itself short, and *English* is itself English, an English word. Let us call such self-descriptive words autological, because they speak about themselves. In addition, let us further say that there is another set of words that do not describe themselves. For example, *monosyllabic,* the word, is not itself monosyllabic, *long* is not itself long, *French* is not itself French. Let us now agree to call this second set of words heterological, because these are words that speak about things besides themselves—allegorical words, because they speak about the Other (*allos,* other; *agoreuein,* to speak), a *logos* of the *heteros,* or, in Lacan's phrase, a discourse of the Other. Having stipulated these two sets, the autological and the heterological, the question then emerges: is the word *heterological* itself autological or heterological? And here we discover the paradox, for simply asking the question forces upon us the odd conclusion that if *heterological,* the word, is itself heterological, then it is autological, whereas, in some kind of contrast, if it is autological, then it is heterological. That is to say, given the definitions and a classical system of logic, the heterological can only be what it is on condition that it is what it is not, and it can only be what it is not on condition that it is what it is.

Thus formulated, the paradox possesses both an elegance and a banality, and in proportions that rather directly correspond to the brittle yet mandarin tenor and texture we associate with Wilde's farce. So too, the paradox very neatly summarizes the plot of *The Importance of Being Earnest,* since Ernest will himself be earnest only when he isn't, just as he will not be earnest only when he is. This paradoxical alternation and oscillation of the subject, a phenomenon to which the play gives the general label Bunburyism, but which Lacan would call *autodifférence,* is resolved at the end of the play when Ernest consults the book of the name of the fathers and discovers that his name "naturally is Ernest," and that therefore to his surprise, "all his life he has been speaking nothing but the truth."[3] Were there time, we would want at this point to conduct both a phonological and a phenomenological analysis so as to explain why all the names of the fathers in the list that Ernest reads begin with the name of the mother, "Ma"—Mallam, Maxbohm, Magley, Markby, Migsby, Mobbs, Moncrieff—and we would want also to know why this enumeration of nasal consonants not only spells an end to the labial phonemics of *Bunbury* but also marks the moment when denomination lapses into description, when use turns into mention, and when Truth itself arrives after the fact to validate what it succeeds.[4] Even putting these important questions to the side, however, we can see that the intention of the farce is to resolve the paradox of autology and heterology by enacting it through to its absurd reduction, to the point, that is, where Ernest becomes, literally becomes, his name.

Again, we might want to take this revival of the tradition of Paracelsian signatures, this coordination of signifier and signified, as indicative of the literary *per se.* But we can do so only if we recognize the specific twist or trope that literature gives to this semiotics of correspondence. For Ernest only becomes earnest when he recognizes in the heterology of words the paradoxical representationality of language, and thus discovers *in* the difference between a name and its thing the paradoxical difference *between* himself and his name. Ernest therefore inherits his name only to the extent that its significance is restricted or promoted to its nominality, only to the extent, that is to say, that it becomes a signifier of itself *as* a signifier, not a signified. This is indeed a paradigm of literary language, of language that calls attention to itself as language, just as the pun on *Earnest* in the title possesses its literary effect precisely because it *doesn't* mean its double-meaning and thereby forces us to register the word as just a word, significant of just itself, with no meaning beyond its palpability as a signifier. This is also why Wilde's play or farce on names is itself so important, for we may say that the special propriety of a proper name with respect to common nouns corresponds precisely to the specialized charge of literature with respect to so-called ordinary language—"so-called" because there could no more be an ordinary language without its fictive complement than there could be a natural language bereft of its fantasy of the propriety of proper names.[5]

Yet if this is a small-scale model, however general, of the literary, of language which stresses its literality, its letters, it is of course profoundly unlike the kind of ordinary language that philosophy, as opposed to literature, would instead prefer to speak—which is why, where literature depends upon the paradox of heterology, philosophy instead prohibits it, with the notion of "metalanguage," which keeps the orders of reference in their hierarchical place. Logicians are of course entitled to introduce whatever constraints might be required to maintain the coherence of their artificial systems, but this remains a merely logical, not a psychological, necessity, which is why Lacan, recognizing the fact that a subject of discourse might at any moment stumble into heterology, says that there is no such thing as "metalanguage."[6] This is not the place to make the point in any detail, but I would want to argue that philosophy of language has always been autological, and that this can be precisely documented by tracing its attitude towards proper names, from the *Cratylus,* where a name will imitate its thing, through the epoch of representation, where a name will uncomplicatedly point to its thing, through Russell and Frege, where the immediate relation of a word to its referent is replaced by the equally immediate relation of a word to its sense, through to speech act theory, where a word uncomplicatedly reflects its speaker's intention. Of late, there are signs that this realism of nominalism has begun to lose its philosophical prestige, for example, Saul Kripke's devastating critique of Searle's theory of nominality, a critique whose account of reference constitutes the exact inverse of Derrida's equally devastating critique of Searle's hypothesis of expressible intention. On the assumption that the enemy of my enemy is my friend, it seems possible that continental and Anglo-American philosophy might eventually meet in the course of these complementary examinations of the propriety or impropriety of names. Leaving these relatively recent indications to the side, however, we may say that the perennial philosophical dream of true language, of language that always means what it says, stands in marked contrast to literary language which can never mean what it says because it never means anything except the fact that it is saying something that it does not mean.[7]

This traditional difference is worth developing, for it allows us to define the self of "The Self in Writing" as both the cause and the consequence of the paradox subtending the autological and the heterological. That is to say, the self becomes the difference between a discourse of things and a discourse of words, a subject situated midway between the subject of philosophy and the subject of literature, between ordinary and extraordinary language, in short, again, between *Importance* and *Earnest*. Where philosophy self-importantly commits itself to autology so as to make of language a transparent vehicle for the signifieds of which it speaks, literature, in contrast, "Earnestly" forswears signifieds altogether for the sake of the heterological materiality of its signifiers. The self between them constitutes the necessity of their difference, so that the ancient quarrel between philosophy and literature thus takes place over the body of the self in writing, with philosophy wanting to do with its signifieds what literature wants to do with its signifiers, and with the self in writing testifying to the fact that neither can do either. A signifier, says Lacan, is what represents a subject to another signifier. Literature and philosophy are thus the signifiers of each other, names, in this sense, whose "sense," or let us say significance, is what their readers are.

Situated thus, as both elision and bar between these two equally inhuman desires, the self in writing finds his own human desire strictly circumscribed, a desire that we might characterize as a lusting of the autological for the heterological, a desire that leaves something to be desired. "My ideal has always been to love someone of the name of Ernest," but "Bunbury is dead." In psychoanalytic terms this would correspond to the transition from narcissistic to anaclitic object choice, or to the difference between the self before and after what psychoanalysis thematizes as his accession to speech. If we recall, though, that desire too is an effect of the language, that Eros is the consequence of Logos, then our paradox will produce the appropriate Freudian paradigm without recourse to the Freudian lexicon. For now, remembering their etymology, we may rechristen the autological as the autosexual, or rather, the homosexual, and we may equally revalue the heterological as the heterosexual. This leaves us with the psychoanalytic conclusion that the fundamental desire of the reader of literature is the desire of the homosexual for the heterosexual, or rather, substituting the appropriate figurative embodiments of these abstractions, the desire of the man to be sodomized by the woman. This is a specifically obsessional desire, but it is one that Freud luridly locates at the center of his three major case histories: Ratman, Wolfman, Schreber. This would also explain why the only word that ends up being naturally motivated in *The Importance of Being Earnest* is not *Earnest* but *Bunbury* itself, which was not only British slang for a male brothel but is also a collection of signifiers that straightforwardly express their desire to bury in the bun.[8]

With this cryptographic reference to the death that we always find buried in the logos of desire we are very close to the impulse to death that Freud assimilated to the wanderings of Eros. There is no time to pursue this connection further, but I would like in conclusion at least to draw the moral. In our literature the heterological is the trope of the autological, just as the heterosexual is the trope of the homosexual, just as woman is the trope of man. This accounts, respectively, for the semiotics, the syntax, and the semantics of our literature. So too does it account for its ethics. Asked to summarize her novel, the novel whose loss is responsible for the subject of the play, Miss Prism, the governess, says, "The good ended happily, and the bad unhappily. That is what Fiction means." So it does, but this embedding of the moral in a necessarily fictive register equally measures the cost of what we must therefore call the fiction of meaning, at least for so long as both the Self and Writing are accorded an authority that even Wilde's farce thus fails to deconstruct.[9]

Notes

Reprinted from *October*, no. 15 (Winter 1980), 79–90.

1.   This paper was delivered at the 1979 convention of the Modern Language Association, at one of the several panels associated with the forum on "The Self in Writing." The essay on *The Importance of Being Earnest* has now grown into a chapter on Wilde which will take its place in a projected book on literary names. The notes have been added for this publication.

2.   See, for example, *The Question of Being*, or "The Temporality of Discourse" in *Being and Time* (IV,68,d). Derrida's project is effectively to apply Heidegger's critique of Western metaphysics to Heidegger himself (e.g., "Ousia and Grammè: A Note to a Footnote in *Being and Time*," in *Phenomenology in Perspective*, ed. F. J. Smith, The Hague, Martinus Nijhoff, 1970; also, "The Ends of Man," *Philosophy and Phenomenological Research*, 30, no. 1 (1969), also in *Marges de la philosophie*, Paris, Minuit, 1972), so as to show that even Heidegger repeats, rather than revises, traditional metaphysical assumptions. For this reason, Derrida argues, even Heidegger's being must be put under further erasure as part of an ongoing, ever-vigilant, vaguely messianic, deconstructive Puritanism. There is no doubt that Derrida makes this point persuasively; the question is whether this measures a blindness or an insight on Heidegger's part, for what is important to Heidegger is the specificity of his history of Western philosophical speculation. What for Derrida is the mark of Heidegger's failure is also a measure, or so Heidegger would no doubt respond, of *necessary* metaphysical limits, a determination of the way it is and is not, or, more modestly and historically, the way it has always been and seems still to be. I am here assuming, following Derrida himself, that it is one of Western metaphysics' special and perennial pleasures to have itself deconstructed, and that for this reason we must register Derrida's always already predetermined *différance* within the horizon of its always eventual determinate recuperation. This is not a static balance: it has a direction, from pre-beginning to end, and this directionality also has its obvious metaphysical—not to mention its more obvious psychological—consequences.

3.   See "Le clivage du sujet et son identification," *Scilicet*, nos. 2,3, Paris, Editions du Seuil, 1970, 127. Note that the fracture is imaginary, not symbolic.

4.   I have elsewhere argued that the first phonemes, labial /papa/ or /baba/ and nasal /mama/, are acquired in accordance with a structure that determines specific literary themes. See "The Structure of Allegorical Desire," *October,* 12 (Spring 1980), 47–66 [reprinted in this volume]. This "Pa/Ma" model phonologically instantiates what Heidegger describes more generally in terms of the question whose asking renders metaphysics possible: "In the service of thought we are trying precisely to penetrate the source from which the essence of thinking is determined, namely *alētheia* and *physis,* being as unconcealment, the very thing that has been lost by 'logic'" (*An Introduction to Metaphysics,* trans. R. Manheim, New York, Anchor Books, 1961, 102). In the same way that Heidegger's *alētheia* is forsworn by *logos,* the babbling /papa/ through which speech is thought is irrevocably lost at the first moment of its meaningful articulation. So too, as Heidegger predicts, the hidden unconcealment of truth always reemerges in literature as death, farcically so in *The Importance of Being Earnest*: "Bunbury is dead. . . . The doctors found out that Bunbury could not live, that is what I mean—so Bunbury died." This has ramifications for the metaphorics of literary sexuality, a point to which I refer briefly above.

5.   I am assuming here Jakobson's "structuralist" definition of the literary function as that message which stresses itself as merely message, and I am assimilating this, for reasons discussed in the next footnote, to proper names, for these are nominal only because they stress their nominality. The opposition of meaningful words to meaningless proper nouns is therefore one instance of a more general system of opposition in *The Importance of Being Earnest* that manages consistently to juxtapose the serious against the trivial in such a way as to destabilize the integrity of meaningful binary antithesis. This is an obvious theme of *The Importance of Being Earnest,* which Wilde subtitled *A Trivial Comedy for Serious People* so as to make the very fact of farce a problem for whatever might be understood to be its opposite. In this way, by mentioning itself, Wilde's theme defends its own expression by referring the formal force of farce to an ongoing repetition internal to itself. This is, as it were, the asymptotic height of farce, which, because it is the genre that, as Marx suggested, imitates or repeats tragedy, is therefore the genre whose literary self-consciousness is formally most acute because thematically most empty.

The generic point is important because it shows us in what sense Wilde took his play seriously. For Aristotle, as for the serious literary tradition that succeeds him, tragedy is the imitation of a logically unified action, with the result that the hero of tragedy, his character subjected to his destiny, becomes a subjectivity as unified as the action he enacts. Hence Oedipus, whether Sophocles' or Aristotle's or Freud's, and the necessity historically attaching to the coherence of his person. It is this unity that makes tragedy, for Aristotle, the most important (and therefore the most "philosophical," see *Poetics,* chs. 9 and 26) of literary genres, just as this unity explains why, for Aristotle, Oedipus is both the perfect tragic object and the perfect tragic subject. In contrast, farce presents itself as the imitation of tragic imitation, as the action of imitation rather than an imitation of action, and the result of this double doubling is that the unifying logic of tragedy, which depends on imitation, is put into question by its own duplication. This sounds paradoxical, but it simply characterizes (1) the literary function as Jakobson describes it theoretically, i.e., the essential structural feature of literature, its recursive reflexivity, (2) the actual historical practice of a literary tradition that unfolds towards increasingly self-conscious forms and themes, i.e., the mocking mechanism, usually mimetic, by means of which literature regularly revives itself by calling attention to its conventions, for example, the way *The Importance of Being Earnest* (as do most of Wilde's plays) parodies what were in Wilde's theater established proprieties of stock and pointed melodrama (the crossed lovers, the bastard child, the discovery of origins that predetermine ends). On the one hand, this explains why farce is, again according to the tradition, of all poetic genres least important, for where tragedy is serious because it imitates something, farce is trivial because it imitates imitation (literature or literariness), which is nothing. (This is the case even if another principle of aesthetic meaning is substituted for imitation, for any notion of importance will be undone when it remarks itself.) But this is also why, on the other hand, because his play makes fun *of* tragedy, the farcically divided Jack-Ernest constitutes the most serious possible critique of Aristotle's tragically unified

Oedipus, which explains why a critical tradition dominated by Aristotle and by Oedipus finds nothing funny in the play's humor—Shaw, for example, who hated the play because he thought its wit was unimportant, or, more generally, the way the play is labeled marginal *because* the perfect farce.

As serious tragedy to trivial farce, so philosophy to literature, and for the same reasons. We know that this is historically the case if we recall that Plato condemns sophistic rhetoric for the way it mimes philosophy, or the way Plato objects to literature for being but an imitation of a more substantial truth. Again the same problem: if any given tragedy might be a perfect farce, how does philosophy defend itself from what would be its perfect imitation, for example Gorgias's parody of Parmenides, which "proves" through nominal negative existentials that "nothing exists." In this paper, therefore, I am not simply assuming that Wilde's farce reenacts, or represents within a literary mode, the traditional quarrel of literature with philosophy. More specifically, I am arguing, first, that Wilde's play on names, the play's thematic matter, is the objectification of its parodic manner; second, that it is by a commitment to the propriety of names that philosophy has historically defended itself against the possibility that it is its own dissimulation—a weak defense, given the historical failure, to this day, of the philosophy of proper names. Gorgias's onto-logical name-play is what makes rhetoric a *necessary* mockery of philosophy (as Gorgias describes it in one of the few surviving fragments)—"to destroy an opponent's seriousness by laughter and his laughter by seriousness"—just as it is the earnestness of "Earnest" that makes Wilde's "philosophy of the trivial" serious (as Wilde described it in an interview just prior to the play's premiere):

> What sort of play are we to expect?
>> It is exquisitely trivial, a delicate bubble of fancy and it has its philosophy.
>> Its philosophy?
>> That we should treat all the trivial things of life seriously, and all the serious
> things of life with sincere and studied triviality.

The relevant contemporary example is Derrida's parody, iteration, citation, quotation of Searle's defense of Austin (see "Limited Inc," *Glyph,* 2, Baltimore, Johns Hopkins University Press, 1977). Derrida not only makes fun of Searle's speech act theory and its notion of "copyrightable" proper names (for naively supposing some innocent principle of difference with which to distinguish a serious legitimate utterance from its nonserious illegitimate repetition); he also "proves" the point by making fun—a serious joke about corporeal anonymity—of "Searle-Sarl's" name itself.
6.   See "D'une question préliminaire à tout traitement possible de la psychose," in *Ecrits,* Paris, Editions du Seuil, 1966, 538. See also Jacques-Alain Miller, "U ou 'Il n'y a pas de meta-langage,'" *Ornicar?,* 5 (1975–1976), 67–72.
7.   Gwendolen and Cecily both give voice to this philosophical-philological, idealist dream of a true word: "My ideal has always been to love someone of the name of Ernest. There is something in that name that inspires absolute confidence." Or, "You must not laugh at me, darling, but it had always been a girlish dream of mine to love someone whose name was Ernest. There is something in that name that inspires absolute confidence." Here we can only briefly allude to the complications that make this confidence problematic. The traditional account of names—as formulated, for example, in Mill—is that a proper name has a denotation but not a connotation, in contrast to common nouns which have both. This is a muted version of Socrates' original philosophical desire for a language whose words would necessarily metaphysically correspond with things, a language, as it were, where words literally *are* the things they speak, for example the way *R,* as Socrates says in the *Cratylus,* is the letter of motion. The history of philosophy of names—from Aristotle's *Categories* on, through Stoic grammar, through medieval sign theory (via the incipient nominalism of Abelard, the modified realism of Aquinas, the straightforward nominalism of Ockham)—is a continual attempt somehow to nourish and to satisfy this initial philosophical desire for true language (for a truth *of* language, an *etymos* of *logos*) by lowering the ontological stakes to something merely nominal, for example, Mill's denotation theory where names merely indicate the things that formerly they were. The covert metaphysical assumptions embedded even in so modest a claim as Mill's were

brought out by Frege and Russell in their well-known criticisms of denotation theory, first, with the instance of negative existentials, where there is no referent to which a name might point (Odysseus, golden mountains, etc.), second, with the instance of identity propositions, which give off information even though the names they contain share the same referent (e.g., "The Morning Star is the Evening Star," "Cicero is Tully"—these being the traditional examples, as though philosophy can only think the problem under the aegis of the queen of desire, Venus, and the king of rhetoric, Cicero). For these reasons, lest language call things into being simply by denominating them, Frege and Russell, in somewhat different ways, introduced between a name and its referent a third term which is its "sense," arguing that while a name must have a sense in order to refer, it need not have a referent in order to make sense. As a result, no longer the essence of things, names now will merely mean them; they are truncated definite descriptions, to use Russell's phrase, and so not really names at all, but abbreviated bundles of meaning which are only contingently related to a referent.

There are several difficulties with this account of names which understands them to refer by means of what and how they mean. (Neither does such an account eliminate metaphysics by transferring its claims to the register of meaning. Cf. Quine: "Meaning is what essence becomes when it is divorced from the object of reference and married to the word," in "Two Dogmas of Empiricism," in *From a Logical Point of View,* Cambridge, Mass., Harvard University Press, 1961, 21.) First of all, it must be decided which aspects of nominal sense will be essential in determining a name's referent, for two people might well have entirely different senses of "Aristotle" and yet surely refer to the same person when they use his name (my "Aristotle" may only have written the *Poetics* whereas yours may have only tutored Alexander, and the real Aristotle might in fact have done neither). So too, there is an intuitive difficulty that comes of thinking names like *John* or *X* in fact possess a sense; this is to truncate description to a grotesque degree. These difficulties are not resolved even when the Russell-Frege account is "loosened up," as it is by Searle when, following Wittgenstein, he collates description and identification in a speech act theory of names. (See J. Searle, "Proper Names," *Mind,* 67 [1958]; see also the criticism of this in S. Kripke, "Naming and Necessity," in *Semantics of Natural Language,* ed. D. Davidson and G. Harman, Dordrecht, D. Reidel, 1972; also K. Donellan, "Speaking of Nothing," *The Philosophical Review,* 83 [1974]. Searle's essay should be read so as to notice the continuity subtending speculation about names in philosophy's *démarche* or retreat from ontology to psychology: first, names are the things to which they refer, then they imitate them, then they point to them, then they mean them, and then, in speech act theory, they "intend" them.) These difficulties, and others associated with them, have been much discussed in recent Anglo-American philosophy of language, by, amongst others, Donellan, Putnam, and, most influentially, Kripke. There is a good introduction to the topic, with bibliography, in *Naming, Necessity, and Natural Kinds,* ed. S. Schwartz, Ithaca, Cornell University Press, 1977. We cannot here discuss the technical issues involved, which begin primarily with the way names rigidly designate the same thing in all possible worlds (e.g., "The author of the *Iliad* might not have been born and might not have been the author of the *Iliad*" makes sense, but, substituting a name for the description, as in "Homer might not have been born and might not have been Homer" does not), but the force of this recent theory is to oblige philosophy, for the most part, to give up a strong sense theory of nominal reference. Instead, as a possible alternative, Kripke proposes to explain nominal reference by appealing to history, relating every use of every name to a series of hypothetical causal chains which reach back to every name's original moment of ostensive baptism. The consequences of Kripke's novel account are subtle and far-reaching, and they remain important even though, still more recently, their argument has itself run into difficulties. Here we must be content simply to allude to the problem, and to mention these two points relevant to our discussion above.

First, though Kripke can demonstrate that a name cannot have a sense in a strong way such that it determines its referent, he must still account for the information we receive in identity propositions. Here, as N. Salmon suggests, the only sense a name conveys is of itself as a name. See Salmon's review of L. Linsky's *Names and Descriptions,* in *The Journal of Philosophy,* 76, no. 8 (1979). This is why I feel justified in assimilating proper names to Jakobson's account of literariness.

Second, Kripke has recently discovered a paradox built into his theory of causal chains, for he imagines a situation in which a single origin legitimately produces a divided name. See "A Puzzle about Belief," in *Meaning and Use,* ed. A. Margalit, Dordrecht, D. Reidel, 1979. Kripke confesses himself unable to resolve the paradox even though it calls his entire account of proper names into question (and, as Putnam points out, the paradox also infects a theory of natural kinds; see Putnam's "Comment" on Kripke's puzzle, also in *Meaning and Use*). Kripke's puzzle is an inversion of Derrida's differentiated, reiterated origin, which is why I suggest in this paper that the two philosophers, though neither speaks to or of the other, share a common criticism of Searle, and also why I say that Anglo-American philosophy of language and continental phenomenology are now drawing together in their discovery of the impropriety of proper names. This is also why they both share an interest in the ontological status of the fictive. This is a point to be developed elsewhere. The history of philosophy of names should, however, be of special interest to students of literature, for in many ways the progressive and increasingly dogmatic subordination by philosophy of nominal reference, first to extension, then to expression, then to intention, and finally to a historicity that postpones its temporality, in many ways parallels the development and eventual demise of an aesthetics of representation. That is to say, the perennial awkwardness philosophy discloses in the collation of word and thing is closely related to the uneasy relation our literary tradition regularly discovers when it connects literal to figurative literary meaning. So too, there is an obvious affinity between what are the topoi of a long philosophical meditation on names—e.g., the integrity of a clear-cut distinction between analytic and synthetic propositions, or the possibility of an overlap between *de dictu* intensional meanings and *de re* extensional truth values—and what are the corresponding chestnuts of hermeneutic concern—e.g., the relation of an autonomous text to its external context, or the imbrication of form with content, or medium with message. In this paper, however, I am more concerned with the difference, rather than the similarity, between philosophical and literary names, for this difference possesses a specificity of its own, and it can be identified, as I say above, with the significance (which is to be distinguished from the meaning) of literature. We assume (with De Man) that all literary texts share the same indeterminate meaning, but we further argue (with Lacan) that this indeterminacy of meaning in turn determines a specific literary significance.

8.   Again we cannot develop the point adequately, but we would begin our psychoanalytic account with Freud's essay on "The Uncanny" (which concludes, by the way, with a reference to Wilde), and we would conclude it with Lacan's discovery that there is no such thing as woman. See "Aristote et Freud: L'autre satisfaction," also "Dieu et la jouissance de la femme," in *Le Seminaire, Livre XX, Encore: 1972–1973,* Paris, Editions du Seuil, 1975. We thus assume, in traditional psychoanalytic fashion, that the subject of Western literature is male, that its object, which exists only as an effect which puts existence into question (in the same way that Wilde gives us *Being* flanked by punning), is female, and that its project is therefore the representation of desire. We deal here with the metaphorics of literary sexuality, with the way the male is historically a subject undone by its female sub-version. Hence our epigraph, or the way Wilde's farce repeats the erotic melodrama through which it is thought: "It is called *Lady Lancing* on the cover: but the real title is *The Importance of Being Earnest*," letter to George Alexander, October 1894, printed in *The Letters of Oscar Wilde,* ed. R. Hart-Davis, New York, Harcourt, Brace, and World, 1962, 375–376. For a summary of the proposed *Lady Lancing,* a cuckoldry plot which Wilde describes as "A sheer flame of love between a man and a woman," see the letter to Alexander, August 1894, *The Letters of Oscar Wilde,* 360–362.

9.   Because the moral is imaginary it has that much more force. This speaks to an old psychoanalytic ambiguity, that the precursor of the super-ego is the ego-ideal. This raises a problem for Lacan's psychoanalytic topography, suggesting the possibility that Lacan's "Symbolic" is itself "Imaginary," the last lure of the "Imaginary." To discuss this problem properly we would necessarily consider a different literary genre: romance, which is not tragedy and is not farce, neither Oedipus nor his courtly derision.

"The Pas de Calais":
Freud, the Transference and
the Sense of Woman's Humor

If your four negatives make your two
affirmatives, why then the worse for my
friends and the better for my foes.

(*Twelfth Night* V.i.21–3)

For Freud and for Lacan both, transference is a theoretical idea initially developed to account for specific practical failures.[1] Freud thought out his first thoughts on transference in relation to the irresolute conclusion of the Dora case, the failure of which Freud attributed to his inadequate and belated appreciation of the nature and force of Dora's transference to his own person. Lacan developed his ideas about the transference in the course of a polemical attack on the analytic practice of ego psychology, where the stress on an interpersonal relation between two potentially autonomous egos, along with an accompanying concern for a neat—Lacan thought an inane—symmetry or complementarity between the patient's transference and the analyst's countertransference, provokes and secures, according to Lacan, an imaginary identification between patient and analyst that, of necessity, orients the direction of the treatment towards an exercise of power.[2] For Lacan, such a regime of power is the inevitable result of an inability to sustain a *praxis,* specifically an analytic practice, "in an authentic manner," and it is possible, of course, to see evidence of Lacan's claim—i.e., an instance of a psychoanalytic rush to power that derives its motivation from an inauthentic psychoanalytic practice—in Freud's treatment of Dora. At any rate, Freud's manhandling of Dora's transference has often been criticized on just these grounds.

Apart from the connection to the question of therapy, however, there is nothing at all theoretically new about the idea of transference. That affectively charged events in the present recapitulate, that they repeat, the psychic reality of infantile experience goes, so to speak, without saying in any psychoanalytic discourse, and it is only because this repetition can be put to use in therapy, when subjected to what both Freud and Lacan call "interpretation," that the phenomenon of transference deserves and receives any special theoretical attention.

As a phenomenon of repetition, however, the logic of the transference seems, at least at first glance, at odds with the logic of a therapy. It is assumed by psychoanalysis that the patient is compelled to repeat, Freud sometimes says "to act out," in his analysis precisely that which brings him to analysis, the patient thereby living out the nosographic past in the therapeutic present. This repetition is the essence of transference, its most urgent and insistent motivation, and this is irreducibly the case, since Freud characteristically gives an absolute quality to transferential repetition, as in the discussion of the repetition compulsion in *Beyond the Pleasure Principle,* the primary evidence for which Freud draws from the phenomenon of transference. But if transference in analysis is an enjoined, necessary repetition in the present of the past, how is it possible that any therapeutic innovation can ever be achieved? According to the theory of transference, every moment of analysis, from beginning to interminable end, is assimilated to, is fed into, a machinery of recapitulation such that the interventions of the treatment, the surprises of analysis—indeed, the very cure that analyst and patient together are embarked on—are nothing more than symptomatic repetitions of the illness they address. Hence the theoretical problem, a problem of recursive, replicating repetition, that the transference poses to the practice of psychoanalysts. Written out as transference, the therapeutic present necessarily becomes another chapter in the same old story, a story that already includes, and thereby renders secondary, the interpretative novelty that sees the way in which the story it interprets and partakes in is a repetition of the past.

This is why, for Freud and Lacan both, the *interpretation* of the transference becomes so central an issue. For there to be any consequence whatsoever of any analytic treatment, there must be a way in which the repetition of the transference becomes a repetition with a difference, one that makes a difference to or in a patient who would otherwise stay the same. For Freud this difference comes when the analyst, interpreting the therapeutic present, "obliges [the patient] to transform his repetition into a memory." "By that means," says Freud, "the transference, which, whether affectionate or hostile, seemed in every case to constitute the greatest threat to the treatment, becomes its best tool, by whose help the most secret compartments of mental life can be opened."[3] For Lacan, who conceives the process Freud called "Repeating, Remembering, and Working Through" in a somewhat different way, therapeutic innovation also derives from the interpretation of the transference, for, as Lacan puts it, "In order to decipher the diachrony of unconscious repetitions, interpretation must introduce into the synchrony of the signifiers that compose it something that suddenly makes translation possible—precisely what is made possible by the function of the Other in the concealment of the code, it being in relation to that Other that the missing element appears."[4] This is how Lacan explains the fact that the analyst, frustrating the patient's infinite demand, resisting the patient's seduction, opens up a way, through the interpretation of the transference, for the patient to speak the signifier of an unconscious desire. But again, for Lacan as for Freud, it is only through the translation opened up by the interpretation of the transference that the therapeutic process can come up with something novel: "My doctrine of the signifier is first of all a discipline in which those I train have to familiarize themselves with the different ways in which the signifier effects the advent of the signified, which is the only conceivable way that interpretation can produce anything new."[5]

How is it, though, that the interpretation of the transference, an active construction on the part of the analyst—whether understood as Freud's translation of unconscious material into conscious material, or as Lacan's account of the emergence, through "the different ways in which the signifier effects the advent of the signified," of an hitherto unspeakable signifier of desire—can escape the vicious hermeneutic circle traced out by the logic of transferential repetition? The question must be asked, for the very possibility of therapeutic practice hinges on its answer. Without an account of the way in which a psychoanalytic interpretation can be something other than a repetition of the same, the analytic patient will be thoroughly determined by the past that he perpetually and, in fact, in principle, *ab ovo* reenacts.[6] And this is a political as well as a clinical question, for the possibility of any psychoanalytic *political* practice—the possibility of any psychoanalytic intervention making any difference whatsoever—also hinges on a way of understanding how a psychoanalytic interpretation of the transference can be something other than a repetition of the same.

I put this point in this way in order to address the practical question of the relation in psychoanalysis of interpretation to transference. This is Lacan's question when he asks in "The Direction of the Treatment" "What is the place of interpretation?"[7] As answer, I want to suggest that the "place" of psychoanalytic interpretation, i.e., the *topos* of psychoanalytic interpretation—somewhat more strongly, the commonplace of psychoanalytic interpretation—is more strictly circumscribed by the structure of the transference than is usually recognized and that, for this reason, the effect of any psychoanalytic interpretation, regardless of its content, will always be the same, even when, and just because, it introduces something novel. I take as an exemplary example a dream Freud took from his analysis of what he called "a skeptical woman patient." Freud first reports this dream in *The Introductory Lectures,* but he was quite struck by the example, so much so that he added it to the 1919 edition of *The Interpretation of Dreams,* as a footnote at the beginning of chapter 7, where it is supposed to serve as confirmation of Freud's claim in the text that "one can reconstruct from a single fragment not, it is true, the dream—which is in any case a matter of no importance—but all the dream-thoughts."[8] Freud reports the dream as follows:

> A skeptical woman patient had a longish dream in the course of which some people told her about my book on jokes and praised it highly. Something came in then about *a "channel," perhaps it was another book that mentioned a channel, or something else about a channel . . . she didn't know . . . it was all so indistinct.*

As it stands, the dream presents a mystery, a mystery compacted in the vague amorphous "channel" which is all the woman patient carries with her as the residue of her dream. Following out his standard practice, however, Freud then asks the woman for her associations to this single fragment she remembers, and though, at first, registering resistance, nothing occurs to the woman in the context of "channel," the next day she comes up with a joke to the following effect. An Englishman and a Frenchman are on the ferry between Dover and Calais. For some reason or another, the Englishman, speaking French, announces: *"Du sublime au ridicule il n'y a qu'un pas."* "Yes," says the Frenchman, who is also a well-known author, *"le Pas de Calais,"* meaning, Freud takes the trouble to point out, that the Frenchman thinks France sublime and England ridiculous. As far as Freud is concerned, this joke resolves the mystery of the fuzzy "channel" of the dream. Freud explains:

> The *Pas de Calais* is a channel—the English Channel. You will ask whether I think this had anything to do with the dream. Certainly I think so; and it provides the solution of the puzzling element of the dream. Can you doubt that this joke was already present before the dream occurred, as the unconscious thought behind the element "channel"? Can you suppose that it was introduced as a subsequent invention? The association betrayed the skepticism which lay concealed behind the patient's ostensible admiration; and her resistance against revealing this was no doubt the common cause both of her delay in producing the association and of the indistinctness of the dream element concerned. Consider the rela-

tion of the dream-element to its unconscious background: it was, as it were, a fragment of that background, an allusion to it, but it was made quite incomprehensible by being isolated.[9]

Quite apart from the fact that this little story provides an excellent allegory of the relations between French and English psychoanalysis, there are many things to say about the way Freud takes this joke about his joke-book as corroborating confirmation of the fact that from a single fragment "one can reconstruct all the dream thoughts." To begin with, Freud's reconstructing story, his interpretation of the lady's transference, demonstrates the way in which Freud characteristically commits himself to a posture of hermeneutic authority and interpretive totality in the face of, or in response to, what is essentially enigmatic, constitutively shrouded, foundationally opaque—e.g., the "navel" of every dream that Freud refers to in *The Interpretation of Dreams,* which is where the dream "reaches down into the unknown," and which corresponds here to the lady's "indistinct channel."[10] Thus, equally characteristically, on the basis of his reconstruction, Freud can see the lady's resistance to psychoanalysis, objectified in the indistinctness of her "channel," as the proof of the psychoanalytic pudding, so that the lady's skepticism with regard to psychoanalysis becomes for Freud the symptomatic witness of psychoanalytic truth. We can recall that Freud does exactly the same in his analysis of Dora, another example of a skeptical woman patient whose resistance Freud's interpretations energetically resist, and another case in which Freud's interpretations work to transform ridicule of psychoanalysis into admiration.

At the same time, however, Freud's story about the story of the *Pas de Calais* does more than enable him, through interpretation, to get the last laugh out of and on the lady's skeptical derision. For the little joke about the *Pas de Calais* not only thematizes but also acts out both Freud's and Lacan's understanding of the psychoanalytic transference, to the extent, at any rate, that the skeptical lady's story about the crossing of the channel is the story, precisely, *of* the transference, the *Übertragung,* the *transferre,* the crossing over, back and forth, between patient and analyst that Freud's interpretation of the story says the story is about. It is necessary to understand this point quite literally, for it is not only at the level of the plot that the Frenchman's English Channel is something to be crossed. More concretely, the *"pas"* of the *"Pas de Calais"* functions, at the level of the letter, as the signifier that occasions and sustains the desire of the narrative in which it plays a part, and it does so precisely as Lacan says it should when he speaks about the way in which "interpretation must introduce into the synchrony of the signifiers that compose it something that makes translation [*la traduction*] possible." In a merely etymological sense, "transference" and "translation" here translate each other; they are the same word, meaning "to carry over," "to carry across," both of these being translations of the same idea in Greek, where such crossing over is called "metaphor," *metaphorein*.[11] The coherence and consistency of this metaphoric constellation allows us to say, speaking thematically, that the crossing of the *Pas de Calais*—from France to England, from the sublime to the ridiculous—is the metaphor of the Freudian transference, and this because such crossing amounts to the metaphor of metaphor itself. Accordingly, we can also say—but, again, only on the basis of this etymological derivation—that Freud's interpretation (his account of the skeptical deep meaning of the *Pas de Calais* joke) of the lady's indistinct "channel" makes "translation possible" by directly introducing metaphor into transference.

Grounded only in etymology, however, such an interpretation remains a merely thematic intervention, one that cannot carry any psychoanalytic weight, since the unconscious, for Freud as well as for Lacan, is concerned with signifiers not with signifieds. But with *pas,* as we hear it doubly articulated in the joke about the way the *pas* which is not but a step is not the same as the *pas* of the *Pas de Calais,* we have a situation in which, as Lacan puts it, "the signifier effects the advent of the signified, which is the only conceivable way that interpretation can produce anything new." Specifically, we have an instance of the consequential operation of metaphor as Lacan has formally defined it, as the substitution of one signifier by another signifier such that the signified of the first signifier is assimilated to the second signifier at the cost of the remarked exclusion of the initial signifier, whatever it might be, from the entirety of the signifying chain.[12] Lacan's well-known algorithms for the reciprocally constitutive interrelationship obtaining between the linguistic axes Roman Jakobson called metaphoric (paradigmatic selection) and metonymic (syntagmatic combination) formalize this point with only slightly comic over-precision. On the one hand, according to Lacan,

$$f\left(\frac{S'}{S}\right) S \cong S(+)s$$

expresses "the metaphoric structure, indicating that it is in the substitution of signifier for signifier that an effect of signification is produced that is creative or poetic, in other words, which is the advent of the signification in question. The sign + between ( ) represents here the crossing of the bar – and the constitutive value of this crossing for the emergence of signification."[13] On the other hand, according to Lacan,

$$f(S \ldots S')S \cong S(-)s$$

expresses "the metonymic structure, indicating that it is the connection between signifier and signifier that permits the elision . . . [of the original signifier, and where] the sign – placed between () represents here the maintenance of the bar – which, in the original algorithm [$\frac{S}{s}$, or signifier over signified; this is how Lacan represents Saussure's understanding of the sign] marked the irreducibility in which, in the relations between signifier and signified, the resistance of signification is constituted."[14] Taken together, the formulae explain why, as Lacan says—here speaking against a naively nominalist account of metaphor—"The creative spark of the metaphor does not spring from the presentation of two images, that is, of two signifiers equally actualized." Rather, "It flashes between two signifiers one of which has taken the place of the other in the signifying chain, the occulted signifier remaining present through its (metonymic) connection with the rest of the chain."[15] In this way, through the association of the signified of one signifier with an altogether different signifier, we can understand, on the one hand, how it is that a metaphor manages to signify anything whatsoever, at the same time as we understand, on the other, through a metaphor's necessary metonymic evocation of an absent or occulted signifier, what it is about a metaphoric signification that will strike us as peculiar, i.e., what Lacan here calls its "creative spark."

For Lacan, this metaphoric-metonymic correlation describes the generalized and normative operation by means of which "the signifier effects the advent of the signified," but the most explicit demonstration of this normative occurrence can be seen in that which makes a joke a joke. Thus, explaining his understanding of metaphor as a function of the substitution of one signifier for another, Lacan observes, "We see, then, that metaphor occurs at the precise point at which sense emerges out of non-sense, that is, at the frontier which, as Freud discovered, when crossed the other way produces the word that in French is *the* word *par excellence,* the word that is simply the signifier *'esprit.'*"[16] And it is in this inspired or spiritual comic sense that, we can say, the thematics etymologically embedded in the lady's jokes about the crossing of the English Channel are immanent to Freud's very registration of the transferential meaning of the joke. For the novelty produced by Freud's interpretation of the joke about the *Pas de Calais* and of the joke's relation to the skeptical lady's report of her dream consists in the way the metaphoric slippage it discloses between two "*pas*"s—again, the *pas* which is not but a step and the *pas* of the *Pas de*

Calais—is shown to correspond to the way the lady betrays "the skepticism which lay concealed behind her ostensible admiration." This is the translation *of* metaphor which is precisely that which the interpretation of the transference is supposed to bring about. Between the one and the other, between skepticism and belief, *il n'y a qu'un pas,* but for this very reason, as Freud interprets the joke, one moves, in one directed direction, *from* one *to* the other, i.e., from skepticism to belief because something missing is revealed. As skeptical dreamer, the lady dreams of a boat that travels derisively from France to England, from the sublime to the ridiculous, but because Freud gets the *point* of her joke, he can thereby reverse the lady's skeptical direction: to France and the sublime from England and the ridiculous. Passing from one *pas* to another, therefore, Freud's interpretation, which puts the lady in her trans-ferential place, translating her ridicule into admiration, exemplifies at least one of "the different ways in which the signifier effects the advent of the signified, which is the only conceivable way that interpretation can produce anything new."

The point that seems important to stress is that the scope of this interpretative novelty is very strictly determined, whether understood perfomatively or themati-cally. Coming from *passus, pas* is a simultaneously spatial and temporal figure of pas-sage as such, passage in a double sense, first, as the movement across a distance, a passage or a passing, second, at the same time, passage as the very distance, space, breadth, opening—again, the passage—that passage passes over. *Pas* is thus, at once, not only the place but also the movement of the transference, its own *double entendre* making a place, within itself, for the movement of the transference or, the other way around, motivating a movement that traces out a transferential place. Given the etymology of *pas,* this is obviously the case thematically, but the point to emphasize is that, when metaphoricity is understood as substitution, this is also the case performatively, for the moment there are two "*pas*"s—and that there are two "*pas*"s is the point of the joke (not to mention the fact that it takes two feet to take one step)—then there is metaphor, and where there is metaphor there is necessarily one *pas* missing that metaphor, as metaphor, will metonymically evoke. We arrive, therefore, at a rule or regulation: if there are two "*pas*"s—*pas-pas*—then there is always one *pas* missing, a principle of *pas-pas* → p̶a̶s̶-pas that Lacan characterizes as "the function of the other in the concealment of the code, it being in relation to that other that the missing element appears." This is why Lacan also says that the structure of metaphor determines for the subject the structure of desire, a desire, precisely, for the signifier whose loss presents the pace, footstep, track, the *pas,* of *translatio* itself.[17] According to Lacan, this lost signifier, present only in the echo that remarks its absence, both constitutes and sustains the desire of a subject who, entering language through metaphor, subjected to and by metaphor, thereafter comes continually upon this missing signifying link whose loss reverberates throughout the signifying chain. Lacan makes this point directly when he glosses the metonymy formula, in a passage that I earlier elided, namely: "It is the connection between signifier and signifier that permits the elision in which the signifier installs the lack-of-being in the object relation, using the value of 'reference back' possessed by signification in order to invest it with the desire aimed at the very lack it supports."[18]

In the terms presented by the skeptical lady's dream, we can say that *pas,* because it metaphorically traverses itself, necessarily surpasses itself, thereby motivating, in itself, its own crossing over upon or through itself, so as to leave over, as testamentary ruin of itself, as mark of its own internal diversion, the indistinct fragment of the "channel" from which, Freud says, "it is possible to reconstruct all the dream thoughts," i.e., from which it is possible—according to Freud's fundamental definition of what it means to interpret a dream—to identify the wish or desire that motivates the dreaming of the dream in the first place.[19] Correspondingly, this is also how "interpretation," for Lacan, "in order to decipher the diachrony of unconscious repetitions," "must introduce into the synchrony of the signifiers that compose it something that suddenly makes translation possible." Again, the "something" that makes translation possible, suddenly, is the substitutive structure of metaphor—*pas* for *pas,* one for the other, *pas de deux*—that precipitates the *pas du tout* or even the *pas tout*—the one which is not altogether one—whose noticed absence motivates the metonymic temporality of erotic yearning. It is not surprising, therefore, that psychoanalytic interpretation, introducing metaphor into transference, will find in every indistinct channel the double and divergent articulation of *pas*—a *pas de chat*—as it here emerges in what Freud says is the point of the lady's joke: a two-step *pas-pas* that always serves to initiate a single step in the right psychoanalytic direction, a direction we can identify, moreover, using the title of Lacan's essay on the transference, as "The Direction of the Treatment and the Principles of Its Power." *Pas,* as the passage over passage, carves out within itself, as the point of *any* joke, a signifying gap or opening across which and within which desire will always find its motive and also find its path. The structure of metaphor, in this way generating a novel signifier—a signifier not only of another signifier's signified but also of that other signifier's loss—thus necessarily, inexorably, provides the Freudian and Lacanian sense of the lady's humor.

It is important to notice the straightforward way in which the double *pas* of the *Pas de Calais* joke, as the smallest minimal unit of psychoanalytic wit, an "equivoceme," thus recapitulates and calls out for the central thematics of psychoanalytic therapeutics: the arrival of the symbolic name of the father—*PaPa*—whose "No"—*pas*—is also for Lacan "the function of the other in the concealment of the code, it being in relation to that other that the missing element appears." The predetermined appearance of this missing element, its predetermined appearance *as* missing—in the dream the indistinctness of the "channel," in the interpretation of the dream what Freud reveals as the lady's "resistance against revealing"—is what guarantees or warrants the Heideggerian erotics that makes the psychoanalytic truth into a fetish. Thus, the doubt of Woman—Freud's skeptical lady—functions as both frustrating object and animating impulse of Freud's hermeneutic want, something that keeps the analysis moving to and toward its interminable end. In either case, thinking of Truth or of Woman, the interpretation of the transference yields familiar topoi—the Truth of Woman or the Woman as Truth—in accord with the scenario of translation sketched out by the passage of *pas* through the detour of its round-trip passage through itself (that these topoi are typically marked with question-marks—"What is Truth?" "What does Woman want?"—follows from the way the punctuating structure of metaphor puts its own signification into question).[20] As his practice in the Dora case makes clear, Freud is true to this truth when he verifies psychoanalysis by reference to that which he insists escapes psychoanalysis, Dora's lesbian relation to Frau K., which "exists" as the excess to the phallocratic that the phallocratic presupposes.[21] But so too is Lacan true to this truth when in "Intervention on Transference," his commentary on the Dora case, Lacan puts his faith in the way the psychoanalyst, simply through his presence, brings dialogue to therapeutic discourse. "A subject," says Lacan, "is strictly speaking, constituted through a discourse. Whatever irresponsiblity, or even incoherence, the ruling conventions might impose on the principle of this discourse, it is clear that these are merely strategies of navigation intended to insure the crossing of certain barriers, and that this discourse must proceed according to the laws of a gravitation peculiar to it, which is called truth."[22]

This is the regulating, orientating truth of the psychoanalytic interpretation of the transference, the truth that guides the captain of the psychoanalytic loveboat as he ferries back and forth between the sublime and the ridiculous, and a truth that is measured by the force of its titanic effect. What we see here, however, in the story of the *Pas de Calais* story, if this story is in fact exemplary, is that the effect of the interpretation of the transference, its truth or the effect of its truth, is the specific clinical symptom of transference itself. And if it is the case that the very indeterminacy of the transference is what determines the truth of its interpretation as something determinate, as a question which, *as* question, is an answer one can always count on, then it becomes reasonable to wonder, after Freud, whether the repetition with a difference produced by the metaphoricity of *pas* is not, as such, a repetition of the same, a difference now that makes no difference precisely because it tells the same old story of difference itself. If so, this would explain why even the authentic practice of psychoanalysis is itself "inauthentic," which in turn would explain what seems to be a characteristically psychoanalytic rush to power. To put the point yet more bluntly and summarily, we can say that the *Pas de Calais* story is a narrative of metaphor that recounts the master narrative that specifically literary language always tells about its own figurality. To the extent that Lacan and Freud's theories of the transference recapitulate this story, we can say that psychoanalysis interprets and partakes in a very traditional literariness—and saying this tells us something important, for it helps to account, at least in part, for psychoanalytic power. For the same reason, however, we can also say that, in doing so, the novelty of psychoanalysis by no means introduces something new.

But, we must add, it is not only psychoanalysis that is thus constrained; so too is the skeptical lady, at least in so far as she is caught up in her reading of the psychoanalysis she wants to put down, as in the lady's dream, where "some people told her about my book on jokes and praised it highly." I have been arguing that the structure of metaphor that governs the transference also governs the interpretation of the transference, and that this accounts for the topical complicity that obtains between the transference and its interpretation. For the same reason, however, it can also be assumed that an engaged resistance to psychoanalysis will be equally subjected to the rule of metaphor. I say this bearing in mind Derrida's well-known "post-structuralist" criticisms of the "structuralism" of Lacanian psychoanalysis.[23] As I have meant to imply throughout, Lacan's account of the reciprocally constitutive correlation of spatializing metaphor (selection from a code of signifiers that are structured as a code by binary differentiation) and temporalizing metonymy (combination over time of metaphorically selected signifiers) formulates, using the now somewhat dated vocabulary of structuralist linguistics, the same logic of displaced spacing and deferred timing that Derrida attempts to give a name to with his neologism "*différance.*"[24] That such a theoretical homology joins Derrida to Lacan, and through him to a determined Freud, no doubt requires far more rigorous demonstration than can be presented here, but at the level of topoi it is relatively easy to adduce what seem to be instructive repetitions of the same. Leaving commonplaces such as Truth and Woman to the side, we can take "*pas*" as a convenient example, since this is the title Derrida gave to his reading of Blanchot. Commenting on a sentence of Blanchot—

"L'éloignement est ici au coeur de la chose" ("Distancing here is at the heart of things") from *"Les deux versions de l'imaginaire,"* in *L'Espace littéraire*—Derrida remarks:

> *La proximité du proche n'est pas proche, ni propre donc, et tu vois s'annoncer, de proche en proche, toutes les ruptures de sécurité. Quand je dirai* éloignement, *désormais, quand je le lirai dans l'un de ses textes, entends toujours le trait invisible qui tient ce mot ouvert sur lui-même, de lui-même é-loigné: d'un pas qui éloigne le lointain de lui-même. Pas est la Chose.*[25]

The proximity of the near is not near; nor, then, is it proper to itself, and you see revealed, nearer and nearer, all ruptures of security. When, henceforth, I say *distancing,* when I read it in his texts, you should always hear the invisible stroke that holds this word open upon itself, distanced from itself by a step which distances the distant from itself. Step and stop is the thing.

If this *"Pas,"* which *"est la Chose"*—*"cet étrange 'pas' d'éloignement"* (p. 124)—is not what Lacan called *"La chose freudienne,"* it nevertheless emerges as the same kind of intervening and interventive "interval."

> *Cet intervalle a la forme de l'absence qui permet le pas et la pensée, mais il intervient d'abord comme rapport du pas au pas ou de la pensée à la pensée, comme inclusion hétérologique de pas à pas, de pensée à pensée, pas sans pas ou "pensée sans pensée." Ce jeu (sans jeu) du sans dans ses textes, tu viens de voir qu'il désarticule toute logique de l'identité ou de la contradiction et qu'il le fait depuis "le nom de mort" ou la non-identité du double dans le nom.*[26]

This interval has the form of an absence that permits stepping (stopping) and thought, but it first intervenes as the link of step to step, or of thought to thought, as the heterological inclusion of step within step or of thought within thought, step without step or "thought without thought." You have just seen how this play (without play) of the "without" in his texts disarticulates any logic of identity or of contradiction, and how it does so commencing with "the dead-name" or with the non-identity of the double in the name.

And this is not for Derrida a contingent or an accidental or an anecdotal fact, for, as Derrida goes on to explain:

> *Il y a* toujours deux *pas. L'un dans l'autre mais sans inclusion possible, l'un affectant l'autre immédiatement mais à le franchir en s'éloignant de lui. Toujours deux pas, franchissant jusqu'à leur négation, selon le retour éternel de la transgression passive et de l'affirmation répétée. Les deux pas, le double pas désuni et à lui-même allié pourtant, l'un passant l'autre aussitôt, passant en lui et provoquant dès lors une double prétérition instantanée, mais interminable, voilà qui forme une limite singulière entre la garde et la perte, entre le souvenir aussi et l'oubli. Ils ne s'opposent pas plus dans leur différence infinie, que le pas à l'autre pas. Selon ce simulacre de cercle—retour éternel du double pas—celui qui dit "Viens" n'inaugure qu'à répondre déjà. Il suit celle qu'il paraît appeler et dont lui souvient son appel. "Faux-pas" du désir, comme il est dit dans* Le Pas au-delà, *et franchissement du cercle (pas de cercle). Pas est l'oubli, pas d'oubli doublement affirmé (oui, oui).*[27]

There are *always two* steps. One within the other but without any possible inclusion, one affecting the other immediately but by overstepping it while distancing itself from it. Always two steps, overstepping even their negation, in accordance with the eternal return of passive transgression and repeated affirmation. The two steps, the double step disunited and yet conjoined to itself, one immediately passing the other, passing within it and thereby provoking a double *praeteritio,* instantaneous but interminable: this is what forms the singular limit between keeping and losing, and between memory and forgetting as well. These are no more opposed in their infinite difference than is the one step to the other step. According to this simulacrum of the circle—eternal return of the double step—he who says "Come" only inaugurates by already replying. He follows her whom he seems to call and of whom the call recalls him. *Faux-pas* of desire, as it is put in *Le Pas au-delà,* and step outside the circle (no circle, circle step). *Pas* is the forgetting, the step and stop of forgetting doubly affirmed (yes, yes).

Again, there is more that must be said here, a lot more; but the quotations allow the suggestion that between the psychoanalytic *pas-pas* and the Derridean *"oui, oui"* il *n'y a qu'un pas,* which in turn would explain why Freud's "reconstruction" and Derrida's deconstruction both tend to circle (no circle) around the same fragmented point of difference. Men of *La manche,* the theory of the one plays (*"sans jeu"*) an old practical joke on the theory of the other.

Notes

Reprinted from *On Puns: The Foundation of Letters,* ed. Jonathan Culler (New York: Basil Blackwell, 1988), 100–114.

1.   This chapter was originally delivered, in somewhat different form, to a conference on "Lacan and the Transference" at The University of Massachusetts at Amherst, 14–16 June 1985.

2.   "I hope to show how the inability to sustain a *praxis* in an authentic manner results, as is usually the case with mankind, in the exercise of power." Jacques Lacan, "The Direction of the Treatment and the Principles of Its Power," *Ecrits,* trans. Alan Sheridan (New York, 1977), 226.

3.   Sigmund Freud, *The Complete Introductory Lectures on Psychoanalysis,* trans. J. Strachey (New York, 1966), Lecture 27, 444.

4.   Lacan, "Direction of the Treatment," 233.

5.   Ibid.

6.   *Ab ovo,* given the principle of deferred action, whereby a traumatic first time becomes such only retroactively, after the fact of itself, when activated by a second time that makes the first time primal.

7.   "Direction of Treatment," 232.

8.   Freud, *Introductory Lectures,* Lecture 7, 118; Freud, *The Interpretation of Dreams,* trans. J. Strachey (New York, 1965), 556.

9.   Ibid., 556–7.

10.   Ibid., 564. For Freud, skeptical jokes such as the lady's raise fundamental epistemological questions, *as* jokes, about the truth of the transference. The famous example is the joke about the two Jews in a railway carriage. "'Where are you going?' asked one. 'To Cracow,' was the answer. 'What a liar you are!' broke out the other. 'If you say you're going to Cracow, you want me to believe you're going to Lemberg. But I know you're going to Cracow. So why are you lying to me?'" Freud says of this joke: "The more serious substance of the joke is the problem of what determines the truth. The joke, once again, is pointing to a problem and is making use of the uncertainty of one of our commonest concepts. Is it the truth if we describe things as they are without troubling to consider how our hearer will understand what we say? Or is this only jesuitical truth, and does not genuine truth consist in taking the hearer into account and giving him a faithful picture of our own knowledge? I think that jokes of this kind are sufficiently different from the rest to be given a special position. What they are attacking is not a person or an institution but the certainty of our knowledge itself, one of our speculative possessions. The appropriate name for them would therefore be 'skeptical' jokes." *Jokes and Their Relation to the Unconscious,* trans. J. Strachey (New York, 1960), 115.

11.   Freud especially liked "translation" jokes, e.g., *"Traduttore—Traditore."Jokes,* 34 and 121.

12.   The chronology involved here—first and second signifiers—is, of course, merely heuristic, the subject's sense of successivity, which justifies affective terms such as "loss," being a function of structural retrospection.

13.   Jacques Lacan, "The Agency of the Letter in the Unconscious or Reason since Freud," *Ecrits,* 164.

14.   Ibid. For Lacan, the occultation of the original signifier is what makes this signifier the constitutive cause of the subject's desire for what this signifier signifies, structurally occasioned, by the operation of metaphor, as something lacking, and registered as such by metonymic resistance. For this reason, in the full explication of the formula for metonymy, which I have abbreviated above for the sake of clarity, Lacan explains the occultation of the original signifier in subjective terms. Meta-

phorization, through which the subject accedes to language, accounts for the production of the subject as a desiring subject; thus: "the metonymic structure, indicating that it is the connection between signifier and signifier that permits the elision in which the signifier installs the lack-of-being in the object relation, using the value of 'reference back' possessed by signification in order to invest it with the desire aimed at the very lack it supports. The sign – placed between ( ) represents here the maintenance of the bar – which, in the original algorithm, marked the irreducibility in which, in the relations between signifier and signified, the resistance of signification is constituted" (164).

15.   Ibid., 157.

16.   In a passage on the problematics of translation, Lacan footnotes this point so as to make the connection to Freud's joke-book explicit. "'*Esprit*' is certainly the equivalent of the German *Witz* with which Freud marked the approach of his third fundamental work on the unconscious. The much greater difficulty of finding this equivalent in English is instructive: 'wit' burdened with all the discussion of which it was the object from Davenant and Hobbes to Pope and Addison, abandoned its essential virtues to 'humour,' which is something else. There only remains the 'pun,' but this word is too narrow in its connotation" (ibid., 177).

17.   Related to this is the implicit foot fetishism informing Freud's account of Jensen's *Gradiva—"gradus"*: "step," "walk," "gait."

18.   Ibid., 164. See note 14 above.

19.   This is why the interpretation of the dream is complete when we arrive at its "navel," where it "reaches down into the unknown."

20.   Consider Freud's "specimen dream" of Irma's injection, where the question of Irma's desire elicits from Freud the uncanny image of the printed formula for "Trimethylamin," which Freud would have understood to formulate literally the chemistry of female sexuality (*Interpretation of Dreams*, 140). See also the question-mark whose punctuation interrupts normal syntax in Dora's dream of a letter she received from Frau K: "if you would like? you can come." Freud, *Dora: An Analysis of a Case of Hysteria*, trans. J. Strachey (New York, 1963), 114. The same question-mark governs Lacan's understanding of the relation of analyst to patient in the transference: "man's desire is the *désir de l'Autre*. . . . That is why the question *of* the Other, which comes back to the subject from the place from which he expects an oracular reply in some such form as '*Che vuoi?*' 'What do you want?,' is the one that best leads him to the path of his own desire—providing he sets out, with the help of the skills of a partner known as a psychoanalyst, to reformulate it, even without knowing it, as 'What does he want from me?' It is this superimposed level of the structure that will bring my graph (cf. *Graph III*) to completion, first by introducing into it as the drawing of a question-mark placed in the circle of the capital O of the Other, symbolizing by a confusing homography the question it signifies." Lacan, "The Subversion of the Subject and the Dialectic of Desire in the Freudian Unconscious," *Ecrits*, 312.

21.   "The longer the interval of time that separates me from the end of this analysis, the more probable it seems to me that the fault of my technique lay in this omission: I failed to discover in time and to inform the patient that her homosexual (gynaecophilic) love for Frau K. was the strongest unconscious current in her mental life. . . . Before I had learnt the importance of the homosexual current of feeling in psychoneurotics, I was often brought to a standstill in the treatment of my cases or found myself in complete perplexity" (*Dora*, 142). As Suzanne Gearhart observes, Freud eventually, at least sometimes, promotes this failure into a theoretical necessity, to a point where it precludes the possibility of a positive transference between a male analyst and a female homosexual, as in Freud's "Psychogenesis of a Case of Homosexuality in a Woman." See S. Gearhart, "The Scene of Psychoanalysis: The Unanswered Questions of Dora," in *Dora's Case: Freud—Hysteria—Feminism,* ed. C. Bernheimer, C. Kahane (New York, 1985) 117.

22.   Jacques Lacan, "Intervention on Transference," trans. J. Rose, in *Dora's Case*, 93.

23.   As in "The Purveyor of Truth," *Yale French Studies* 52(1975) (expanded on in *La Carte postale de Socrate à Freud et au-delà* (Paris, 1980)), *Positions,* trans. A. Bass (Chicago, 1981), *Spurs: Nietzsche's Styles,* trans. B. Harlow (Chicago, 1979).

24.   Arguing that every structuralist metaphor establishes the temporal metonymy of its own origin, and taking as example the way Roman Jakobson understands /pa/ to be the first phoneme of all speech, I have elsewhere discussed the way the "post" of Derridean "post-structuralism" is predicated by a specifically structuralist understanding of rhetorical figurality, in "The Structure of Allegorical Desire," *Allegory and Representation: Selected Papers from the English Institute, 1979–80,* ed. S. Greenblatt (Baltimore, 1981), 26–60 [reprinted in this volume].

25.   Derrida, "Pas (préambule)," *Gramma,* 3/4 (1978), 120.

26.   Ibid., 139.

27.   Ibid., 153–4.

The History of the Anecdote: Fiction and Fiction[1]

The sexual impasse exudes the fictions that rationalize the impossible within which it originates. I don't say they are imagined; like Freud, I read in them the invitation to the Real that underwrites them.

(Jacques Lacan, *Television*)[2]

A letter for me! it gives me an estate of seven years' health, in which time I will make a lip at the physician. The most sovereign prescription in Galen is but empiricutic, and, to this preservative, of no better report than a horse-drench.

(William Shakespeare, *Coriolanus*)[3]

This will be an informal, not a formal, talk, because when it happens, if it happens, that I give what I originally thought would be the practical illustration of what I have to say about the New Historicism—a discussion of the way Stephen Greenblatt's essay, "Fiction and Friction," anecdotally collates traditional, Galenic, gynecological medical theory with a reading of Shakespeare's *Twelfth Night,* an essay I take to exemplify the relation of what is called the New Historicism to, on the one hand, what is called literature and, on the other, what is called history—I will be speaking, for the most part, informally from notes rather than reading a paper.[4]

I say "if it happens" I speak about Greenblatt's essay because what I have to say about that essay builds on and derives from more general considerations, both formal and historical, regarding the anecdote, and so, as prefatory prolegomenon to what I want to say about Greenblatt's "Fiction and Friction," I am obliged to develop, in a general, programmatic, and schematic way, some introductory material. As a result, my presentation today will be somewhat ill-proportioned and promissory. In effect, I will be reporting on the early stages of a research project concerned both with the formal operation of the anecdote, understood as a specific literary genre, with peculiar literary properties, and also with a practical literary history of the anecdote insofar as the formal operation of the anecdote bears on the history of historiography, i.e., on the history of the writing of history. Initially, I want to argue, on formal grounds, that the anecdote, in significant ways, determines the practice of historiography, but, as can readily be imagined, such a formal argument will necessarily look to derive its evidentiary exemplifications from a practical literary history of the history of historiography. Accordingly, because what I have to say about the New Historicism only makes sense within the general context of this twofold project, formal and historical, I must spend some considerable amount of time rehearsing, sketching out, and summarizing the main lines of reasoning guiding my research. Hence the following, rather extended, set of preliminary remarks—quite extended; they will likely take up the entirety of the time I am allotted. If so, when time will tell, I plan at the end of these preliminary remarks very quickly to sketch out what it was I wanted to say about Stephen Greenblatt's essay, "Fiction and Friction," and its relation to the New Historicism, in the paper that, finally, in the event, I may not get to deliver today, a paper that is called "The History of the Anecdote: Fiction and Fiction."

When the idea of participating in this panel of the New Historicism first arose— it was as a panel of the New Historicism that this occasion was first described to me, and I am assuming this has some relation to the session's subsequently revised or further specified scope, "The Boundaries of Social History"—it was my plan to approach the topic in terms of what I will be calling the history of the anecdote, taking Thucydides's *History of the Peloponnesian War* as an exemplary text with which to illustrate the operation of the history of the anecdote, and taking Thucydides as an historically significant, because the first, example of a New Historicist. "New Historicism" is, of course, I need hardly say, a recently developed term or name, probably coined on the model of an older rubric, "The New Criticism," but perhaps also affected or inflected by leftover memories of 1950s and 1960s, maybe even earlier, philosophical discussions of history and historicism—e.g., Karl Popper on *The Poverty of Historicism* (which dates back to the thirties, but was published in the forties and was influential in the fifties), or R. G. Collingwood's *The Idea of History* (1946, but based on lectures delivered in the 1930s), or Thomas S. Kuhn's *The Structure of Scientific Revolutions,* published in 1962, which initiated, through what it had to say about the history of science, a popular debate about the scientificity of science, a debate that not only had considerable currency in the sixties and seventies but one that inspired a remarkable amount of interest outside the relatively narrow world of the philosophy of science (in many ways what Kuhn had to say about scientific paradigms and paradigmatic shifts really did, as has often been said to be mistakenly said, condition and prepare for the later, American reception of Michel Foucault).[5] Primarily designed to mark out or off a methodological and self-described interdisciplinary approach to the embedding—"embedding" being the metaphor regularly put into play—of cultural artifacts, primarily literary artifacts (what was then still called literature), within the particularity of their social context, the term, the New Historicism, was also intended to function more urgently as a rallying cry calling out for an increasingly explicit thematic concern with the historical as such in the professional practice of American academic literary criticism. In principle, therefore, because addressed to the entire field of literary studies, New Historicism was intended to sound out a very general appeal, across the disciplinary board, for an historiographic consciousness and conscience, but, in fact, for reasons the significance of which I will later want to consider, the first and central projects of the New Historicism, so-called, and understood in the restricted and restricting sense to which I have just referred, were materialized primarily in studies of the Renaissance, in studies of the English literary Renaissance in particular. We can add that the term "New Historicism" initially carried with it a somewhat polemical air, for the literary criticisms and literary histories that pronounced themselves New Historicist, and that thereby understood their own critical practices to amount to actions performed, quietly enough, in the name of history, presented themselves as overdue corrections of, or as morally and politically motivated reactions against, the formalism—more precisely and more pejoratively, the "mere formalism" (which, as such, as something merely or purely formal, was thought to be apolitical, sexist, hermetic, elitist, etc.)— that, for one good or bad reason or another, had come to be associated with everything from the kind of close, immanent textual readings said to be endemic to the New Criticism, to the scientistic, agentless, essentialist, cross-cultural typologizations said to be characteristic of what was called Structuralism, to the kinds of deconstructive, but still mandarin and still strictly textual, and therefore still formalist, and therefore still objectionable, formulations—mere formulations—identified with either the phenomenologically or the rhetorically conceived versions of what came to be called Post-Structuralism: Jacques Derrida, for example, on the one hand, Paul de Man, for example, on the other, not that these two hands did not let each other know what they were up to.

In the context of so relatively recent, datable, even dated, a derivation of the New Historicism—and here I will assume the inadequacies, both historical and intellectual, of this genealogical account, developed from the point of view of the history of ideas, of the emergence of the New Historicism as one merchandisable rubric amongst others in the not so free marketplace of academic ideas, are more or less obvious—my characterization of Thucydides as the first New Historicist might seem either overcoyly playful or anachronistically misplaced, especially if we recall the quite particular institutional demographic and economic factors that effectively conditioned and enabled the New Historicism to emerge as an identifiable intellectual posture in the first place.[6] But if the New Historicism, despite its programmatic refusal to specify a methodological program for itself—its characteristic air of reporting, haplessly, the discoveries it happened serendipitously to stumble upon in the course of undirected, idle rambles through the historical archives—can be identified in this way with the specificity of a particular moment in recent American academic intellectual history—i.e., if, in addition to pronouncing its name, "The New Historicism," we can also locate for that name a very local habitation within the extended apparatus of the University—it is still the case that it is also possible to relate the specificity of the New Historicism, as a practice, however amorphous, to a far more general, but still historically specifiable, impulse towards the historical; it is possible, that is to say, to relate the New Historicism to an historical tradition of historicity or of historicizing within which it, the New Historicism, can be understood to occupy a coherent time and place. In this more general context, it makes sense, for several reasons, to turn to Thucydides, or to what goes on in the name of Thucydides, for Thucydides, quite apart from questions of his historical influence, is not only exemplary of, but also constitutive of, in an historically significant way, Western historiographic consciousness.[7]

I will not really be turning to Thucydides in any detailed, pressured way, but it is important to recall, in a very general way, that Thucydides is usually taken to be, and praised for being, the very early, if not the first, historian who takes a scientific view of history; explicitly and implicitly, he introduces, discovers, presupposes—for my purposes there is no need to decide or to determine just which—regularizing, normativizing, essentializing laws of historical causation by reference to which it becomes possible to fit particular events into the intelligible whole of a sequential, framing narrative—a whole that then becomes a pattern in accord with which one can understand an altogether different set or sequence of historical events, again on the assumption these events are also subject to or exemplary of one or another principle of nomological historical succession. For Thucydides the identification of such recurrent patterns defines the eternal usefulness of his history, or, in the famous words with which he announces and defends the novelty of his historical project, novel, in comparison, say, to the memorializing, commemorative, more or less epideictic, historiography of Herodotus: "And it may well be that the absence of the fabulous from my narrative will seem less pleasing to the ear; but whoever shall wish to have a clear view both of the events which have happened and of those which will someday, in all human probability, happen again in the same or a similar way—for these to adjudge my history profitable will be enough for me. And, indeed, it has been composed, not as a prize-essay to be heard for the moment, but as a possession for all time."[8]

A clear view of particular events which have, in fact, happened, plus a way of understanding the happening of these events through a general or generic logic of succession such that how they happened is predictably recurrent thus defines the double focus of Thucydides's history—but a double focus necessarily directed towards a single end. To the extent Thucydides's successivity is successful, his characteristic "*meta touto*," "after this," i.e., the way Thucydides modulates within his history from one moment to another, will become the model for connecting any *touto*, any particular "this," to another, through some logic of sequential and transitional necessity that gives to every individual and singular event its representative historical significance. Only through the mutual coordination of a particular event and its genericizing narrative context—a coordination such that the particularity of the *touto*, the "this," and the generic, representative urgency of the logic of the *meta* reciprocally will call each other up—is it possible to identify or to attribute an historical significance either to a "this" or to a *meta*, for the specifically historical importance of either depends upon the way they each co-constitute or co-imply each other. We can say this more simply, in more familiar theoretical terms, by saying that Thucydides's "*meta touto*," his "metahistory"—to use, but with a different inflection, Hayden White's carefully considered phrase—works by collating structure and genesis.[9] Thus it is, for famous example, that Thucydides can frankly admit that the versions he reports of the speeches delivered at one or another particular deliberative or forensic occasion are not verbatim records of what, in fact, was said, but are nevertheless historically representative, i.e., historically significant examples of what was called for, at the occasion, by the logic of events: "The speeches are given in the language in which, as it seemed to me, the several speakers would express, on the subjects under consideration, the sentiments most befitting the occasion, though at the same time I have adhered as closely as possible to the general sense of what was actually said."[10] The Greek here translated as "the sentiments most befitting the occasion" is *ta deonta,* i.e., "the things necessary," and, as scholars have noted, for Thucydides the reconstruction of this occasional "necessity," the necessity of the historically significant occasion, is more important than, though not necessarily at odds with, "the general sense of what was actually said"—this kind of necessity, we can add, reappears within the rhetoricity of the speeches that are reported, which develop, scholars generally agree, arguments based on probability and plausibility, likelihood, generic types and situations, etc., in accord with sophistic modes introduced to the deliberative protocols and forensic atmosphere of the Athens of Thucydides's youth.[11]

Thus understood, as representative historiography of significant historical events—of events joined together by a narrative formation, where events derive historical significance because they fit into a representative narrative account, and where the narrative account derives its historical significance because it comprehends significant historical events—familiar questions relating to such an historiographic enterprise immediately arise. On the one hand, how, in principle, does one identify an event within an historical frame, first, as an event, second, as an event that is, in fact, historically significant? These are two questions because, in principle, there are events that are not historically significant events. Correspondingly, on the other hand, how do singular events warrant or call out for the contextualizing, narrative frame within which they will individually play their collectively intelligible parts, i.e., how does one arrive, from a multiplicity of occurrences, first, at a single and coordinating story, second, at an historically significant story, for, again, there are stories that are not, as such, historically significant?

Here the question of the apparently incomplete state of Thucydides's manuscript, the way, for example, it seems to trail off at its end, and the way this fact affects a determination of just when Thucydides wrote his history, acquires a more than biographical historiographic interest. In his very first paragraph, Thucydides recalls, retrospectively, that he began to write his history "at the very outset of the war," anticipating that this war would be "great and noteworthy above all the wars that had gone before."[12] Accordingly, we can, on the one hand, imagine Thucydides writing up his history as its events occurred and deriving or observing the overriding logic of their historical occurrence, the logic of their *meta,* in the course of their occurrence, guided here by his historian's foreknowledge of what would come to pass.

Alternatively, on the other hand, we can imagine Thucydides writing up his history at the end of the war, when the final scheme of its unfolding had at last revealed itself to him, i.e., after the fact of its facts, and that, like the owl of Minerva at dusk, or like Hegel at the end of history, he then returns to his historiographic beginning with its concluding and historically significant end already clearly in his retrospective sight. We can no doubt reasonably presume that Thucydides did both, that he wrote his history both backwards and forwards, in retrospection and prospection, but whether he did both, or more of the one or more of the other, his biographical relation to the history he lives through foregrounds the general questions I have mentioned regarding the way events and framing context are to be related to, derived from, or thought through each other.

I mention the biographical version of this familiar problematic relating to the intersection of event and context because it repeats the terms and situation of the medical historiographic model that, it is sometimes said, is an important influence on Thucydides's conception of historiographic method and succession.[13] Here I refer to the medical writings associated with the name of Hippocrates (what will later become Stephen Greenblatt's Galen), and to the stylistic, lexical, and procedural affinities that can be identified between them and the practice of Thucydides in his history. Thus, scholars have noted that Thucydides adopts the specifically semiological language and method of the Hippocratic doctor who is concerned to interpret the signs of disease for the sake of diagnosis and prognosis; Thucydides does the same with political, military, and social facts, and does so with the same language of diagnosis, prognosis, and natural cause, *prophasis*. So too, there are stylistic affinities between Thucydides's compressed and stressedly antithetical prose style and the noticeably aphoristic manner of the Hippocratic corpus—e.g., "Life is short, Art long," to quote the famous opening of the medical treatise that goes under the name *Aphorisms*—and it is possible to show that these stylistic patterns at the level of the sentence also correspond with larger architectural patterns in Thucydides's narrative, e.g., the balanced disposition of one speech against another, and related contrapuntal symmetries and formal arrangements that serve to organize the narrative. Finally, it seems clear Thucydides conceives his history under the model of the medical case history, so that the generic frame of Thucydides's events is imagined in conformity with the organic form of an Hippocratic illness that passes through significant events, i.e., symptoms, which appear in a coherent, chronological succession—one that starts from some zero-degree of vulnerable healthiness, that then builds up, through a series of significant symptoms, to a predictable dramatic climax at a moment of required "crisis" ("crisis" being a technical medical term), after which the disease completes its predetermined and internally directed course, when the patient either dies or returns to health.

In such medical case histories, which, in sufficient number, will generate a natural history of particular diseases, an abstract model for the integration of event within a context is straightforwardly disclosed, for it is within the frame of a natural and teleologically governed progress, passing inexorably from a beginning through a middle to an end, that the individuated, symptomatic moments of any given disease acquire their historical—in this case their medical historical—significance—in Thucydidean terms, the *logos,* or principle, of the facts, the *erga.* Thus the Hippocratic doctor, writing up a case history—of which there are many examples, e.g., in the treatise on *Epidemics*—will selectively report, for example, the acute fever of the third day, the bilious stools of the seventh, the yellow vomit of the sixteenth, the sedimented urine of the seventeenth, the crisis on the twentieth, the death or cure thereafter, and all these individuated moments, the days omitted as well as those selected, the items noticed as well as those ignored, acquire their specifically medical significance insofar as they are understood to articulate in their appearance or omission what are coherently segmented moments in the fluid and continuous unfolding of the internal logic of disease, just as their appearance is what circularly corroborates the doctor's nosological description of disease—his nomological narrative or *meta*—that turns the disease into an abstract, reified entity with its own representative, medical significance.[14] This double articulation is what allows the doctor to diagnose the disease, so that he can account for its events in terms of one medical explanation as opposed to another; this is what allows him to make, in similar cases, predictive prognoses of the course of an illness before it runs its course; and, in general, this is what allows him to believe in medical laws controlling the historical unfolding of beginning, middle, and end. For shorthand evidence of all this, especially evidence of the doctor's concern with establishing a continuous, seamless narrative of beginning, middle, and end, I quote the savvy opening of the Hippocratic treatise called *Prognostic*:

> I hold that it is an excellent thing for a physician to practice forecasting. For if he discover and declare unaided by the side of his patients the present, the past, and the future, and fill in the gaps of the account given by the sick, he will be the more believed to understand the cases, so that men will confidently entrust themselves to him for treatment. Furthermore, he will carry out the treatment best if he know beforehand from

the present symptoms what will take place later. Now to restore every patient to health is impossible. To do so indeed would have been better even than forecasting the future. But as a matter of fact men do die, some owing to the severity of the disease before they summon the physician, others expiring immediately after calling him in—living one day or a little longer—before the physician by his art can combat the disease. It is necessary, therefore, to learn the natures of such disease, how much they exceed the strength of men's bodies, and to learn how to forecast them. For in this way you will justly win respect and be an able physician. For the longer time you plan to meet each emergency the greater your power to save those who have a chance of recovery, while you will be blameless if you learn and declare beforehand those who will die and those who will get better.[15]

It is here, where the logic of event and context established by the historiography of the medical case history of the aphoristic Hippocratic corpus coincides with the logic of event and context as this is developed by Thucydides, that the anecdote, a specific literary form, is important, and this because, I want to argue, the anecdote determines the destiny of a specifically historiographic integration of event and context. The anecdote, let us provisionally remark, as the narration of a singular event, is the literary form or genre that uniquely refers to the real. This is not as trivial an observation as might at first appear. It reminds us, on the one hand, that the anecdote has something literary about it, for there are, of course, other and nonliterary ways to make reference to the real—through direct description, ostention, definition, etc.—that are not anecdotal. On the other hand, it reminds us also that there is something about the anecdote that exceeds its literary status, and this excess is precisely that which gives the anecdote its pointed, referential access to the real; a summary, for example, of some portion of a novel, however brief and pointed, is, again, not something anecdotal. These two features, therefore, taken together—i.e., first, that the anecdote has something literary about it, but, second, that the anecdote, however literay, is nevertheless directly pointed towards or rooted in the real—allow us to think of the anecdote, given its formal if not its actual brevity, as a *historeme,* i.e., as the smallest minimal unit of the historiographic fact. And the question that the anecdote thus poses is how, compact of both literature and reference, the anecdote possesses its peculiar and eventful narrative force.

Before addressing the question it is necessary to recall, however, as no doubt many of you have already recalled to yourselves, that everything I have said so far in

a loose, informal way about the integration of event and context has of course been
said before in far more formal and more pressured fashion in the philosophical
reflections on history, historiography, and historicism that come out of the experienced aftermath of Hegel's end of history. It is often said these days—I am thinking
here, in particular, of Jean-François Lyotard's remarks on the subject—that we live
now, especially when it comes to historiography, after the age of the *grand récit,* i.e.,
in an epoch for which the large story of the exigent unfolding of beginning, through
middle, to end, no longer carries any urgency.[16] Hegel's philosophy of history, with
its narration of the spirit's gradual arrival at its own final self-realizing self-reflection,
is the purest model of such an historical *grand récit,* and, from Dilthey on, the problem posed to history by such an absolutely and inevitably determined integration of
historical event and historical context has been, precisely, that, properly speaking,
such a history is not historical. Governed by an absolute, inevitable, inexorable teleological unfolding, so that, in principle, nothing can happen by chance, every moment
that participates within such Hegelian history, as the Spirit materially unfolds itself
into and unto itself, is thereby rendered timeless; such moments, we can say—and
here I am influenced by Jean-Luc Nancy's discussion of this issue in a paper on Hegel
and "Finite History"[17]—exist, for all intents and purposes, precisely because they are
intentional and purposeful, outside of time, or in a timeless present, and this because
their momentary durative appearance is already but the guaranteed foreshadow, the
already all but realized promise of the concluding end of history towards which ten-
dentiously, as but the passing moments in a story whose conclusion is already written, they tend.[18]

We can say, still speaking at a considerable level of generality, that it has been
the project of post-Hegelian philosophy, insofar as it remains Hegelian, and concerned therefore with history, to find some way to introduce into the ahistorical historicality of Hegelian philosophy of history some break or interruption of the
fullness and repletion of the Spirit's self-reflection, so as thereby to introduce to history the temporality of time. Thus Husserl, to take the central instance, attempts—I
am thinking of *The Origin of Geometry,* but the theme arises elsewhere, notably in
The Crisis of European Science—at the final limits of his phenomenological deduc-
tion of the transcendental ego's relation to its own necessary historicity, to find a way
to root the structural a priori of universal historicality in a natural, not a transcendental, origin, so as thereby to return the transcendental subject to an origin in time,
and to establish thereby a practical "universal teleology of reason."[19] This is Husserl's
late great turn to History—when the transcendental ego reflects alternatively on his

place in a specific tradition of philosophical reflection or, instead, on the natural attitude that is necessarily pregiven, as life-world, to his transcendental subjectivity—that marks the novelty of Husserl's late writings, distinguishing them from his earlier—in principle, ahistorical—eidetic, phenomenological reductions of ideas. So too with Heidegger, who attempts in *Being and Time,* which is dedicated to Husserl, to establish what he calls "authentic historicality" by developing the broken self-reflection by means of which the subject, through his opening to the finitizing futurality of death, appropriates his tradition, his past, and thereby enters into an existential relation to the temporality of *Dasein:*

> Only an entity which, in its Being, is essentially futural so that it is free for its death and can let itself be thrown back upon its factical "there" by shattering itself against death—that is to say, only an entity which, as futural, is equiprimordially in the process of having-been, can, by handing down to itself the possibility it has inherited, take over its own thrownness and be in the moment of vision for "its time." Only authentic temporality which is at the same time finite, makes possible something like fate—that is to say, authentic historicality.[20]

And, for Heidegger, what is true for the subject of history is also true for the methodology of the discipline thereof:

> The question of whether the object of historiology is just to put once-for-all "individual" events into a series, or whether it also has "laws" as its objects, is one that is radically mistaken. The theme of historiology is neither that which has happened just once for all nor something universal that floats above it, but the possibility which has been factically existent. This possibility does not get repeated as such—that is to say, understood in an authentically historiological way—if it becomes perverted into the colourlessness of a supratemporal model ... Even historiological disclosure temporalizes itself *in terms of the future.* The *"selection"* of what is to become a possible object for historiology *has already been met with* in the factual existential *choice* of Dasein's historicality, in which historiology first of all arises, and in which alone it *is.*[21]

(We should recall in passing that Heidegger's description of the individual's fateful history—*Schicksal*—is supposed to become collective with the idea of a communal Destiny—*Geschick*—and Being-in-the-world.)[22]

And so too with Jacques Derrida, whose deconstruction of Husserl's natural origin (the origin whose necessity Husserl develops in *The Origin of Geometry*) shows how such a transcendentally required natural origin (as the need for this natural origin is established by Husserl's phenomenological account of the historical a priori), is, *as origin,* necessarily conceived as a deferment, as a structural deferment, and must be so for history to happen:

> On the condition that the taking seriously of pure factuality follows after the possibility of phenomenology and assumes its juridical priority, to take factuality seriously as such is no longer to return to empiricism or nonphilosophy. On the contrary, it completes philosophy. But because of that, it must stand in the precarious openness of a question: the question of the origin of Being as History. . . . Here delay is the philosophical absolute, because the beginning of methodic reflection can only consist in the consciousness of the amplification of *another* previous, possible, and absolute origin in general. Since this alterity of the absolute origin structurally appears in *my living Present* and since it can appear and be recognized only in the primordiality of something like my *living Present,* this very fact signifies the authenticity of phenomenological delay and limitation. . . . Could there be an authentic thought of Being *as* History, as well as authentic historicity of thought, if the consciousness of delay could be reduced? But could there be any philosophy, if this consciousness of delay was not primordial and pure? . . . The impossibility of resting in the simple maintenance [nowness] of a Living Present, the sole and absolute origin of the De Facto *and* the De Jure, of Being *and* Sense, but always other in its self-identity: the inability to live enclosed in the innocent undividedness of the primordial Absolute, because the Absolute is *present* only in being *deferred-delayed* [*différant*] without respite, this impotence and this impossibility are given in a primordial and pure consciousness of Difference. Such a *consciousness,* with its strange style of unity, must be able to be restored to its own light. Without such a consciousness, without its own proper dehiscence, nothing would appear.[23]

(I cite Derrida at such length in part to recall the way he fits into or participates within a relatively familiar historical tradition of reflection on historicity, but also to make the point that people who criticize Derrida for ignoring history—and there are, lately, many such people—simply have not read him carefully enough, in my opinion, since history and the possibility of historicality have been central concerns for

Derrida, and also emphatically explicit thematic issues, in almost everything he has written.) In all these cases—Husserl, Heidegger, Derrida, and, let me say, what goes without saying, that I mention these three names only as a way of pointing to a larger continuity of concern—the self-completing self-reflecting of Hegelian historicity is turned over on itself, turned over and turned inside out, so as to open up in space a space for space to take its place, and to open up the temporality of time so that time can have its moment. (I will parenthetically add, for reasons that will become clearer later, that Jacques Lacan's category of the Real for the subject—different both from the Imaginary and the Symbolic—a Real that can be neither specularized nor represented, identifies the same kind of genuinely historical opening.)[24]

In this philosophical context, to which, of course, necessarily I here simply gesture, we can see the good historicizing heart and the good historicizing intentions of the New Historicism, of the New Historicism that is properly so-called. The oxymoron, if that is the right word for it, embedded in the rubric—the cheery enthusiasm with which the New Historicism, as a catchy term or phrase, proposes to introduce a novelty or an innovation, something "New," into the closed and closing historiography of successive innovation, "Historicism"—however unreflectingly or naively this oxymoron may initially have been intended, and whatever it was the old and unreformed "Historicism" of the New Historicism may have been supposed to have been before its supplanting renovation—this oxymoron is witness to or earnest of an impulse to discover or to disclose some wrinkling and historicizing interruption, a breaking and a *realizing* interjection, within the encyclopaedically enclosed circle of Hegelian historical self-reflection. This is why the term, "The New Historicism," as a term, is different in kind from the "New Criticism," the term that may have been its model. As a title, the New Historicism strives to perform and thereby to enable the project it effectively entitles, and thus to earn thereby its access to the real through the excess of its name. In this sense, if only in name only, the New Historicism amounts to a gesture which is the very opposite of Fredric Jameson's essentially ahistorical injunction in *The Political Unconscious* to "always historicize."[25]

All this brings us back both to Thucydides and to the anecdote, and, then, eventually, though in the mode of deferment, to Stephen Greenblatt. Given what I have said just now, and using Heidegger's topoi because they are familiar, we can propose the following provisional definition of history: History is what happens, I shall say, provisionally, when you combine Being and Time, the problem with this definition being—what makes it provisional—that it is necessary immediately to recognize that it is not necessarily the case that something happens when you combine Being and Time. To be sure, if it is the case that something necessarily happens when you com-

bine Being and Time, then you do indeed get history, but, specifically, what you get is the history of philosophy, i.e., the story of a philosophically exigent historical *démarche*—in this case, given the topoi with which we began, we get Heidegger's somewhat portentous, melodramatic rehearsal of the inexorable falling off, in Time, from Being, an ontological decline that, according to Heidegger, begins in the West the day after the pre-Socratics, and from which, according to Heidegger, we still deeply suffer in our Greco-German souls. But, again, such a history of philosophy is, as such, not historical, and again, this is the case because the story it reports is one that leaves no room for chance. It is necessary, therefore, to revise, at the start, our provisional definition of history, by saying that history is what happens when it happens—but as it only sometimes, in particular cases, happens—that something happens when you combine Being and Time.

And I specify the definition in these terms because this is how I propose to understand both the formal literary-referential peculiarity of the anecdote as well as the historical effects of the anecdote on the writing of history—these two features establishing, when they are taken together, what I am calling the history of the anecdote. In formal terms, my thesis is the following: that the anecdote is the literary form that uniquely *lets history happen* by virtue of the way it introduces an opening into the teleological, and therefore timeless, narration of beginning, middle, and end. The anecdote produces the effect of the real, the occurrence of contingency, by establishing an event as an event within and yet without the framing context of historical successivity, i.e., it does so only in so far as its narration both comprises and refracts the narration it reports. Further, I want further to maintain, still speaking formally, that the opening of history that is effected by the anecdote, the hole and rim—using psychoanalytic language, the orifice—traced out by the anecdote within the totalizing whole of history, is something that is characteristically and ahistorically plugged up by a teleological narration that, though larger than the anecdote itself, is still constitutively inspired by the seductive opening of anecdotal form—thereby once again opening up the possibility, but, again, *only* the possibility, that this new narration, now complete within itself, and thereby rendered formally small—capable, therefore, of being anecdotalized—will itself be opened up by a further anecdotal operation, thereby calling forth some yet larger circumcising circumscription, and so, so on and so forth.[26] Understood in this way, we can distinguish the anecdote from a strictly or restrictively literary formation in which what I am calling the anecdotal opening of narrativity either does not occur to begin with or, what turns out to be the same thing, occurs as a prescriptive opening that forever forecloses any

finalizing or finitizing closure. Correspondingly, understood in this way, we can distinguish the anecdote from nonliterary forms of reference (e.g., direct description, ostention, definition, etc.) that, relatively speaking, do not call up the narration of beginning, middle, and end, in which, therefore, there can be no dilation of narrative successivity, and from which, therefore, there exudes no effect of the real.

This double intersection, the formal play of anecdotal hole and whole, an ongoing anecdotal dilation and contraction of the entrance into history through the opening of history that lets history happen, leads me also to what is intended as a large, but nevertheless straightforwardly historical investigation regarding the historical collation of, on the one hand, the anecdote, or, as it is called in French, *la petite histoire,* the little story, and, on the other, the *grand récit,* where the *grand récit* must be understood as a symptomatic system of enveloping, narrativizing encapsulations called forth as response to the historical effect—the opening of history that lets history happen—that is first disclosed by, but that is then closed up by, anecdotal form. On the basis, therefore, of this formal theory of anecdote, I propose, then, to understand the history of historiography as the history of the effect of anecdotal form on the writing of history, a history that would follow out a traceable, genealogical progression from the medical case history of the aphoristic Hippocrates, through Thucydides, through collections, both in late antiquity and in the middle ages (where, in fact, Thucydides is not really powerfully present), of anecdotal historiography— not just things like chronicles or anthologies of narrative exempla, lives of saints and holy men, parables, collected sequences of stories that take place in larger frames, and the like, but also compilations such as dictionaries, riddles, jest-books, etc.— through the Renaissance, up to the present, up to, through, and, therefore, perforce, beyond the New Historicism.[27]

In this large history of historiography, Thucydides, I think, occupies not only an exemplary but also an historically significant place. Exemplary, because it would be possible to show that specific events and figures in Thucydides's historiography illustrate the effect of the operation of the aporetic anecdote on the writing of history—I refer here, in particular, to the way Thucydides discusses the plague, but also to the way Thucydides develops Alcibiades as a trickster figure who is never more Athenian than when he betrays Athens, these being central instances of the way the anecdotal works to introduce historicizing chance into Thucydides's otherwise, would-be Hippocratic history.[28] Exemplary, then, but also historically significant, however, or moreover, because Thucydides in this way, as a writer of the history of the anecdote, thereby stands, despite his totalizing historiographic intentions, for the

appearance of contingency, and therefore of History, in the very Athens that at this very moment is inventing and collating, as complicitous alternatives, a programmatically ahistorical Philosophy and Literature of the noncontingent.[29]

So too, in this grand, recognizably comic, universal history of historiography, the Renaissance would also occupy a crucial place, because, as is often said, it is in the Renaissance that there begins to develop a thematic historical consciousness— the subject as a subject *of* history—at the same moment that there begins to develop a correspondingly thematic scientific consciousness as well—Vico, say, on the one hand, Galileo, on the other—though it is important to recall that there also appears in the Renaissance, at least in the English Renaissance, though it only appears very briefly, an intentionally antiquarian historicism that sees itself as a refreshing alternative to large-scale moralizing, narrative historiography.[30] Here I am guided, historiographically, by Husserl, for whom the Renaissance marked the inauguration of what he called "The Crisis of European Science" because this is when the language of science, exemplified by Galileo's mathematical physics, grows so formal that the sedimented meanings embedded within it grow too faint to recall (in contrast to what happens with less formalized language) their origination in the natural lifeworld—for prime historical example, and from whence derives the significance of Husserl's *Origin of Geometry,* the way the magnitudes of Euclidean geometry are rewritten by Diophantus and Viete in algebraic terms (here I should say that I am very influenced by Jacob Klein's book on the history of mathematics, which is called *Greek Mathematical Thought and the Origin of Algebra,* and also by what Klein elsewhere wrote on Husserl and the history of science).[31] For Husserl, this forgetfulness nestled within formal scientific language marks the beginnings of crisis—a crisis no doubt conceived in medical terms—for the European spirit, for this is what initiates a specifically European tradition of empiricist, technicist scientism that works to divorce knowledge from experience. It is possible, however—indeed, given Husserl—it is *almost* necessary to imagine a corresponding crisis in historical consciousness inaugurated by the emergence in the Renaissance of a correspondingly technicist historicism that carries as its cost its unspoken sense of estranged distance from the anecdotal real. This locates what for me is the primary issue of my research project, at the same time as it suggests why the New Historicism is at once a symptom of and a response to a specifically Renaissance historiographic crisis. It is my suspicion or hypothesis that we can identify in the passage from the early to the late Renaissance, from the first humanist enthusiasm for the revival or rebirth of the past to the subsequent repudiation of the ancients in the name of science—e.g., Francis

Bacon—how it happened that historiography gave over to science the *experience* of history, when the force of the anecdote was rewritten as experiment. This is why, if ever it were to happen I give my paper, I want to consider the relation between Bacon's aphoristic essay style, along with the aphorisms of *The New Organon,* and Bacon's formulation in *The New Organon* of the idea of the crucial experiment for science, i.e., the experiment that would allow one to decide, if such an experiment could ever be devised, between competing theories. This is the type of "Prerogative Instance" Bacon calls *Instantiae Crucis*—traditionally translated as "Instances of the Fingerpost," i.e., what happens when one stands upon or at (and, hence, ex-ists) the intersecting "crossroads"—because, as with Oedipus's "crossroads," this marks the point where one decides which road to travel.[32] There is obviously much more to say about this, but I think this explains why the Renaissance is both a period and a period term, like the period and period term of the New Historicism, haunted by its failure to sustain the historical aspirations of its self-pronounced and new histori-cizing name. In Shakespeare's words—sonnet 59—"If there be nothing new, but that which is / Hath been before, how are our brains beguil'd, / Which laboring for inven-tion bear amiss / The second burthen of a former child."[33]

Finally, in this large history or historiography that I propose to develop in the light of the history of the anecdote, the New Historicism, as such, also occupies an exemplary and historically significant place, if not quite so crucial a place as that of Thucydides at the beginning of the history of historiography, or as that of the Renais-sance at a crucial moment of its development. (I should say that, as a period term, the "New Historicism" is less important than the "Renaissance.") For the aporetic operation of anecdotal form not only allows us to understand the chracteristic writ-ing practice of the New Historicism—those essays that begin with an introductory anecdote that introduces history, followed by amplification, followed by a moralizing conclusion that serves to put an end to history, this then sometimes followed by another anecdote that strives to keep things open (and here I will just assert that it is the prosaic and considerable achievement of the New Historicism to have rein-vented for our time the essay form invented by Francis Bacon in the Renaissance), but also helps us to understand why the initially eager reception of the New His-toricism was and is followed almost immediately by yet more eager and profoundly antihistorical impulse to reject it in the name of one or another presumptively more scientific or more idelogically secured and closed, and closing, historiographic approach. To see why this is the case, however, why in both the practice and recep-tion of the New Historicism the opening of history occurs for but a moment, it is necessary to look more carefully at an illustrative and representative example. Turning, therefore, from large things—Thucydides, the Renaissance, the history of historiography—to different—i.e., to Stephen Greenblatt's essay, "Fiction and Friction"—I here conclude my introductory remarks to the talk I will now not finally deliver, "The History of the Anecdote: Fiction and Fiction."[34]

Notes

Reprinted from *The New Historicism,* ed. Harold Veeser (New York: Routledge, Chapman & Hall, 1989), 49–76.

1.   This paper was originally delivered as a talk at a conference on "The New Historicism: The Boundaries of Social History," at the West Coast Humanities Institute, Stanford University, Oct. 9, 1987; I have retained the marks of oral presentation but have added and amplified some footnotes for the sake of publication in this anthology.

2.   Jacques Lacan, "Television," trans. Denys Hollier and Rosalind Krauss, *October,* 40 (Spring, 1988), 34.

3.   William Shakespeare, *Coriolanus,* 2.1.113–19; all subsequent Shakespeare quotations are from *The Riverside Shakespeare,* ed. G.B. Evans et al. (Boston: Houghton Mifflin, 1974).

4.   For the most part, I will be referring to the essay, "Fiction and Friction," as this originally appeared in *Reconstructing Individualism: Autonomy, Individuality, and the Self in Western Thought,* ed. Thomas C. Heller, Morton Sosna, and David Wellbury (Stanford: Standford University Press, 1986), 30–63. A somewhat revised version of this essay appears as a chapter in Stephen Greenblatt's *Shakespearean Negotiations: The Circulation of Social Energy in Renaissance England* (Berkeley: University of California Press, 1988), 66–93.

5.   Karl Popper, *The Poverty of Historicism* (New York: Harper and Row, 1977); originally published in *Economica* (1944/5. R. G. Collingwood, *The Idea of History* (Oxford: Clarendon Press, 1946; this book was published posthumously and is based on a lecture delivered at Oxford in 1936); Paul Ricoeur characterizes the way Collingwood conceives history as "reenactment" of the past as a history of the Same, this in contrast to, on the one hand, an exoticizing history of the Other or of individuated Difference, which Ricoeur associates with the work of Michel de Certeau and with poststructuralist historicisms in general, and, on the other, to what Ricoeur calls the history of the Analogous, i.e., tropological history, which he associates with the work of Hayden White; see *Time and Narrative,* vol. 3, trans. K. Blamey and D. Pellauer (Chicago: University of Chicago Press, 1988), esp. ch. 6, "The Reality of the Past," 142–156. Thomas S. Kuhn, *The Structure of Scientific Revolutions* (Chicago: University of Chicago Press, 1962); for a characteristic conjoining of Kuhn with Foucault, see Hilary Putnam, "Philosophers and Human Understanding," in *Scientific Explanation,* ed. A. F. Heath (Oxford: Clarendon Press, 1981), 106. For what is a traditional pejorative criticism of anecdotal historicism, see Benedetto Croce, *History as the Story of Liberty* (New York: W.W. Norton, 1941), chs. 3 and 4, 118–132.

6.   For responses to the New Historicism, understood as an academic event, see Louis Montrose, "Renaissance Studies and the Subject of History" and Jean Howard, "The New Historicism in Renaissance Studies," both in ELR, 16, no. 1 (Winter 1986). In general, it seems right to think of the New Historicism as an academic phenomenon specific to the U.S.A., something that is also true of what is called deconstruction. As with deconstruction, New Historicist criticism is regularly concerned with the "textuality" of its texts, something very foreign to the practical literalism of U.K. "materialism," on the one hand, and, on the other, the theoretical literalism one associates with Derrida. As has often been suggested, this is probably the result of the textualizing legacy left or left over by New Criticism, which opens up a specifically U.S.A. space for "textuality." As with a deconstructive

critic such as Paul de Man—who is profoundly influential in the U.S.A., but who has no urgent currency in either England or France—one suspects New Historicism, as a specific critical practice, will remain firmly rooted in the sensibility of the U.S.A. literary academy.

7.   One should note in this contextualizing context "The New History" (*Nea Historia*) of Zosimus, the sixth-century pagan historian of the decline of the Roman empire; see *Zosimus: New History*, trans. and ed. R. T. Ridley (Canberra: Australian Association for Byzantine Studies; Australian National University Press, 1982).

8.   Thucydides, *History of the Peloponnesian War*, C.F. Smith (Boston: Harvard University Press, 1962), 1.22.4; unless otherwise noted, all subsequent reference to Thucydides will be to this four-volume edition of *The Loeb Classical Library*.

9.   The terms are familiar from Jean Hippolyte's *Structure and Genesis in Hegel's Phenomenology*, trans. S. Cherniak and J. Heckman (Evanston: Northwestern University Press, 1974).

10.   Thucydides, Loeb, 1.22.4; an alternate translation, by John H. Finley, Jr., makes the point more clearly: "As for the speeches delivered by the several statesmen before and during the war, it proved difficult for me to report the exact substance of what was said, whether I heard the speeches myself or learned of them from others. I have therefore made the speakers express primarily what in my own opinion was called for under the successive circumstances, at the same time keeping as close as possible to the general import of what was actually said," *Thucydides* (Ann Arbor: University of Michigan Press, 1963), 94–95. Thucydides's practice should be contrasted to the way Livy, for example, stylistically and characterologically individuates the voices of particular speakers. In this connection, consider Freud's remarks at the beginning of his report of the case of Dora:

> The wording of these dreams was recorded immediately after the sitting, and they thus afforded a secure point of attachment for the chain of interpretations and recollections which proceeded from them. The case history itself was only committed to writing from memory, after the treatment was at an end, but while my recollection of the case was still fresh and was heightened by my interest in its publication. Thus the record is not absolutely—phonographically—exact, but it can claim to possess a high degree of trustworthiness. Nothing of any importance has been altered in it except in several places the order in which the explanations are given; and this has been done for the sake of presenting the case in a more connected form.

Sigmund Freud, *Dora: An Analysis of a Case of Hysteria* (1905), trans. J. Strachey (New York: Collier Books, 1963), 24.

11.   Finley, cited above, discusses *ta deonta*, p. 95. For discussions of Thucydides's style and its relation to the Sophistic tradition, see also John H. Finley, Jr., *Three Essays on Thucydides* (Boston: Harvard University Press, 1967), esp. ch. 2; Michael Grant, *The Ancient Historians* (New York: Charles Scribner's Sons, 1970), 88–101. In this context, Francis M. Cornford's objections to the absence of social or cultural history in Thucydides's strictly military history of the war amount to a criticism of Thucydidean style as well as of substance, ([*Thucydides Mythhistoricus*] London: E. Arnold, 1907).

12.   Thucydides, 1.1.1; as does Herodotus, Thucydides begins his history by marking his own proper name, describing himself—though this was not exactly the case—as an Athenian.

13.   On the relation of Thucydides to the Hippocratic corpus, see C.N. Cochrane, *Thucydides and the Science of History* (London: Oxford University Press, 1929); also Grant and Finley cited above; also Roland Barthes, "The Discourse of History," in *The Rustle of Language*, trans. R. Howard (New York: Hill and Wang, 1986), 127–140; see also, though in a somewhat different context, Carlo Ginzberg, "Morelli, Freud and Sherlock Holmes: Clues and Scientific Method," *The History Workshop*, 9 (1980), 5–36.

14.   Hippocrates, the Loeb Classical Library, ed. E. Capps et al., trans. W.H.S. Jones, vol. 1 (London: William Heinemann; NY: G.P. Putnam's Sons, 1923), 227–229.

15.   Hippocrates, the Loeb, vol. 2 (London: William Heinemann; Cambridge, MA: Harvard Univ. Press, 1923), 7–9.

16.   "In contemporary society and culture—postindustrial society, postmodern culture—the question of the legitimation of knowledge is formulated in different terms. The grand narrative has lost its credibility, regardless of what mode of unification it uses, regardless of whether it is a speculative narrative or a narrative of emancipation," Jean-François Lyotard, *The Post-Modern Condition: A Report on Knowledge* (Minnesota: University of Minnesota Press, 1984), 37.

17.   Jean-Luc Nancy, Lecture delivered at Berkeley, Spring, 1987.

18.   "While we are thus concerned exclusively with the idea of Spirit, and in the History of the World regard everything as only its manifestation, we have, in traversing the past—however extensive its period—only to do with what is *present*; for philosophy as occupying itself with the True, has to do with the *eternally present*. Nothing in the past is lost for it, for the idea is ever present; Spirit is immortal, with it there is no past, no future, but an essential *now*," G.W.F. Hegel, *The Philosophy of History*, trans. J. Sibree (New York: Dover Publications, 1956), 78–79. There is an enormous literature that discusses post-Hegelian philosophy of history; I cite here some works I find especially useful for thinking about the topic: Michael Murray, *Modern Philosophy of History: Its Origin and Destination* (The Hague: Martinus Nijhoff, 1970); Rainer Nägele, "The Scene of the Other: Theodor W. Adorno's Negative Dialectic in the Context of Postsructuralism," in *Postmodernism and Politics*, ed. Jonathan Arac (Minnesota: University of Minnesota Press, 1986), 91–111; Rodolphe Gasché, "Of Aesthetic and Historical Determination," in *Post-Structuralism and the Question of History*, ed. Derek Attridge, Geoff Bennington, and Robert Young (Cambridge: Cambridge University Press, 1987), 139–161. Stanley Cavell, criticizing Paul Ricoeur's criticism of the would-be "eventless" history of *Annales* school history, develops what in this context is an extraordinarily suggestive distinction between the "eventless" and the "uneventful"; see "The Ordinary as the Uneventful: A Note on the *Annales* Historians," *Themes out of School; Effects and Causes* (San Francisco: North Point Press, 1984), 184–194. I have also greatly benefited from discussions of the concept of "event" with John Rajchman; see his "Lacan and the Ethics of Modernity," *Representations*, 15.

19.   "If the usual factual study of history in general, and in particular the history which in most recent times has achieved true universal extension over all humanity, is to have any meaning at all, such a meaning can only be grounded upon what we can here call internal history, and as such upon the foundations of the universal historical a priori. Such a meaning necessarily leads further to the indicated highest question of a universal teleology of reason." "The Origin of Geometry," trans. David Carr, 378, included as appendix to Edmund Husserl, *The Crisis of European Sciences and Transcendental Phenomenology* (Evanston: Northwestern University Press, 1970), 353–378.

20.   Martin Heidegger, *Being and Time*, trans. John Macquarrie and Edward Robinson (New York: Harper and Row, 1962), 437.

21.   Heidegger, *Being and Time*, 447.

22.   It can certainly be said, especially if one recalls Heidegger's relation to fascism, that this idea of a communal destiny is too fateful indeed; similar objections can be raised to Gadamer's Heideggerian approach to hermeneutics and literary history; see Hans-Georg Gadamer, *Truth and Method* (New York: The Seabury Press, 1975).

23.   Jacques Derrida, *Edmund Husserl's "The Origin of Geometry": An Introduction*, trans. John P. Leavey, Jr. (Stony Brook, New York: Nicolas Hays Ltd., 1978), 151–153.

24.   I cite Lacan in order to account for a specifically psychologistic subject of history and to explain thereby a corresponding fetishization of time, e.g., the tidal wave of history; Lacan helps us to understand why the phenomenological experience of historicity is eroticized; see footnotes 26 and 34, below. Lacan's formulation of an unimaginable and unspeakable "real" accounts for my use of the word "anecdote," which, at least etymologically, means that which is "unpublished." For an anecdotal history that lives up to the erotics of its name, see Procopius's *Anekdota*, usually referred to as *Secret History*. On the erotics of the contingent real, see also the end of Jean-Paul Sartre's *The*

Psychology of Imagination where Sartre explains that the perfectly beautiful woman is not desirable because she does not elicit contingency (New York: Citadel Press, 1961 [c. 1948]), 282.
25. This is the opening sentence and also, Jameson says, the "moral" of *The Political Unconscious: Narrative as a Socially Symbolic Act* (Ithaca: Cornell University Press, 1981), 9.
26. Cf. Jacques Lacan's account of the *objet a* and the mark of the real:

> The very delimitation of the "erogenous zone" that the drive isolates from the metabolism of the function (the act of devouring concerns other organs than the mouth— ask one of Pavlov's dogs) is the result of a cut (*coupure*) expressed in the anatomical mark (*trait*) of a margin or border—lips, "the enclosure of the teeth," the rim of the anus, the tip of the penis, the vagina, the slit formed by the eyelids, even the horn-shaped aperture of the ear. . . . Observe that the mark of the cut is no less obviously present in the object described by analytic theory: the mamilla, faeces, the phallus (imaginary object), the urinary flow. (An unthinkable list, if one adds, as I do, the phoneme, the gaze, the voice—the nothing.) For is it not obvious that this feature, this partial feature, rightly emphasized in objects, is applicable not because these objects are part of a total object, the body, but because they represent only partially the function that produces them? These objects have one common feature in my elaboration of them—they have no specular image, or, in other words, alterity. It is what enables them to be the "stuff," or rather the lining, though not in any sense of the reverse, of the very subject that one takes to be the subject of consciousness. For this subject, who thinks he can accede to himself by designating himself in the statement, is no more than such an object.

"The Subversion of the Subject and the Dialectic of Desire in the Freudian Unconscious," *Ecrits: A Selection,* trans. A. Sheridan (New York: W.W. Norton, 1977), 314–315.
27. For example, it is generally agreed that the *Chronicle* (*chronikoi kanones*) of Eusebius, the fourth-century historian of the church, is the first attempt to compile a universal history of history, beginning with Abraham and extending up to the relatively recent past. Passed on through St. Jerome's Latin translation, Eusebius's history is enormously influential; it is not too much to say that Eusebius's *Chronicle is* the history of the West *in* the historiography of the West for the next twelve hundred years. What is worth remarking is that, though Eusebius's *Chronicle* is designed to unfold in tabular form the exigencies of providential history, its very format seems to call forth what I above characterize as the aporetic structure of the anecdote. Eusebius's *Chronicle* appears originally to have been organized so as to line up in its left-hand column events from sacred history, Jewish and Christian, and in its right-hand column what are chronologically corresponding events from secular or pagan history. Between the two columns, vertically descending down the page, were columns of numbers marking or dating successions of Olympiads, the reigns of different kings, etc., (for the sake of brevity, my description here somewhat distorts and very much oversimplifies the layout of Eusebius's manuscript). In principle, therefore, one reads the resulting table both vertically and horizontally, reading down the page for the progress of time, and across the page so as to compare and to contrast events in sacred and pagan history. Collating horizontal and vertical axes, one can thus behold the calendaric display of providential Christian history. However, in the light of scholarly reconstructions of Eusebius's original manuscript (the oldest extant version of the manuscript is not reliable), it is possible to see, at least for some crucial dates, the operation of an aporetic chiasmus in the horizontal collation of sacred and pagan events, with the result that the intersection of paradigmatic and syntagmatic axes seems to stand at odds with, rather than to confirm, straightforward Christian teleology. My remarks here are perfunctory (I intend to discuss Eusebius's *Chronicle* in more detail elsewhere, so too its relation to the Aristotelian idea of time as numbered, countable motion); I cite the example, however, for the sake of what I say later about a specifically Renaissance translation of the real of history into the real of science. For, speaking historically, it is

significant that Eusebius's history receives its first deeply critical revision when subjected to the pressure of Humanist, scientific philology—Joseph Scaliger's *Thesaurus temporum* (1606), a genuine instance of "New Historicism"—which is something that eventually will altogether undo "canonical" history as such. For a marvelously detailed account of the history of scholarly attempts to reconstruct Eusebius's original manuscript, see Alden A. Mosshammer, *The "Chronicle" of Eusebius and Greek Chronographic Tradition* (Lewisburg: Bucknell University Press, 1979); for Scaliger's revision of Eusebius, see Anthony T. Grafton, "Joseph Scaliger and Historical Chronology: The Rise and Fall of a Discipline," *History and Theory,* 14 (1974), 156–185; also, Anthony T. Grafton, *Joseph Scaliger: A Study in the History of Classical Scholarship* (Oxford: Clarendon Press, 1983).

28.   With regard to the plague what is important to note is that Thucydides both suffers and survives it, as opposed to the doctors who, Thucydides stresses, were especially and mortally susceptible to the disease: "For neither were the physicians able to cope with the disease, since they at first had to treat it without knowing its nature, the mortality among them being greatest because they were the most exposed to it, nor did any other human art avail," 11.47.3. Thucydides's description of the plague is usually taken to be the most Hippocratic moment in his history: hence, according to my argument, Thucydides's description of the plague is a precise Hippocratic description of what exceeds the Hippocratic, i.e., the doctor's account of what, as doctor, the doctor does not understand. Moreover, Thucydides stresses the surprising and chance appearance of the plague, introducing its report immediately after Pericles's "Funeral Oration," so that the plague appears as the diegetic surprise that determines, by inexorable chance, the history and "The History" of the Peloponnesian war. The inevitability of this accident corresponds to the equivocal prediction and retrospection with which Thucydides codes the plague. Thus, discussing the plague, Thucydides reports the following prophecy: "'A Dorian war shall come and pestilence with it'"; Thucydides then elaborates: "A dispute arose, however, among the people, some contending that the word used in the verse by the ancients was not *loimos*, 'pestilence,' but *limos*, 'famine,' and the view prevailed at the time that 'pestilence' was the original word; and quite naturally, for men's recollections conformed to their sufferings. But if ever another Dorian war should visit them after the present war and a famine happen to come with it, they would probably, I fancy, recite the verse in that way," 2.54. The always available indeterminacy of the determining prophecy establishes what I call the historeme as an equivoceme that generates the aporetic structure of the anecdote. Compare the fungibility of Thucydides's *loimos-limos* with Greenblatt's "the simple change of one letter" in the example of Marie/Marin that I discuss in footnote 34, below.

      What I say above about the anecdotal Alcibiades—i.e., Alcibiades as Mr. Anecdote—is intended to refer to the traditional question raised by Thucydides's characterization of this famous hero-villain: i.e., is the personality of Alcibiades representative of the personality of Athens? The answer to this question is yes, but this is precisely *because* Alcibiades betrays Athens, his person and his city both being the essence of that which lacks essence; this is related to traditional characterizations of democracy in terms of the lawless and unstable.

29.   The question at issue is the historical specificity of the invention in fifth-century Athens of the concatenated interrelationship between Philosophy, Literature, and History, each of these categories calling for or forth what will eventually become fixed forms of formal narration, i.e., the eventual and consequential striation of *logos* (Philosophy), *muthos* (Literature), and *historia* (History). This concatenation in turn establishes a specific psychology, which is why I speak of a psychologistic "subject of history." Thus, for example, anticipating what I say later about Bacon, the *De Augmentis Scientiarum* begins by "dividing" and "deriving" "human learning" "from the three faculties of the rational soul, which is the seat of learning. History has reference to the Memory, Poesy to the Imagination, and Philosophy to the Reason," *The Works of Francis Bacon,* ed. James Spedding, Robert Ellis, vol. 4 (London: Longman's and Co., 1875), 292. Bacon's anatomy here is traditional, but it suggests why invocations of, or appeals to, what is called "History," regularly presuppose, whether this is recognized or not, a particular faculty psychology that predetermines the results of what is called historical investigation; we can call this presupposition the subjective "burden of 'History.'" (Note

to deconstructionists: Bacon is careful in his next sentence further to subdefine "poesy" as "nothing else than feigned history or fables," but this does not freeze him in his tracks.) It is often said that the historical invention of "History" in fifth-century Athens is one consequence of the arrival of writing: e.g., "History becomes possible only when the Word turns into words. Only verbatim traditions enable the historian to reconstruct the past. Only where words that were lost can be found again does the historiographer replace the storyteller. The historian's home is on the island of writing. He furnishes its inhabitants with subject matter about the past. The past that can be seized is related to writing." Ivan Illich and Barry Sanders, *The Alphabetization of the Popular Mind* (San Francisco: North Point Press, 1988), ix. It is surely the case that the invention of writing is an instrumental or material cause of the invention of "History," but this is why it is all the more plausible, as I say below, to recognize in the Renaissance, which is when the invention of the typographic printing-press makes its mark, a decisive reinflection of historiographic textuality.

30.   On Renaissance antiquarian historicism, see D.R. Woolf, "Erudition and the Idea of History in Renaissance England," *RQ*, 60, no. 1 (Spring 1987), 11–48. We should also note that it is in the Renaissance that Thucydides returns to the history of historiography; thus, as M. I. Finley notes, Lorenzo Valla produces the first Latin translation in 1450–52, the first vernacular translation (in French, from Valla's Latin) appears in 1527, and the first English translation appears in 1550 (also, Hobbes's first publication is his translation of Thucydides, 1628); see M. I. Finley's introduction to *Thucydides: The Peloponnesian War* (New York: Penguin Books, 1972), 31. There are other indications of a Thucydidean revival, e.g., Boccaccio's paraphrase in the *Decameron* of Thucydides on the plague, the many references to Thucydidean events in various historiographic projects (e.g., by Raleigh and Bacon). In general, there is a movement or development in Renaissance Humanist historiography away from a markedly rhetorical historicist tradition (Isocrates, Livy, Plutarch) to what would be conceived, instead, as a more "scientific," presumptively Thucydidean, historicism, e.g., Machiavelli. It is in this context that Bacon can establish, as an impetus to scientific discovery, "A Catalogue of Particular Histories by Titles," e.g., "History of the Heavenly Bodies; or Astronomical History," "History of Rainbows," "History of Flame and of things ignited," etc., or, under the subcategory of "Histories of Man," such items as "History of Humours in Man; blood, bile, seed, etc.," "History of Excrements," "History of the Generation of Man," "History of Life and Death," or—thinking of Greenblatt's "Fiction and Friction"—"History of Venus, as a species of Touch," "Catalogue of Particular Histories," *Works,* ed. Spedding and Ellis, vol. 4, 265–270.

31.   Jacob Klein, *Greek Mathematical Thought and the Origin of Algebra,* trans. Eva Brann (Cambridge, MA: MIT Press, 1968) (in the same volume, see also Winfree Smith's introduction to this translation of Viete, printed as appendix); also, Jacob Klein, "Phenomenology and the History of Science," in *Philosophical Essays in Memory of Edmund Husserl,* ed. Marvin Farber (New York: Greenwood Press, 1968), 164–186.

32.   Francis Bacon, *The New Organon,* ed. F. H. Anderson (New York: The Liberal Arts Press, 1960), Book 2, sec. 36: 191:

> Among Prerogative Instances I will put in the fourteenth place *Instances of the Fingerpost,* borrowing the term from the fingerposts which are set up where two roads part, to indicate the several directions. These I also call *Decisive and Judicial,* and in some cases, *Oracular* and *Commanding Instances.* I explain them thus. When in the investigation of any nature the understanding is so balanced as to be uncertain to which of two or more natures the causes of the nature in question should be assigned on account of the frequent and ordinary concurrence of many natures, instances of the fingerpost show the union of one of the natures with the nature in question to be sure and indissoluble, of the other to be varied and separable; and thus the question is decided, and the former nature is admitted as the cause, while the latter is dismissed and rejected. Such instances afford very great light and are of high authority, the course of interpretation sometimes ending in them and being completed. Sometimes these instances of fingerpost meet us accidentally among those already noticed, but

for the most part they are new, and are expressly and designedly sought for and applied, and discovered only by earnest and active diligence.

Bacon's method, it will be recalled, is to be applied to "everything":

> It may also be asked (in the way of doubt rather than objection) whether I speak of natural philosophy only, or whether I mean that the other sciences, logic, ethics, and politics, should be carried on by this method. Now I certainly mean what I have said to be understood of them all; and as the common logic which governs by the syllogism, extends not only to natural but to all sciences, so does mine also, which proceeds by induction, embrace everything. For I form a history and table of discovery for anger, fear, shame, and the like; for matters political, and again for the mental operations of memory, composition and division, judgement and the rest; not less than for heat and cold, or light, or vegetation, or the like. But nevertheless, since my method of interpretation, after the history has been prepared and duly arranged, regards not the working and discourse of the mind only (as the common logic does) but the nature of things also, I supply the mind such rules and guidance that it may in every case apply itself aptly to the nature of things. And therefore I deliver many and diverse precepts in the doctrine of interpretation, which in some measure modify the method of invention according to the quality and condition of the subject of the inquiry.

Organon, Book 1, sec. 127.

In such quotations we can glimpse the force of the much remarked movement towards scientific method in the Renaissance—Port Royal, the Royal Society—a methodism or "doctrine of interpretation," that not only encompasses "natural philosophy" but also what will eventually come to be called "the sciences of man": "logic, ethics, politics," and all "the mental operations of memory, composition and division, judgement and the rest; not less than for heat and cold, or light, or vegetation, or the like." Hence, as Husserl noted, the scientism of seventeenth-century psychologism—Locke or Hume, or any purely "natural history of ideas"—a scientism that, according to Husserl, inexorably grows increasingly dissatisfying, to the point at which it potentiates a "crisis." It is in the context of this, for Husserl, historically momentous event that Bacon's identification of "*instantiae crucis*" is important, for it is precisely the idea or idealization of the so-called "crucial experiment" that will subsequently come to pose the greatest problem in the philosophy of science for establishing the scientificity not only of science but, specifically, of the *history* of science.

The classic essay on the matter is Pierre Duhem's essay of 1906, "Physical Theory and Experiment," in which he argues that "A 'crucial experiment' is impossible in physics" because it is never possible to devise an experiment that will unambiguously falsify a theory; trans. P. Weiner, reprinted in *Can Theories Be Refuted? Essays on the Duhem-Quine Thesis,* ed. Sandra G. Harding (Boston: D. Reidel, 1976), 1–40. For this reason, for Duhem, "*In the course of its development,* a physical theory is free to choose any path it pleases provided that it avoids any logical contradiction; in particular, it is free not to take account of experimental facts" (27). For this reason also, the history of science becomes a matter of ethical rather than experimental judgment, as Duhem says in conclusion: "The sound experimental criticism of a hypothesis is subordinated to certain moral conditions; in order to estimate correctly the agreement of a physical theory with the facts, it is not enough to be a good mathematician and skillful experimenter; one must also be an impartial and faithful judge." (39).

Subsequent to Duhem, and often discussed in relation to the famous Michelson-Morley experiments regarding the properties of light, the very idea of a crucial experiment has grown increasingly problematic. Despite a variety of attempts to support the idea of experimental falsification (e.g., Karl Popper, Adlof Grünbaum), philosophers of science for the most part strive, though in very different ways—e.g., the "(w)holism" of W.V.O. Quine and Carl Hempel, the "research programs" of Imre Lakatos, the "paradigm shifts" of Kuhn, the "Dadaism" of Paul Feyerabrand—to draw the moral for science that follows from the fact that there is no such thing as a "crucial experiment," i.e., that it is not possible to devise an experiment capable of deciding between competing theories (because the interpretations of the results of any such experiment are themselves "theory-laden" and because there is no unambiguous way to resolve the differences between "incommensurable theories"). In general, therefore, philosophy of science translates the logical or epistemological problems associated with the crucial experiment into a discussion of the sociology or the psychology or the politics of knowledge, and it is by no means clear such problems are altogether resolved by thus changing the merely thematic register of the discussion. What *is* clear, however, is that the aporias embedded in the idea of the crucial experiment—which I take to unpack the aporetic, chiastic structure of the anecdote, as I discuss it above—have obliged science to replace the idea of an inexorable *démarche* of scientific history with, instead, an ethics of the real. This was clearly not the case for Bacon, whose simple faith in inductive reasoning led him to see in the crossroads of the crucial experiment a way of establishing the inevitable narration of scientific history. For Bacon, scientific "history" functions as a version of "Sacred History"; like divine prophecy, the predictions of the scientist, as "history," report a "memory" of the future: "Prophecy, it is but a kind of history: for divine history has this prerogative over human, that the narration may be before the event, as well as after," *De Augmentis Scientarum,* 426. Contemporary philosophy of science, which possesses the courage of the convictions that give it its intellectual coherence, no longer believes in such "memory of the future"—it certainly distinguishes between prediction and prophecy—and this is a loss of faith that properly responds to the paradoxes embedded in the idea of the crucial experiment. It remains for historicism, which still for the most part believes in the crux of the crucial experiment, to do the same with its equally pious fidelity to the memory of the past.

33.   As I have argued elsewhere, the "second burthen of a former child," defines the "re-" of the late Renaissance as a baby born *as* abortion, i.e., as the issue of the "invention" *of* secondariness, *Shakespeare's Perjured Eye: The Invention of Poetic Subjectivity in the Sonnets* (Berkeley: University of California Press, 1986), 48, 145–146.

34.   Gesturing towards the paper to which the above stands as introduction, I would like here briefly to remark both what I disagree with and what I admire in Stephen Greenblatt's essay, "Fiction and Friction." First, however, it is necessary to rehearse the argumentative movement of Greenblatt's essay, which begins by recounting a striking story—indeed, an anecdote—about a certain Marie le Marcis, a household servant in Rouen, who, in 1601, surprises a fellow woman servant, a woman named Jeane le Febvre, with the revelation that she, Marie, is not the woman she appears to be but, in fact, a man. Following out the story, as its outlines emerge from surviving documentary evidence, Greenblatt goes on to narrate how, subsequent to Marie's revelation, the two servants, Marie and Jeane, engage in sexual relations, including penetrative copulation, fall in love, and propose publicly to marry, an announcement that not only scandalizes the local community but also provokes from the relevant ecclesiastical and juridical authorities an inquisitorial investigation designed to identify the gender of Marie. For all concerned, the consequential question at issue is at once medical and juridical: either Marie is a woman who with her prodigiously enlarged clitoris has committed what would have been understood as sodomy, a serious crime punishable by death, or, instead, Marie is a man, although a peculiar one, and, as such, his proposed marriage to Jeane is neither unnatural nor illegitimate. To resolve the question, one way or the other, a number of doctors are called in, among them Jacques Duvall, a doctor with a special interest in hermaphroditism, who, more conscientiously and carefully than the other doctors, examines Marie's sexual organs—though Marie now calls herself by a man's name, Marin—and is able thereby successfully to establish that he/she is indeed a man, for, as Greenblatt puts it, "the friction of the doctor's touch caused Marin to ejaculate" (p. 32). At least for Duvall, this medically manipulated outcome amounts to a piece of decisive evidence, one that settles the gender question once and for all.

More narrative attaches to the incident but what primarily interests Greenblatt in the story is the way, as he understands it, the example of Marie/Marin serves to illustrate a system of paradoxes and tensions informing what, Greenblatt claims, is a perennial biological or medical imagination of how the two sexes, despite the differences between them, stand to each other, at least with regard to the anatomy of the sexual apparatus, in a relation of introverted homology. Greenblatt cites Galen on the matter—"Turn outward the woman's, turn inward, so to speak, and fold double the man's, and you will find them the same in both in every respect'" (p. 39)—and he also cites some contemporary Renaissance gynecological commentary—e.g., Ambrose Parey (who is translated into English in 1634)—that discusses and conceives the issue in similar terms. What specifically interests Greenblatt in this model of the introverted collation of the anatomical sexuality of the two sexes is the way the model's topographic homology, its depiction of an essential anatomical similarity obtaining between the two sexes, calls forth a developmental principle or dynamic through which to explain the differences—not just the anatomical differences but so too the different social and cultural valuations—also understood to obtain between the sexuality of the two sexes. Hence the "friction" in the title of Greenblatt's essay, for it is the presence of greater or lesser amounts of heat—of specifically bodily heat, as the formation and operation of such heat is imagined by gynecological orthodoxy—that accounts not only for the translation, as the foetus develops, of the inferior sex into the superior (a movement from female to male) but also for the experienced phenomenality, by both men and women, of erotic affect and effect.

In persuasive and suggestive ways, Greenblatt then teases out a series of typological gender consequences packed into this caloric model of anatomic sexual destiny and psychophysiologized desire, all the outcome as Greenblatt puts it, of the way "the topographical account imagines gender as the result of the selective forcing out by heat of an originally internal organ—like reversing a rubber glove—so that where there was once only one sex, there are now two" (p. 41). And this is of critical interest to Greenblatt not simply for what it suggests about a purely medical imagination but also because, for Greenblatt, the same model of transformative, effective heat also informs Shakespeare's "representation of the emergence of identity in the experience of erotic heat" (p. 48). Accordingly, towards the end of his essay, Greenblatt turns briefly to *Twelfth Night* in order to advance and to argue the thesis that the gynecologist's heat or erotic "friction" is "figuratively represented" (p. 49) by Shakespeare, "fictionalized" (p. 49), in the "chaffing," "sparring" (49) language through which Shakespeare's lovers both express and come to experience their erotic life. As exemplary evidence, Greenblatt quotes the playful, punning, bickering dialogue that takes place between Viola and the Clown in the third act of *Twelfth Night,* where we find the same metaphor of the inside-outside glove ("chev'ril" now, not "rubber") as was already deployed by Greenblatt in his explication of the gynecological tradition:

> *Clown,* You have said, sir. To see this age! A sentence is but a chev'ril glove to a good wit. How quickly the wrong side may be turn'ed outward!
> *Viola,* Nay, that's certain. They that dally nicely with words may quickly make them wanton.
> *Clown,* I would therefore my sister had had no name, sir.
> *Viola,* Why, man?
> *Clown,* Why, sir, her name's a word, and to dally with that word might make my sister wanton. (*TN.* 3.1.11–20)

Greenblatt's argument here is straightforwardly New Historicist literary criticism insofar as it is concerned to establish a specific relation between a field of medical discourse, on the one hand, and Shakespeare's literary representations of human relations, on the other. Greenblatt is careful to avoid simplistic, naturalizing reductions and associated New Historicist clichés about the so-called social–cultural construction of the body; instead, he wants to identify how a particular medical discourse—a "discursive field," to use Foucault's somewhat incoherent and reifying concept—influences Shakespeare's literary imagination of the erotic, as this appears in characteristically Shakespearean literary language. The influence Greenblatt describes is fluid but pointed. Greenblatt does not say the biological discourse decisively determines Shakespeare's literary or linguistic imagination; neither does he say a traditionary conceptualization of biological erotic friction is responsible for the erotic "friction," to use Greenblatt's metaphor, of Shakespeare's language; nor does he attempt to establish an opposition between two "discursive fields"—the biological and the Shakespearean—by reference to which either can be seen as either cause or consequence of the other. Rather, Greenblatt is concerned to identify what he will later, in his book, call a "negotiation" between the two, a set of reciprocities and exchanges, one set among many others, through which we can understood how it happens each discourse achieves some of its independent force and charge. Thus, Greenblatt says, "at moments the plays seem to imply that erotic friction originates in the wantonness of language, and thus that the body itself is a tissue of metaphors or, conversely, that language is perfectly embodied" (p. 49). This reciprocal negotiation—Greenblatt's "conversely"—is not, on Greenblatt's part, a way of absolutizing or compromising the difference between two altogether comprehensive or preclusive alternatives; rather, the emergence, in this particular case, of this particular reciprocal negotiation amounts to the substance, modestly restricted, of Greenblatt's "New Historicist" claim.

I stress this point because it is with the substance of this claim—Greenblatt's "conversely"—that I disagree, and on historical grounds, for, as I have argued elsewhere (in connection, precisely, with this "love-glove" in *Twelfth Night*), it is Shakespeare's historical achievement, in literature, to have derived desire from the "wantonness" of words, and to have done so in a way that precludes the possibility of putting things the other way around, i.e., as though the erotic charge of language might be derived from the experience of desire (see, *Shakespeare's Perjured Eye*; also my "Shakespeare's *Will*: The Temporality of Rape," *Representations*, 20 [Fall, 1987], 25–76). For Shakespeare, I have argued, language, either as a theme or as a performed practice, does not figure or "embody," to use Greenblatt's metaphor, some biologized erotic impulse (however it happens such impulsion is thematically conceived); rather, for Shakespeare, desire is the very literal consequence of the figurality of language—a figurality or "wantonness" that Shakespeare characteristically imagines in terms of the "duplicity" of language, where "duplicity" not only carries with it the erotic metaphorics of the anatomic double "fold" but is at the same time the motivating mechanism of erotic intentionality. Greenblatt says this too, and says it explicitly, when he relates the Marie/Marin anecdote to the quoted passage from *Twelfth Night*: "It is as if the cause of Marin le Marcis's sexual arousal and transformation were now attributed to the ease—the simple change of one letter—that turns Marie into Marin: Her name's a word, and to dally with that word might make my sister wanton" (p. 49). But Greenblatt also says "conversely," i.e., he says that the gynecologists' erotic heat is figuratively represented by Shakespeare's language, and in doing so Greenblatt loses, as I understand it, the historical particularity of the fact that, and also the novelty of the particular way that, Shakespeare introduces personhood or subjectivity into literature by registering desire as the particular and specifiable effect of the duplicity of speech. My objection to Greenblatt's claim, therefore, is that I want to say only half of the two things Greenblatt says, but I want to say that half univocally rather than to put the two halves together, as does Geenblatt, for the sake of an equivocal "negotiation."

This is not the place to argue in extended detail the point about the relation of desire to language in Shakespeare; nor is it the place to attempt historically to situate this post-idealist, Renaissance recharacterization of the language of desire—though one gets some sense of the historical novelty attaching to the insight in the lines that continue what Greenblatt quotes from *Twelfth Night*:

> *Clown,* Why, sir, her name's a word, and to dally with that word might make my sister wanton. But indeed, words are very rascals since bonds disgrac'd them.
> *Viola,* Thy reason, man?
> *Clown,* Troth, sir, I can yield you none without words, and words are grown so false,
> I am loath to prove reason with them. (*TN.* 3.1.19–25)

It is important, however, in the context of what I have argued above about the New Historicism's subjective relation to the anecdotal Real to note that Greenblatt's essay gains its own powerful authorial voice from a mechanism very similar to the one through which, as I see it, Shakespeare's literary subjects come to be the desiring agents of their speaking voice. I have already noted that when Greenblatt explicates the gynecological commentaries on the anatomy of the sexual apparatus he introduces, on the basis of what seems to be his own volition, the metaphor of the inside-outside rubber glove, a metaphor that then subsequently appears to be historically significant when it reappears in the quotation from *Twelfth Night.* (We can find the same glove, by the way, folded inside out, in Auguste Dupin's description of the disguised purloined letter: "'In scrutinizing the edges of the paper, I observed them to be more *chafed* than seemed necessary. They presented the *broken* appearance which is manifested when a stiff paper, having been once folded and pressed with a folder, is refolded in a reversed direction, in the same creases or edges which had formed the original fold. The discovery was sufficient. It was clear to me that the letter had been turned, as a glove, inside out, re-directed and re-sealed'"; italics in the original, "The Purloined Letter," *The Complete Tales and Poems of Edgar Allan Poe* (New York: Vintage Books, 1975), 221. But because the metaphor comes to Greenblatt from Shakespeare, and not from the gynecologists—leaving aside the not insignificant difference between leather and rubber—it seems very clear that it is Shakespeare's literary text that controls Greenblatt's reading of the history of medicine, and that, correlatively, it is not the case that the history of medicine opens up, on this reading, a novel way to read Shakespeare. Hence the subtitle of my paper, "Fiction and Fiction," a way of noting that the medical texts Greenblatt discusses, and so too their "friction," are as "fictive" as is *Twelfth Night,* which is just another way of saying that the medical texts are, for Greenblatt, nothing but Shakespearean. Quite apart from the question of Shakespeare, however, it is important to notice this because, if this is the case, then we can conclude that the literary exigencies that determine the ways in which Shakespeare writes his literary subjects not only write the medical texts that are supposed to have influenced Shakespeare but, in addition, so too, the "Stephen Greenblatt" who in his turn will come to write about those medical texts. (It should also be noted that, given the predeterminative force of these literary exigencies—i.e., that they precede Shakespeare, the gynecologists, and Stephen Greenblatt—objections to Greenblatt's essay such as E.A.J. Honigmann's "The New Shakespeare?" in *The New York Review of Books,* vol. 35, no. 5 (March 31, 1988), 32–35, which complain that the gynecological texts Greenblatt cites are posterior to the Shakespeare texts they are supposed to influence, rather completely miss the point).

"A signifier," says Lacan, in his famous definition, "is what represents the subject for another signifier." "The Subversion of the Subject," *Ecrits,* 316. For Lacan, this accounts not only for the intrinsic figurality of language (i.e., that language begins with the primal metaphoricity that substitutes, from the beginning, the signifier of one signified for another signifier) but also for the constitution of the subject as a desiring subject in relation to the signifying motion of these fungibly sliding signifiers. Lacan also speaks of this subjectivizing process in terms of the capture of the imaginary by the Symbolic, in the course of which capture, as both condition and consequence, something slips out; that something which is elided by the achievement of representation is what Lacan calls the "Real," a "Real" that, because left out, can be neither imaginatively specularized nor symbolically represented. For Lacan, this Real, neither here nor there but always elsewhere, accounts for the fact that "there is no sexual relation," which in turn accounts both for the arrival and for the endurance of desire. See *Television,* 12. Hence the relevance of the passage from Lacan's *Television* that I take as my first epigraph, for it seems clear that the Marie/Marin anecdote Greenblatt relates—"the simple change of one letter"—is for Greenblatt an instance or insistence of the way a signifier represents the subject—in this case, "Greenblatt"—for another signifier, a substitution that leaves over as remainder only the mark of the Real, "*Marin le Marcis*" (49), to which Greenblatt's essay wants to give a meaning. Accordingly, we can conclude, in accord with the Lacanian formula I take as epigraph, that Greenblatt's essay amounts to one of those "fictions"—in this case, the empiricized "friction"—exuded by the sexual impasse in an attempt to rationalize the impossible "Real" from which it orginates. On the one hand, the persistent insistence of this "Real" accounts for what calls forth the authorial voice of Greenblatt's essay, just as it accounts for the way the essay stands as ongoing invitation to the Real that underwrites both it and what, by convention, we can call its author. By the same token, however, but on the other hand, this accounts for what is comic about the "empiricutic" in the lines from Shakespeare's *Coriolanus* that I take as complementary epigraph; this is something Menenius says early in the play, when he looks forward to the return of the conquering Coriolanus, and when he can still eagerly anticipate, because he does not know what is going to happen, the triumphant display of the hero's "wounds."

II   Toward the Release of Shakespeare's Will

Shakespeare's "Perjur'd Eye"

In the first portion of his sonnet sequence—in the subsequence of sonnets addressed to a young man—Shakespeare writes a matching pair of sonnets that develop the way in which his eye and heart initially are enemies but then are subsequently friends. The first sonnet of the pair begins: "Mine eye and heart are at a mortal war, / How to divide the conquest of thy sight" (46).[1] In contrast, the second sonnet, relying on a "verdict" that "is determined" at the conclusion of sonnet 46, begins: "Betwixt mine eye and heart a league is took, / And each doth good turns now unto the other" (47).

Taken together and in sequence, the two sonnets compose an argument *in utramque partem,* with their poet placing himself on both sides of a rhetorical question that is a commonplace in the tradition of the Renaissance sonnet.[2] Despite the conventional opposition, however, the two sonnets confidently argue to what is the same, and equally conventional, conclusion: namely, that their poet's eye and heart do "good turns now unto the other" (47). Thus, in the first sonnet, after meditating on the war between his eye and heart, the poet syllogistically and Neoplatonically derives the moral that: "As thus: mine eye's due is thy outward part, / And my heart's right thy inward love of heart." In turn, in the second sonnet, from thinking on the amity between his eye and heart, the poet reassuringly discovers that "thy picture in my sight / Awakes my heart to heart's and eye's delight." Taken together and in sequence, therefore, the two sonnets respond to the rhetorical question that they raise by juxtaposing a *concordia discors* and a *coincidentia oppositorum* each against the other. Both sonnets speak to the fact that their poet's eye and heart, however much they differ from or with each other, are equally "delighted." In both sonnets, eye and heart will peacefully "divide the conquest of thy sight," as though, from the ideal perspective shared by the two sonnets, eye and heart are complementary and coordinated aspects of each other.

In a straightforward way, the rhetorical wit of these two sonnets consists of thus hendiadystically arriving, from different starting points, at a common destination, for in this way the two sonnets manage to resolve, or to beg the question raised by, a traditional *débat.* Yet, however witty, the poems take seriously the equivalence of the conclusions that they share. In both cases the relationship of eye and heart, whether initially antipathetic or sympathetic, leads immediately, via complementary antithesis, to a recuperative and benign assessment of yet other differences adduced. In war or peace the sonnets' several binaries combine to generate a clarity of eye and purity of heart whose own discrete proprieties and properties in turn reciprocally establish, or are established by, the integrity and integration of the other categorical oppositions to which the poems refer. In the first sonnet, for example, sonnet 46, the difference between "outward" and "inward" is secured and reconciled because the vision of the eye and the "thinking" of the heart can be harmoniously apportioned between the clear-cut opposition of "The clear eye's moiety and the dear heart's part." In the second sonnet, 47, the absence of the beloved is converted or transmuted into presence because: "So either by thy picture or my love, / Thyself away are present still with me." This systematic complementarity—whereby opposites either are the same or, as opposites, still somehow go compatibly together—speaks to a general, indeed, a generic, homogeneity subtending both sonnets, something that informs them more deeply than the thematic heterogeneity that the two sonnets only provisionally or momentarily evoke. In the first sonnet it is the difference between eye and heart that establishes the concord between them, whereas in the second sonnet the concord derives from their similarity. But this difference, which is the difference between difference and similarity, turns out not to make much difference. In both sonnets the eye is "clear" and the heart is "dear" by virtue of a governing structure of likeness and contrast, of identity and difference, of similarity and contrariety, that both sonnets equally and isomorphically employ.

What these two young man sonnets, 46 and 47, share, therefore, as Lévi-Strauss might say, is the sameness of their differences: what joins them together is a structural identity, or a structure of identity that is yet more fundamental and more powerful than their apparent opposition. At the level of theme and of poetic psychology, this yields the Petrarchan commonplace in accord with which the poet's eye and heart come instantly to complement each other, moving from war to peace, from antipathy to sympathy, in a progress that constitutes a kind of shorthand summary of the amatory assumptions of ideal admiration, e.g., the way Cupid shoots his arrows through the lover's eye into the lover's heart.[3] This is a specifically *visual* desire, for in both sonnets it is as something of the eye that the young man's "fair appearance lies" within the poet's heart. In both sonnets "thy picture in my sight" indifferently "Awakes my heart to heart's and eye's delight."

Such homogenizing visual imagery, applied to the poet's love, to his beloved, and to his poetry, pervades the sequence of sonnets addressed to the young man, and this imagery is regularly employed, as in sonnets 46 and 47, to characterize a material likeness or sameness that conjoins or renders consubstantial two distinctive yet univocally collated terms: not only the poet's eye and heart, but, also, the poet and his young man (e.g., "Tis thee (myself) that for myself I praise, / Painting my age with beauty of thy days" [62]), the young man and, in the opening sonnets which urge the young man to procreate, *his* young man (e.g., "Look in thy glass and tell the face thou viewest, / Now is the time that face should form another" [3]), as well as the poet's poetry and that of which the poetry speaks (e.g., "So long as men can breathe or eyes can see, / So long lives this, and this gives life to thee" [18]). In general, the poet identifies his first-person "I" with the ideal eye of the young man—"Now see what good turns eyes for eyes have done" (24)—and then proceeds to identify these both with the "wondrous scope" (105) of his visionary verse: "So till the judgement that yourself arise, / You live in this, and dwell in lovers' eyes" (55).

In all these cases the visual imagery that Shakespeare employs is, of course, nothing but conventional. Indeed, the sonnets addressed to the young man regularly allude to the conventionality of their visual imagery, often characterizing such imagery, as well as that of which it is an image, as something old-fashioned, even antiquated, as in the literary retrospection of sonnet 59:

> O that record could with a backward look,
> Even of five hundreth courses of the sun.
> Show me your image in some antique book,
> Since mind at first in character was done!

There are a good many reasons why the young man's poet might "look" in this "backward" way to specifically visual imagery, to imagery of vision, in order, as sonnet 59 goes on to say, to "see what the old world could say / To this composed wonder of your frame." With regard to the poet's ideal desire, which aims to conjoin poetic subject with poetic object—"thou mine, I thine" (108)—the young man's poet can rely upon a familiar Petrarchist motif, derived from Stoic optics, of eroticized *eidōla* or likenesses, intromissive and extromissive, whose very physics establishes a *special* (from *specere,* "to look at") coincidence of lover and beloved, as, for example, when

Astrophil, at the beginning of Sidney's sonnet sequence, looks into his heart to write, and finds there preengraved or "stell'd" upon it the stylized image or *imago* of the Stella whom he loves. In turn, this physics of the *eidōlon* presupposes an equally familiar and specifically idealist metaphysics of genus and species whereby individual particulars are but subspecies of a universal form or type, declensions of a paradigmatic archetype whose immanent universality is regularly and perennially conceived in terms of light, as in Platonic *eidos,* from *idein,* "to see," or as the end of the *Paradiso,* where Dante sees "La forma universal" in his vision of "luce etterna" and "semplice lume" (in this divine light, we can add, Dante also sees the painted "likeness," the "effige," of himself).[4] Moreover, again in ways that are nothing but conventional, the poetry of idealization, especially as it develops in the self-consciously literary tradition of the Renaissance sonnet, characteristically assimilates such visual imagery, which is its imagery *of* the ideal, to itself, so as thereby to idealize itself as effective *simulacrum,* physical and metaphysical, of that which it admires. As an activity of "stelling"—e.g., "Mine eye hath play'd the painter and hath stell'd / Thy beauty's form in table of my heart" (24)—such poetry is *Ideas Mirrour,* as Drayton called his sonnet sequence, and it is so precisely because, being something visual and visionary, it can claim to be not only the reflection of, but also the objectification of, its idea of its ideal.[5]

Speaking very generally, it is fair to say that this is the regular force of visual imagery in the tradition of the literature or poetry of praise—a tradition that goes back to the praise of love in the *Symposium* or *Phaedrus,* but one that is especially vital in the particular literary genre of the sonnet, where it goes without saying that the poet is a lover who desires only that which he admires. With regard to poetic procedure or, rather, with regard to what is the common and longstanding understanding of poetic procedure, this is a tradition of specifically visionary poetic likeness, either mimetic likeness, whereby poetry is the simulating representation of that which it presents—"ut pictura poesis," speaking picture—or figural likeness, as when Aristotle defines metaphor (whether based on analogy or commutative proportion) as the capacity "to see the same" (*theōrein homoion*), metaphor being for Aristotle, as for the tradition of rhetorical theory that derives from him, an activity of speculative likening that, quite literally, "theorizes sameness."[6] Correspondingly, with regard to poetic subjectivity, this is a literary tradition in which the poet is a panegyric *vates* or seer who, at least ideally, is the same as that which he sees (e.g., Dante's reflexively reflective "effige"), just as, with regard to poetic semiosis, poetic language, as *eikōn, speculum, imago, eidōlon,* etc., is Cratylitically the same as that of which it speaks, for example, the way Dante identifies his own "beatitude" with

"those words that praise my Lady," his "lodano" with "la donna," or the way Petrarch
puns on "Laura," "laud," and "laurel."[7] These are general themes and motifs by reference to which the poetry of praise characteristically becomes a praise of poetry
itself.[8]

It is possible to get some sense of how very familiar, over-familiar, this received
literary tradition is to Shakespeare if we register the formulaic way the young man's
poet in sonnet 105 identifies, one with the others, his "love," his "beloved," and his
"songs and praises":

> Let not my love be called idolatry,
> Nor my beloved as an idol show,
> Since all alike my songs and praises be.

What joins these three together is the ideality they share, an ideality that establishes
a three-term correspondence between the speaking, the spoken, and the speech of
praise. "'Fair,' 'kind,' and 'true' is all my argument," says the poet in sonnet 105, and
these "Three themes in one, which wondrous scope affords" ("Three themes" that
sonnet 105 repeats three times) amount to a phenomenological summary, an eidetic
reduction, of a Petrarchist metaphysical, erotic, and poetic Ideal: "Fair" identifies the
visibility, the *Sichtigkeit,* of an ideal sight (*idein,* "to see"); "kind" identifies the homogeneous categoriality, the formal elementality, of an ideal essence (Platonic *eidos*);
"true" identifies the coincidence of ideal knowledge and knowing (*oida,* which is
also from *idein*). It is by reference to such precisely conceived and conceited ideality,
an ideality that in effect recapitulates the history of ideas up through the Renaissance,
that sonnet 105 manages to identify "my love," "my beloved," and "my songs and
praises," each one of these being "'Fair,' 'kind,' and 'true,'" and therefore, by commutation, each one of these being the same and truthful mirror-image of the other
two. In the same idealizing way, this is how sonnets 46 and 47 manage to eliminate
the difference between their eye and heart, and thereby manage, despite the difference with which they begin, to say the same thing. More generally, we can say that
this is how Shakespeare's poetry of visionary praise, because it is a "wondrous scope"
and because it is addressed to a "wondrous scope," is always, as sonnet 105 puts it,
monotheistically, monogamously, monosyllabically, and monotonously "To one, of
one, still such, and ever so." This is an ideological poetry, as sonnet 105 seems almost
to complain, whose virtue consists in the way its copiousness always copies the same
ideal sameness—"Since all alike my songs and praises be"—a universal and uni-vers-
ing poetic and erotic practice whose very ideality is what renders it incapable of man-
ifesting difference, for, as the poet puts it in sonnet 105:

> Kind is my love to-day, to-morrow kind,
> Still constant in a wondrous excellence,
> Therefore my verse, to constancy confin'd,
> One thing expressing, leaves out difference.

However, as the palpable claustrophobia of sonnet 105 suggests, it would be possible to look more closely at the sonnets addressed to the young man so as to see the way they characteristically resist and conflictedly inflect their most ideal expressions of visionary unity, the way they chafe against the "constancy" to which they are "confin'd," the way that they implicitly "express" the "difference" that they explicitly "leave out." If, as Murray Krieger has suggested, we are supposed to hear the "one" in sonnet 105's "*won*drous scope," then so too do we also hear the "two" in its "T(w)o one, of one, still such, and ever so."[9] So too, the entire sonnet is colored by the ambiguous logic of its opening "Since"—"Since all alike my songs and praises be"—since this concessive particle explains both why the young man is an idol as well as why he is not. Such complications, though they are implicit, have their effect. As complications, they add a reservation or a wrinkle to the poet's otherwise straightforward rhetoric of compliment. In such oblique, yet obvious, ways the young man sonnets will regularly situate themselves and their admiration at one affective and temporal remove from the ideality that they repeatedly and repetitiously invoke, with the peculiar result that in these sonnets an apparently traditional poetics of ideal light comes regularly to seem what sonnet 123 calls "The dressings of a former sight."

This peculiar retrospection is a consistent aspect of the young man sonnets' imagery of the visual and the visible, imagery that is characteristically presented in the young man sonnets as though it were so tarnished with age that its very reiteration is what interferes with the poet's scopic or specular identification of his poetic "I" with the ideal "eye" of the young man: "For as you were when first your eye I ey'd" (104). In general, the young man's poet, *as* a visionary poet, seems capable of expressing only a love at second sight; his identification of his ego with his ego-ideal seems worn out by repetition, as though it were the very practice by the poet of an old-fashioned poetry of visionary praise that effectively differentiates the poet as a panegyricizing subject from what he takes to be his ideal and his praiseworthy object. We can take as an example the mixed-up deictic and epideictic compact of the couplet to sonnet 62 which has already been cited—"'Tis thee (myself) that for myself I praise, / Painting my age with beauty of thy days"—where the confused identification of the poet's "I" and "thou" effectively identifies the first person of the poet with the youth and age of visionary praise. The same thing goes, however, to take another example, for the "stelling" of sonnet 24. At the beginning of the sonnet the poet remembers how, in the past, "Mine eye hath play'd the painter and hath stell'd / Thy beauty's form in table of my heart." At the end of the sonnet, however, speaking in and for the present, the poet observes: "Yet eyes this cunning want to grace their art. / They draw but what they see, know not the heart" (24).

In this context, we can recall the fact that Shakespeare writes his sonnet sequence, for the most part, after the Elizabethan sonnet sequence vogue has passed, in what we might call the literary aftermath of the poetry of praise, when such Petrarchist panegyric has come to seem, to some extent, *passé*. This is the historical literary context within which the sonnets addressed to the young man—which are conceived long after what even Sidney, at the inaugural moment of the Elizabethan sonnet sequence, called "Poor Petrarch's long-deceased woes"—make a personal issue out of their self-remarked literary belatedness, regularly associating what they themselves characterize as their old-fashioned literary matter and manner with their poet's sense of his senescence.[10] In sonnet 76, for example, the poet asks:

> Why is my verse so barren of new pride?
> So far from variation or quick change?
> Why with the time do I not glance aside
> To new-found methods and to compounds strange?

As the poet first poses them, these are rhetorical questions, questions about rhetoric, but these questions then will press themselves upon the poet's person; they define for him his sense of superannuated self:

> Why write I still all one, ever the same,
> And keep invention in a noted weed,
> That every word doth almost tell my name,
> Showing their birth and where they did proceed?

A good many young man sonnets are concerned with just this kind of literary question, and, as in sonnet 76, in these sonnets it appears as though it is the very asking of the question that turns out to empty out the poet's praising self. It is as though, because he is committed to an ancient poetry of praise, the poet feels himself obliged to pay the debts incurred by a bankrupt literary tradition—as though the poet, as a person, is himself entropically exhausted by the tired tropes with which, according to an old poetic custom, he ornaments himself:

> So all my best is dressing old words new,
> Spending again what is already spent:
> For as the sun is daily new and old,
> So is my love still telling what is told. (76)

This is significant because it introduces a new kind of self-consciousness into the already highly self-conscious tradition of the Renaissance sonnet. In familiar ways, the poet in sonnet 76 identifies himself with his own literariness. At the same time, however, it is in an unfamiliar way that the poet's subjectivity here seems worn out by the heavy burden of the literary history that his literariness both examples and extends. For what is novel in a sonnet such as 76 is not so much the way the poet takes the ever-renewed sameness of the sun, its perennially revivified vivacity, as a dead metaphor for the animating *energeia* and *enargia* of an ideal metaphoricity. Rather, what is striking, and what is genuinely novel, is the way the visionary poet takes this faded brightness personally, the way he identifies his own poetic person, his own poetic identity, with the after-light of this dead metaphoric sun. Identifying himself with an aged eternality—which is itself the image of an ideal and an unchanging identity—the young man's poet is like a bleached Dante: he is a visionary poet, but he is so, as it were, after the visionary fact, a seer who now sees in a too-frequently reiterated "luce etterna" a vivid image, an *effige* or an *eidōlon,* of the death of both his light and life, as in sonnet 73: "In me thou seest the twilight of such day / As after sunset fadeth in the west, / Which by and by black night doth take away, / Death's second self, that seals up all in rest." This is the peculiarly inflected imagery of light with which the young man's poet assimilates to his own poetic psychology the self-consuming logic of "Spending again what is already spent," for it is with this imagery of after-light that the poet makes his own poetic introspection into something retrospective:

> In me thou seest the glowing of such fire,
> That on the ashes of his youth doth lie
> As the death-bed whereon it must expire,
> Consum'd with that which it was nourish'd by. (73)

In terms of what we can think of as the conventional visual imagery of the poetry of praise, it as though in Shakespeare's sonnets to the young man *Ideas Mirrour* had now become the "glass" of sonnet 62, a "glass," however, that rather horrifyingly "shows me myself indeed, / Beated and chopp'd with tann'd antiquity," with the subjective consequence of this for the poet being that, as sonnet 62 goes on to say, "Mine own self-love quite contrary I read."

There is much more that might be said about this imagery of tired light, or tired imagery of light, for it can be argued that such imagery not only determines the young man's poet's sense of space and time, but also his erotic sensibility as well (consider, for example, "A liquid prisoner pent in walls of glass" [5]). As it is, however, it seems clear that we cannot overlook—as sentimental readings often do—the novel coloring that Shakespeare's young man sonnets give to their visual imagery, to their imagery *of* the visual, for this is responsible, to a considerable degree, for the pathos of poetic persona that these sonnets regularly exhibit. By the same token, however, it would be a mistake to overemphasize this darkness that informs these sonnets' literary, visionary light. If the young man sonnets are suspicious of their visual imagery, this is not a suspicion that they put directly into words. Quite the contrary, whatever reservations attach to the young man sonnets' imagery of vision, these reservations, like those that shade the poet's various characterizations of the ideality of the young man, are implicit rather than explicit, something we read between what the young man sonnets call their "eternal lines to time" (18).

It is important to insist upon this indirection, upon the fact that the young man sonnets do not explicitly speak against their light, because this accounts for the residual idealism with which the young man sonnets always turn, heliotropically, to "that sun, thine eye" (49). At least ideally, the young man sonnets would like to be like the courtly "marigold" of sonnet 25, whose "fair leaves spread . . . at the sun's eye." Like such flowers of fancy, the young man sonnets would like to look exactly like the ideal that they look at, just as the poet would like his "I" to be "as you were when first your eye I ey'd" (104). Hence the nostalgia of the poet's introspection: the poet sees his difference from an eternal visionary sameness, his difference from a visionary poetics that would always be the same because, as Aristotle says of metaphor, it always "see(s) the same." But this insight serves only to make the poet's ideal bygone vision seem all the more ideal, an image of poetic presence that is always in the past, even when this ancient past is the present in the future tense, as in the prospective retrospection of sonnet 104, where the poet tells "thou age unbred: / Ere you were born was beauty's summer dead." This loyally retrospective visuality, a poetry of re-turn rather than of turn, accounts for the complex texture of the young man sonnets' imagery of vision, a complexity that derives from the fact that the young man sonnets never entirely reject the ideality from which they are estranged. If the young man sonnets characteristically distance themselves from their visual imagery even as they employ it, this distanciation possesses poetic force precisely to the extent that such

imagery of light continues to retain, specifically in retrospect, at a distance, its originary and traditionary ideal connotations.

I stress the vestigial power of such visual ideality in the young man sonnets, its
"present-absent" (45) presence, because this both measures and prepares for the difference between the sonnets addressed to the young man and those addressed to
the dark lady. As is well known, in the subsequence of sonnets addressed to the dark
lady such ideal imagery of light is explicitly—Shakespeare's word here is important—"forsworn" (152). What gives this "forswearing" its power, however, and what
distinguishes it, tonally as well as thematically, from the implicit visual reservations
informing the sonnets addressed to the young man, is the way the dark lady's poet
puts these heretofore unspoken visionary suspicions directly into words. In the
young man sonnets, the young man, whatever his faults, is an "image" whose idealization effectively can represent an ideal that is lost, as in sonnet 31: "Their images
I lov'd I view in thee, / And thou (all they) hast all the all of me," or the young man
is a "shadow" who to the poet's "imaginary sight . . . makes black night beauteous,
and her old face new" (27). In contrast, in the dark lady sonnets, though as something
that is more complicated and more unsettling than a simple opposition, the dark lady
has the "power," as in sonnet 149, "To make me give the lie to my true sight, / And
swear that brightness doth not grace the day."

We broach here what is often called the anti-Petrarchanism of the sonnets to
the dark lady, and it is certainly the case that the dark lady sonnets regularly characterize their literary peculiarity and novelty in terms of the way they differ from the
specular ideality of a previous Petrarchist poetics. When the poet looks at the young
man, he sees "That sun, thine eye" (49). In contrast, when he looks at the dark lady,
what he sees is the way she is unlike the ideal brightness of the young man: "My mistress' eyes are nothing like the sun" (130). On the face of it, this amounts to a straightforward difference, for, on the one hand, there is brightness, whereas, on the other,
there is darkness. What makes this difference complicated, however, is that when the
poet makes an issue of it, when he gives explicit expression to it, he presents the
darkness of the lady as itself the image of this difference, as an image, precisely, of
the difference between the black that it is and the light that it is not.

This is why the difference between the lady's stressedly unconventional darkness and the young man's emphatically conventional brightness produces something that is both more and less than a straightforward black and white antithesis of
the kind suggested by the "anti-" of anti-Petrarchanism. On the one hand, there is
brightness, but, on the other, is a darkness that, in a peculiar or what Troilus calls a
"bi-fold" way, is both these hands together both at once.[11] Such is the strangeness of

a lady whom the poet alternately praises and blames for being other than what at first sight she appears. As an image of that which she is not, the lady is presented as the likeness of a difference, at once a version of, but at the same time a perversion of, that to which she is, on the one hand, both positively and negatively compared, and that to which she is, on the other, both positively and negatively opposed. For this reason, as she is presented, the lady is, strictly speaking, beyond both comparison and opposition. The lady both is and is not what she is, and because she is in this way, *in* herself, something double, the lady cannot be comprehended by a poetics of "To one, of one, still such, and ever so." As the poet puts it in sonnet 130—this the consequence of the fact that his "mistress' eyes are nothing like the sun"—the lady is a "love," just as she inspires a "love," that is "as rare, / As any she belied with false compare." The irrational ratio of the formula defines the peculiarity of the lady. She is a "she" who is logically, as well as grammatically, both subject and object of "belied with false compare," comparable, therefore, only to the way comparison has failed.

From the beginning, this effective doubleness of the lady, defined in specifically literary terms, i.e., in terms of a new kind of poetics, is what the poet finds distinctive about her, as in the first sonnet he addresses to her:

> In the old age black was not counted fair,
> Or if it were it bore not beauty's name;
> But now is black beauty's successive heir,
> And beauty slander'd with a bastard shame. (127)

What we are supposed to recognize here as officially surprising is that the lady's traditional foul is now characterized as something that is fair, just as in later sonnets this novel fair will be yet more surprisingly foul: "For I have sworn thee fair, and thought thee bright, / Who art as black as hell, as dark as night" (147). In either case, however, whether fair or foul, it is always as images of that which they are not, as something double, fair *and* foul, as something duplicitous and heterogeneous, that the lady and her darkness acquire their erotic and their literary charge.

Thus "black" is "now" "beauty's successive heir," now that "beauty" is "slander'd with a bastard shame." In the context of the sequence as a whole, the force of this unconventional "succession" is that it repeats, but with a difference, the themes of reiterated and legitimately procreated likeness with reference to which the young man at the opening of his subsequence is supposed, as an *imago,* to "prove his beauty by succession thine" (2): "Die single, and thine image dies with thee" (3). Instead of the ideal multiplication of kind with kind, the ongoing reproduction of the visual same, by means of which the young man is supposed to "breed another thee" (6)—a breeding implicitly associated in the young man sonnets with a kind of homosexual usury: "that use is not forbidden usury" (6)—the novel beauty of the lady instead exemplifies a novelly miscegenating "successivity"—novel *because* successive to such Platonized "succession"—whereby black becomes the differential substitute, the unkind "heir," of what is "fair."[12] So too with the blackness of the lady's "raven" eyes, a darkness that replaces at the same time as it thus displaces the brightness it sequentially succeeds:

> Therefore my mistress' eyes are raven black,
> Her eyes so suited and they mourners seem
> At such who, not born fair, no beauty lack,
> Slandering creation with a false esteem. (127)

This, in little, defines the structural and temporal relationship of the dark lady sonnets to the young man sonnets. The second subsequence is a repetition of the first, but it is a discordant and a disturbing repetition because the latter subsequence, stressing itself as a repetition, represents the former (as also the former's themes of visionary presence—"So either by thy picture or my love / Thyself away are present still with me" [47]—in such a way that its memorial repetition explicitly calls up the poignant absence of that which it recalls. To the degree that this articulates the silent reservations that darken the idealism of the young man sonnets, to this extent we register the way in which the "black" of the second subsequence is continuous with the elegaically retrospective visuality of the first. Yet there is also an emphatic difference between the two, a difference that derives precisely from the fact that the dark lady's poet explicitly expresses what the young man's poet preferred to leave implicit. For what the dark lady's poet sees in the darkness of the lady's mourning eyes is the death of ideal visionary presence; her darkness is for him an image or *imago* of the loss of vision. But, according to the poet, it is this very vision of the loss of vision that now thrusts him into novel speech—the discourse of "black beauty"— making him now no longer a poet of the eye, but, instead, a poet of the tongue: "Yet so they mourn, becoming of their woe, / That every tongue says beauty should look so" (127).

As Ulysses says of wanton Cressida, therefore, "There's language in her eye."[13] But what is odd about this language is what is odd about the lady's eye, namely, that it is opposed to vision. The difference between this and the way that language is characterized in the young man sonnets is, of course, considerable, and we may say that this difference at once examples and defines the novelty of the way a poet speaks in a post-Petrarchist poetics. In the young man sonnets the poet ideally speaks a visionary speech, and therefore, when he speaks about this speech he speaks of it as something of the eye: "O, learn to read what silent love hath writ: / To hear with eyes belongs to love's fine wit" (23). In contrast, but again as something that is more complicated than a simple opposition, the poet in the dark lady subsequence will speak about his speech *as* speech, and as something that, for just this very reason, is different from a visual ideal. It is in this "forswearing" way that the dark lady, with the "pow'r" of her "insufficiency," will "make me give the lie to my true sight, / And swear that brightness doth not grace the day" (150). The double way the lady looks is like the double way that language speaks, which is why, for example, when the poet looks at the lady's far too common "common place" (137), a place that is at once erotic and poetic, he tells us how "mine eyes seeing this, say this is not" (137).

Thematized in this way, as something radically discrepant to the truth of ideal vision, as the *voice* of "eyes . . . which have no correspondence with true sight" (148), language is regularly presented in the dark lady sonnets as something whose truth consists not only in saying, but in *being,* something false: "My thoughts and my discourse as madman's are, / At random from the truth vainly express'd: / For I have sworn thee fair, and thought thee bright, / Who art as black as hell, as dark as night" (147). Correspondingly, because no longer something visual, because no longer the iconic likeness or the *eidōlon* of what it speaks about, verbal language now defines itself as its forswearing difference from what is "'Fair,' 'kind,' and 'true'": "For I have sworn deep oaths of thy deep kindness, / Oaths of thy love, thy truth, thy constancy, / And to enlighten thee gave eyes to blindness, / Or made them swear against the thing they see" (152). And, as a further and more personal result, the poet now identifies himself with the difference that his language thus bespeaks. He is no longer a visionary poet who identifies his "I" and "eye." Instead, *because* he speaks, the poet comes to inhabit the space of difference between poetic language and poetic vision, a difference generated *by* the speech he speaks. The poet's subjectivity, his "I," is precipitated in or as the slippage between his eye and tongue. The poet becomes, in the phrase I take as title for this paper, the subject of a "perjur'd eye": "For I have sworn thee fair: more perjur'd eye, / To swear against the truth so foul a lie!" (152).

It is fair to say, therefore, that in the dark lady sonnets we encounter a poetics in which true vision is captured by false language, and that the conflict thus engendered—between sight and word, between being and meaning, between poetic presentation and poetic representation—in turn determines specific variations on, or mutations of, traditionary sonneteering claims and motifs. A poetics of verbal representation, stressing the repetition of the *re-,* spells the end of the poetics of visual presentation, thereby constituting the Idea of poetic presence as something that is

lost. To the extent that this is the case, Shakespeare's sonnet sequence marks a decisive moment in the history of lyric, for when the dark lady sonnets forswear the ideally visionary poetics of the young man sonnets, when poetic language comes in this
way to be characterized as something verbal, not visual, we see what happens to
poetry when it gives over a perennial poetics of *ut pictura poesis* for (literally, *so as*
to speak) a poetics of *ut poesis poesis,* a transition that writes itself out in Shakespeare's sonnets as an unhappy progress from a poetry based on visual likeness—
whose adequation to that which it admires is figured by a "wondrous scope" by
means of which "One thing expressing, leaves out difference" (105)—to a poetry
based on verbal difference—whose inadequate relation to that which it bespeaks is
figured by an "insufficiency" that "make(s) me give the lie to my true sight" (150).
In the sequence as a whole, this progress from a homogeneous poetics of vision to
a heterogeneous poetics of language is fleshed out as a progress from an ideally
homosexual desire, however conflicted, for what is "'Fair,' 'kind,' and 'true'" to a
frankly misogynistic, heterosexual desire for what is fair *and* unfair, kind *and*
unkind, true *and* false—a progress, in other words, from man to woman. Here again,
however, it is explicitly and literally as a figure *of* speech that the lady becomes the
novel "hetero-" opposed as such to an ideal and a familiar Neo-Platonic "homo-," as
when: "When my love swears that she is made of truth, / I do believe her though I
know she lies" (138). It is in this way, by making each the figure of the other, that the
poet collates his corrupting Eros with his corrupting Logos. When the poet "credit[s]
her false-speaking tongue," the result is that "On both sides thus is simple truth sup-
press'd" (138). But the consequence of this false correspondence, of this traduce-
ment of the Cratylism of the poetry of praise—e.g., of the "beatitudinizing" power
of Dante's "Beatrice," or of the self-applauding circularities of Petrarch's puns on
"Laura," "laud," and "laurel"—is that the poet comes to express, in terms of a specific
desire of language, the novel duplicity of a specifically linguistic language of desire:
"Therefore I lie with her, and she with me, / And in our faults by lies we flattered be"
(138).

   Again there is more that might be said about the way the dark lady sonnets thematize their lady's and their poet's speech as speech, and draw from this the moral
that such speech is radically excessive to an orthodox poetics of admiration. As with
the implicit reservations that inform the young man sonnets' visionary themes, it
would be possible to show how Shakespeare's explicitly paradoxical version of a
traditionary poetics of praise not only affects the poet's expressions of desire—leading him from a homosexual desire for that which is admired to a heterosexual desire
for that which is not admired—but, again, his sense of space and time as well. If we

could follow this out in sufficient detail we would develop a more textured phenomenology of the psychology of the Shakespearean subject. This would help not only to describe the ways in which poetic person or lyric subjectivity in Shakespeare's sonnet sequence is altogether foreign to the kind of poetic person we find in first-person poetry up through the Renaissance, but also to explain why this novel Shakespearean subjectivity—not only as it appears in Shakespeare's first-person sonnets but also as it manifests itself in Shakespeare's zero-person plays—subsequently becomes (since Shakespeare, which is to say since the decisive conclusion of an epideictic poetics, which is to say since the end of a poetic tradition in which all poetry is a poetry of praise) the dominant and canonical version in our literary tradition of literary subjectivity per se.

For obvious reasons an essay is not the place to develop the details of such an account, an account that necessarily calls for all the particularity and specificity of extended practical and historical literary criticism.[14] However, for the sake of an outline of such an account, one point seems especially important: namely, that this novel Shakespearean subjectivity, for all its difference from that which it succeeds, is nevertheless constrained by the traditionary lyric literariness to which it stands as epitaph. In this sense, we might say that "poor Petrarch's long deceased woes" exert a posthumous power, prescribing in advance the details of their own forswearing. This point, too, can only be developed here in a schematic and perfunctory fashion. But it is possible, by looking at the way the dark lady's poet revises the visionary logic and psychologic of the young man's poet's eye and heart, to get some sense of the way Shakespeare's paradoxical invention of a heterogeneous and heterosexual poetics of paradoxical praise amounts to an orthodox mutation of a conventionally homogeneous and homosexual poetics of orthodox realization:

> Thine eyes I love, and they as pitying me,
> Knowing my heart torment me with disdain,
> Have put on black, and loving mourners be,
> Looking with pretty ruth upon my pain.
> And truly not the morning sun of heaven
> Better becomes the grey cheeks of th' east,
> Nor that full star that ushers in the even
> Doth half that glory to the sober west,
> As those two mourning eyes become thy face.
> O, let it then as well beseem thy heart
> To mourn for me, since mourning doth thee grace,

> And suit thy pity like in every part.
>
> Then will I swear beauty herself is black,
>
> And all they foul that thy complexion lack.

As in sonnets 46 and 47, the general conceit of sonnet 132, with its frustrated lover addressing his pitiless, disdaining beloved, is a Petrarchan commonplace, going back beyond Petrarch to the *rime petrose* of Arnault Daniel. Equally common is the intricate development of the imagery of sympathetically erotic vision. In this sense we deal here with the same poetics Shakespeare presupposes in the young man sonnets, where, for example, he can speak familiarly of "that sun, thine eye" (49) precisely because a long-standing tradition of metaphysical and sexual allegory authorizes an iconographic equating of the two. On the other hand, but in an equally insistent way, sonnet 132 further plays upon this convention and these traditional light-sight metaphors when, as a result of comparing the beloved's eyes to the sun, it turns out not that her eyes are lamps, but that the sun to which they are compared is therefore black. This too is, in part, conventional (e.g., Stella's eyes are black), but what concerns us is the stressed contrast to what has come before. In the young man sonnets the morning is "sacred," "new-appearing" (7), "golden" and "green" (33). Here, instead, "the morning sun of heaven" is obscuring complement to "the grey cheeks of the east," shining in the morning like the evening star at night, because it is a brightness in an encroaching darkness of which it is itself the cause and sign. Where in the sonnets addressed to the young man the sun is a "gracious light" (7) to the morning, here, instead, the morning is a "mourning" whose inversion is a darkening "grace"; "Since mourning doth thee grace." This pun on "mo[u]rning," which explains why in the dark lady sonnets "brightness doth not grace the day," is the kind of motivated homophone that Shakespeare is often either faulted or appreciated for, either the sort for which, in Johnson's phrase, he threw away the world, or the sort with which he generates the resonant ambiguities that critics like to list. The point that is emphasized by the sonnet, however, is that the pun, which must be noticed as such for it to work its poetic effect, does in little what the poem does rhetorically as a whole: repeating itself *in* itself so as to undo itself with its own echo, discovering and producing its own loss at the very moment of calling to our attention the way language, theme, and image displace themselves by folding over upon themselves in paradox. So too, this is precisely the mourning paradox of what is epideictically orthodox for which the poem will sadly say that it was written: "Then will I swear beauty herself is black, / And all they foul that thy complexion lack."

In obvious ways, therefore, all this—morning *and* melancholia—results in something that is much more complex than a simple negation of Petrarchan themes and images, and for this reason the poem possesses a tonality unlike even the most self-consciously witty Petrarchan lovers' complaint. The system of logical oppositions and conventional antitheses into which we might be tempted to organize the sonnet's courtly courtship argument falls to pieces as soon as the sonnet brings antithesis into play. Just as the lady's eyes by turning black express a pity occasioned by her heart's disdain, so too does the poet here thematize the fact that he here expresses his heart's desire with a language of disdain. In the same way that the stain of the lady's eyes is both image of and answer to the disdain of her heart, so too does the poet here amplify the lady's beauty by fouling the conventional images of fairness. The relationship between the lady's eye and the lady's heart, or of the poet to the lady, is a matter, therefore, neither of similarity and contrast nor of pity and disdain, and, for this reason, there is no way either poet or lady might "suit thy pity like in every part." Pity is a figure of disdain just as morning is a version of the night, each of them the homeopathic mirror of the heteropathy of the other. As a result, with likeness emerging as the instance, rather than the antithesis, of difference, with pity the *complement* to disdain, the sonnet forces its reader to deal with oddly asymmetrical oppositions whereby each polarized side or half of every opposition that the sonnet adduces already includes, and therefore changes by encapsulating, the larger dichotomy of which it is a part. With regard to the lady, this means that she cannot treat the poet either with pity or with disdain, or even with an oxymoronic combination of the two. For her "charm" consists precisely of the way these two apparently antithetical modalities, empathy and antipathy, each turn out to be, within their singular propriety, the contrary double not only of its other but also of itself, the two together thus composing a double doubling whose reduplicating logic forecloses the possibility of ever isolating either modality in itself. With regard to the poet, this means that he cannot speak of his lady with a simple rhetoric of similarity and contrast, for his language undercuts the logic of likeness and difference even as it advances complementary contrarieties.[15]

The difference between this and what happens when sonnets 46 and 47 develop their eye-heart topos is pointed enough, a difference now that *makes* a difference. Where the two young man sonnets see both eye and heart as each the figure and occasion of the other, sonnet 132 instead both literally and figuratively describes a desire at odds with itself because at odds with what it sees. Where the two young man sonnets bring out the syncretic identity built into their differences, the dark lady sonnet instead brings out the diacritical difference built into its identities. Where the two young man sonnets develop an ideal logic of sympathetic opposition, the dark lady sonnet gives us instead what is the paradoxical opposite, if we can call it that, to such a logic of sympathetic opposition. In terms of form, of theme, of tone, these are all significant differences. But it is important to realize that these differences derive not only their force but also their specific qualities, their content as well as their contours, from the structurally systematic way in which sonnet 132 understands its language paradoxically to redouble, with a difference, the orthodox dual unities with which it begins—i.e., from the way in which the double doubling of sonnet 132 tropes, re-turns, re-verses, the unifying tropes of an idealizing, homogeneous poetics, this way inverting the reciprocal way that eye and heart in sonnets 46 and 47 "each doth good turns now unto the other" (47). "Mourning" its "morning," the sonnet puts into words, literally puts *into* words, the duplicity of its speech, and this duplicity, thus bespoken, in turn divides the original bright desire and golden poetics presupposed by the young man sonnets. By means of this remarked duplication, the sonnet undoes both erotic and rhetorical identification, and thereby, *through* its language, justifies the chiasmic inversion of the poet's eye and heart. In sonnet 132 the content of "mourning" *is* the loss of "morning," and this hole built into a double language, this difference sounded in a sameness, is what functions both to blind the poet's eye and to break the poet's heart. Developed in this way, as the forswearing double of a visual ideal, as "morning" *manqué,* language acquires in the sonnet, and at the same time also proclaims, its novel motives and motifs, precisely those that the poet defines, logically and psychologically, as "Then will I swear beauty herself is black."

It is language, therefore, conceived and conceited as something linguistic, as something of the *tongue,* as both like and unlike the vision to which it is opposed and on which it is superimposed, that in the dark lady sonnets describes and names the redoubling of unity that leads to division, the mimic likeness of a likeness that leads to difference, the representation of presentation that spells the end of presence. Writing at or as the conclusion of a tradition of poetic idealism and idealization, when poetic imitation no longer functions as *Ideas Mirrour,* when poetic metaphor no longer "see(s) the same," Shakespeare in his sonnets draws the formal and thematic consequences that follow from the death of visual admiration. In the poetics of the sequence as a whole, at the level of its rhetorical figures, the dark lady sonnets explicitly break the amatory metaphorics of "Two distincts, division none" (*The Phoenix and the Turtle*) by substituting for such a unitary duality a tropic system of triangular, chiasmic duplicity: "A torment thrice threefold thus to be crossed" (133).

In the narrative the sequence tells, this figural double duplication, which brings out the difference built into binary identities, is thematically embodied in the ambiguously duplicitous dark lady—darker and older, almost by structural necessity, than the fair young man—and then projected into the double cuckoldry story itself, where the poet is betrayed by both his objects of desire when they couple or cross-couple with each other, and when the sequence as a whole moves from the unity of *folie à deux* to the duality of *ménage à trois*. In terms of the sonnets' own literary self-consciousness, there is an analogous contrast, again thematic, between the traditional poetry of erotic idealization addressed to the young man and the parodic undoing of that tradition by means of the radically *para-*, not *anti-*, Petrarchanism addressed to the dark lady, which repeats, but with a difference, the "sameness" of traditional idealizing themes. Finally, because the self-conscious tradition of the poetry of praise assumes that the language of poetic desire is itself identical to the object of poetic desire—which is why an orthodox poetry of love characteristically writes itself out as a love of poetry—Shakespeare's paradoxical version of the poetry of praise brings out even the difference built into the identity of literary and sexual admiration, which is how the dark lady sonnets describe a poetic desire whose Eros and Logos are themselves thematically out of joint.

It would be possible, of course, to find literary precedents for what seems novel in Shakespeare's sonnets. The kind of chiasmic (not oxymoronic) figurality that governs so many of Shakespeare's sonnets, the darksome light of the young man sonnets and their conflicted response to idealism, the general sense of literary belatedness that runs through the sequence as a whole—such features are already present in Dante, and they are yet more insistently and urgently emphatic in Petrarch, where the intractably heterogeneous relation of poetic signifier to poetic signified defines, to some extent, the central worry of the "scattered" songs to Laura. (In *The Secretum*, Petrarch's private and unpublished imaginary dialogue with Saint Augustine, Augustine accuses Petrarch of having fallen in love with Laura *only* on account of her name). So too, we could readily trace the way the Renaissance sonnet grows increasingly arch in its presentation of the Cratylitic correspondence of signifier to signified. This archness develops in so smooth and continuous a way as to suggest an unbroken line linking Beatrice, through Laura, through Stella (and through others) to, finally, what Shakespeare in several voluptuary sonnets calls his "Will."[16] So too, we could correlate the development of such literary self-consciousness with the increasingly intentional artificiality of the later "golden" sonnet, the way such sonnets strive, quite frankly, to present the conventionally reflexive reflections of orthodox epideixis as something *merely* literary, for prime example, the over-written way that Astrophil looks deep into his heart and in this way underwrites his introspective astrophilia. Even more obviously, we could find in the Renaissance vogue for the mock encomium, in the widespread enthusiasm for comically paradoxical praises of that which is low, not only the hyper-rhetorical temperament that Shakespeare's sonnets presuppose, but, also, a regularly reiterated interest in the specific themes that Shakespeare develops in the sonnets to the dark lady—e.g., the paradoxical praise of blindness, darkness, nymphomania, cuckoldry, false language, and so forth.[17]

The existence of such precedents is evidence of the fact that what Shakespeare "invents" in his sonnets is what he "comes upon" in a literary tradition and a literary history of which he is well aware and to which his sonnets are, again in a conventional way, intended as response. Yet it is important to recognize the genuine novelty that Shakespeare introduces into this literary tradition when he puts into words, as I have put it, his suspicions—truly, *sub-spicere*—of the visual and visionary poetics of idealism. For when Shakespeare thus outspokenly articulates, thematically as well as formally, the "insufficiency" that "make[s] me give the lie to my true sight" (150), when he makes his language literally as well as figuratively "mourn" the "morning," he manages, on the one hand, to render explicit reservations that in the orthodox Renaissance sonnet are serious but always implicit, just as, on the other, he manages to take seriously what in the tradition of the paradoxical mock encomium is explicit but always merely comic. He can do so because the thematic innovation has more than thematic consequence. By "expressing" the "difference" that the idealizing and homogeneous Renaissance sonnet necessarily "leaves out," the peculiar matter of Shakespearean paradox finds itself instantiated, exampled, by the corresponding paradox of Shakespearean poetic manner. Language thus speaks *for* its own gainsaying. The result is a new kind of Cratylism, a second degree of Cratylism, that, like the Liar's Paradox Shakespeare often flirts with in his sonnets—"Those lines that I before have writ do lie" (115), "When my love swears that she is made of truth" (138)—is proof of its own paradoxicality. In this gainsaying way—a speech acquired on condition that it speak against itself—Shakespeare accomplishes a limit case of the correspondence of signifier to signified. As the self-belying likeness of a difference, language becomes in Shakespeare's sonnets the true icon of an idol. Shakespeare's poetics of the word in this way acquires the "power" of its "insufficiency" (150), for every word the poet speaks effectively presents, is demonstration of, the loss of his ideal.[18]

With regard to Shakespearean subjectivity, two points follow from this, one practical, the other theoretical. First of all, the poet who speaks such a "forswearing" speech is no longer the speaking "eye" of the traditional sonnet. As a result, the poetic persona of Shakespeare's sonnets can no longer elaborate his subjectivity in accord with the ideal model of a self composed of the specular identification of poetic ego and poetic ego-ideal, of "I" and "you," or of eye and eyed. Instead, identifying himself with the heterogeneous look of the lady, or with the duplicity of her speech, the poet identifies himself with difference, with that which resists or breaks identification. The result is that the poet's identity is defined, by chiasmic triangulation, as the disruption or fracture of identity: "Me from myself thy cruel eye hath taken, / And my next self thou harder hast engrossed" (133). In terms of poetic erotics, we can say that this is why the poet of Shakespeare's sonnet sequence possesses a doubly divided desire—"Two loves I have of comfort and despair" (144)—and why the one is purchased dialectically, measure for measure, at the expense of the other, as "Th' expense of spirit in a waste of shame" (129). Speaking more generally, we can say that such a poetic self identifies himself with an inescapable, because constitutive, "insufficiency." Built up on or out of the loss of itself, its identity defined as its difference from itself, a hole opens up within the whole of poetic first-person self-presence. This "hole" within the "whole" (and also without, see sonnet 134: "He pays the whole, and yet am I not free") inserts into the poet a space of personal interiority, a palpable syncope, that justifies and warrants poetic introspection. This accounts for the strong personal affect of Shakespeare's lyric persona, what is called its "depth." By joining the rhetorical form of triangular chiasmus to the thematic heartbreak of a "perjur'd eye" (a phrase that, for this reason, we can think of as a "Shakespeareme," i.e., the smallest minimal unit of Shakespearean self), Shakespeare's sonnets give off the subjectivity effect called for by a post-idealist literariness. This is also how Shakespeare produces subjectivity in his plays, where, to take a simple example, the cross-coupling of pairs of lovers, their "star-cross'd" fate regularly explained in terms of a thematic disjunction between vision and language, characteristically generates what are taken to be Shakespeare's deeply realized, psychologistically authentic, dramatic personae. Moreover, to the extent that the characterologies of these characters continue to retain their specifically characterological or subjective appeal, to this extent we have evidence of the abiding, though posthumous, power of the idealism and the idealization to which the logic of their unhappy psychologies attest—an ideality all the more powerful for being constituted retrospectively, as a "remembrance of things past," as "th' expense of many a vanish'd sight," as a "fore-bemoaned moan," "Which I new pay as if not paid before" (30).

This leads, however, to a concluding theoretical observation. It has no doubt already been noticed that this reading of Shakespeare's sonnets, perfunctory as it is, has many affinities with various literary theories that have been labeled, somewhat simplistically, Structuralist and Post-Structuralist. My concern with the way the "languageness" of language is stressed by Shakespeare's sonnets is related to accounts of literariness that have been developed by such formalists as Roman Jakobson, Gérard Genette, Michael Riffaterre. My concern with cross-coupling chiasmus is related in very obvious ways to A. J. Greimas's "semantic square," to Paul De Man's discussions of figural chiasmus, and also to Jacques Lacan's "Schema L," which Lacan draws as a quaternary "Z". So too, my discussion of the way in which an idealist homogeneity is disrupted by a supplementary heterogeneity is in many ways like, and is certainly indebted to, Jacques Derrida's various essays in deconstructive phenomenology. Most obviously and most importantly, my account of a subjectivity precipitated by the paradoxical relationship of language to vision, my understanding of a language of desire and a desire of language, is very much influenced by Lacan's psychoanalytic account of what he calls the capture of the Imaginary by what he calls the Symbolic.

It is possible to recognize, therefore, a considerable overlap between certain contemporary literary, and not only literary, theorizations and both the formal and thematic peculiarities of Shakespeare's "perjur'd eye." This suggests either that Shakespeare was very theoretically acute or, instead, that contemporary theory is itself very Shakespearean. However, before choosing between either of these alternatives, we should recall the fact that contemporary literary theory, as it has thought itself out, has enacted a development very similar not only to the development we can discern in Shakespeare's sonnets as they move from the sonnets addressed to the young man to those addressed to the dark lady, but similar also to the larger literary development within which we can locate the historical significance of Shakespeare's sonnet sequence as a whole. Responding to Husserl's Dantesque phenomenology of *Ideas,* to Husserl's concern with eidetic reduction and a transcendental Ego, Sartre developed a psychology of imagination whose logic and metaphors very much resemble the paranoiac visionary thematics of a good many of Shakespeare's sonnets to the young man. The subjective optics of the Sartrian "gaze" and its melodrama of mutually persecutory master-slave relations subsequently receives in the thought of Merleau-Ponty, especially in late works such as *Le Visible et l'invisible,* an ironically comic revision whose chiasmic marriage of subject and object is reminiscent of more than a few of Shakespeare's most genuinely poignant sonneteering conceits; it was Merleau-Ponty, after all, who introduced "chiasmus" into contemporary critical discourse, as a way to explain the way Cézanne paints the trees watching Cézanne.[19] Lacan, Merleau-Ponty's friend, broke with Merleau-Ponty on just this point, seeing in the fully lived "flesh" and "visibility" of Merleau-Ponty's chiasmus a psychological and a phenomenological sentimentality. Instead, Lacan developed an account of the way subjectivity is born in the place where chiasmus breaks. Lacan's anamorphic "gaze," very different from *"le regard"* of Sartre or of Merleau-Ponty, along with Lacan's account of the way language potentiates and inherits this rupture of the imaginary, rather perfectly repeats the formal as well as the thematic logic of Shakespeare's "perjur'd eye."[20] So too, Derrida's attempt to rupture this rupture, Derrida's putatively postsubjective account of a supplemental *différence,* seems, from the point of view of Shakespeare's sonnets, nothing but another "increase" that "From fairest creatures we desire" (1), assuming we recognize the wrinkle, literally the "crease," that Shakespeare introduces into the perennial poetics of copious "increase."

This is significant because it raises the possibility that current thought works to transfer into a theoretical register a constellated set of literary themes, metaphors, motifs, that Shakespeare introduces into literature, in response to specific literary exigencies, at and as the beginning of the end of the Humanist Renaissance. If so, it is possible that current theorizations are important not because they offer a method or even a point of view with which to look back at Shakespeare, but, instead, because they participate in the very same literary history within which Shakespeare writes his sonnets, emerging now as a symptomatic and epiphenomenal consequence of the way, at the beginning of the modernist epoch, Shakespeare rethinks the literature he succeeds. Putting the question more strongly, we can ask whether, repeating Shakespeare's repetition, it is possible for contemporary theory to do so with a difference.

These are not questions I mean fully either to answer or even to address in this essay. But I would like at least to raise them, for it seems important that such a sense of repetition is itself a distinctive mark of Renaissance sensibility, especially of a good many literary minds for whom the project of their present is to give rebirth to the past. The very great Humanist Leone Ebreo—precursor to Spinoza, and in this way an important influence on Freud—in his dialogue *D'amore e desiderio* distinguishes—the topic is an old one—between love and desire on the grounds that love is an emotion one feels for that which one possesses, whereas desire is the emotion one feels for that which one does not possess.[21] Returning to the subject sometime later, in a dialogue called *De l'origine d'amore,* Ebreo emends his original distinction, reformulating it on the grounds that even that which one possesses, because it is possessed in transient time, carries with it, even at the moment of possession, a sense of loss.[22] This possession of loss, an emotion which is half love and half desire—what we might call a desire for love, but what we cannot call a love of desire—grows increasingly strong when the later and post-Humanist Renaissance returns to rethink a good many other topics relating to the origin of love. In time, in Shakespeare's sonnets, the rebirth of the Renaissance turns into the death of remorse, for in Shakespeare's sonnets "desire is death" (147) *because* "now is black beauty's successive heir" (127).[23]

It is because this is so central a theme in them, because they fully realize their *re-,* that Shakespeare's sonnets possess more than merely local interest. In Shakespeare's sonnets we hear how a literature of repetition, rather than a literature *de l'origine,* explains its desire to itself. With regard to the matter of poetic person, this is important because it allows us to understand how Shakespeare's response to secondariness leads him to introduce into literature a subjectivity altogether novel in the history of the lyric, or, as Shakespeare puts it, "Since mind at first in character was done" (59). For this very reason, however, the constitution of Shakespearean poetic self necessarily recalls the imperatives of a literariness larger even than the Shakespearean:

> If there be nothing new, but that which is
> Hath been before, how are our brains beguil'd
> Which laboring for invention bear amiss
> The second burthen of a former child! (59)

"The second burthen of a former child" very well characterizes the subjectivity fathered in the late Renaissance by the burden of a belated literariness. There is good reason to compare the rebirth of this aborted subject that "invention bear(s) amiss" with "Death's second self, that seals up all in rest" (73). However, to the extent that it is not only Shakespeare who looks, as sonnet 59 puts it, "with a backward look," to see "Your image in some antique book," the revolutionary question raised by such Shakespearean retrospection will continue to retain the ongoing urgency of a perennial and, it seems fair to say, since even Shakespeare now is "nothing new," an increasingly important literary commonplace:

> That I might see what the old world could say
> To this composed wonder of your frame,
> Whether we are mended, or whe'er better they,
> Or whether revolution be the same.
>   O, sure I am the wits of former days
>   To subjects worse have given admiring praise. (59)

Notes

Reprinted from *Representations,* no. 7 (Summer 1984), 59–86.

1.   All Shakespeare references are to *The Riverside Shakespeare,* ed. G.B. Evans et al. (Boston, 1974). Sonnet numbers are indicated within parentheses.

2.   See Lisle C. John, *The Elizabethan Sonnet Sequences: Studies in Conventional Conceits* (New York, 1938), 93–95; J.H. Hanford, "The Debate of Eye and Heart," *Modern Language Notes,* 26:6 (1911), 161–65.

3.   Petrarch, 174; compare to 86 and 87; references are to *Petrarch's Lyric Poems: The Rime Sparse and other Lyrics,* ed. and trans. R.M. Durling (Cambridge, Mass., 1976). *Le Roman de la Rose,* ed. F. Lecoy (Paris, 1914), 1684–87; see notes for background of the motif.

4.   Dante, *Paradiso,* Canto 33, lines 91–131; references are to *Dante's Paradiso,* ed. and trans. John D. Sinclair (New York, 1977).

5.   "Idea" is a sonneteering commonplace: J.W. Hebel, in his edition of *The Works of Michael Drayton* (Oxford, 1961) cites parallels in de Pontoux's *L'Idée,* in du Bellay, Desportes, Daniel; see vol. 5, p. 13. The Quarto prints "steeld"; Stephen Booth summarizes the range of connotations in *Shakespeare's Sonnets* (New Haven, 1977), 172–73. The conflicting ensemble of motifs attaching to "steeld"—visual, metallic, inscriptive, all those also referring to "stolen" and to "styled"—themselves stage the tensions that sonnet 24 develops out of its general visual conceit, especially the sonnet's play on "perspective."

6.   Simonides' saying is already a cliché for Plutarch, *De aud. poet.* 3. In *Elizabethan Critical Essays* (London, 1937), vol. 1, 386–87, G.G. Smith cites the many Renaissance parallels. Aristotle, *Poetics* 1459a 5–8; "But the greatest thing by far is to be a master of metaphor. It is the one thing that cannot be learnt from others; and it is also a sign of genius, since a good metaphor implies an intuitive perception of the similarity in dissimilars *(to gar eu metapherein to to homoion theōrein estin),*" *Aristotle on the Art of Poetry,* ed. and trans. I. Bywater (Oxford, 1909), 71.

7.   "'We beg you to tell us wherein this bliss of yours *(tua beatitudine)* now lies.' And I answered her by saying: 'In those words that praise my lady (In quelle parole che lodano la donna mia)'. . . . Therefore I resolved that from now on I would choose material for my poems that should be in praise of this most gracious one." *La Vita nuova,* (XVIII), F. Chapelli, ed., *Opere di Dante Alighiere* (Milan, 1967); M. Musa, trans., *La Vita Nuova of Dante Alighieri* (Bloomington, Ind., 1965). Acting on this resolve, Dante composes the first canzone of *La Vita Nuova,* "Donne ch'avete inteletto d'amore,"* which later, in *Purg.* 24, 49–63, in conversation with Buonagiunta, will be remembered as marking the beginning of *"le nove rime"* of the *"dolce stil nuovo."* For Petrarch's puns on "Laura," see, for example, *Rime Sparse,* 5, 6, 7, 194, 196, 246, 327, 356.

8.   Because the sonnet begins as a poetry of erotic praise, and because praise is also a central thematic issue in the orthodox Renaissance sonnet, the genre is a particularly focused instance of the poetry of praise. This is a significant fact because from antiquity up through the Renaissance, praise or, more generally, the epideictic (praise or blame), is taken to be the master literary genre of literature as such, the single genre under which all other, more particular, literary genres are properly subsumed. This is the basis for the hierarchy of literary genres or "kinds" in Renaissance literary theory, a typology that goes back to Aristotle, who derived all poetry from primal, epideictic imitation: praise of the high and blame of the low. We can identify the idealist assumptions at stake here by recalling the fact that the only poetry Socrates allows into the republic is "praise of gods and virtuous men."

The epideictic bias of traditional poetics—e.g., reading the *Aeneid* as a praise of Aeneas—is usually understood to reflect a concern on the part of the theoreticians with the didactic function of the poetical and the rhetorical; this is to understand the poetical or rhetorical in terms of effective moral persuasion. There is a more formal reason, however, with which traditional poetic theory accounts for the generic importance of the epideictic. Epi-deictic or de-monstrative rhetoric is called such because it is a rhetoric of "show" and "showing forth." The Greek is *epideiknunai,* "to show," "display"; in the middle voice, "to show off," "to display oneself." The Indo-European root is *deik*, with variant *deig*, "to show," which gives Greek *dikē*, "justice," and the verb *deiknunai*, "bright to light," "show forth," "represent," "portray," "point out," "show," leading to English "deictic," "paradigmatic," "apodeictic," etc. So too, *deiknunai* is also closely related to *deikeilon*, "representation," "exhibition," "reflection," "image," "phantom," "sculpted figure."

Aristotle brings out the significance of this semantic field, the Heideggerean resonance of which is obvious enough, when he distinguishes epideictic rhetoric from the two other kinds, forensic and deliberative, on the grounds that in the former the audience serves as "observer" *(theōron)*, whereas in the latter two the audience serves as "judge" *(kritēn)*, *Rhetoric*, 1358b2. Aristotle's point, brought out by his distinguishing between a rhetoric addressed to vision and a rhetoric addressed to judgment, is that epideictic or demonstrative oratory, as distinct from the transparent language of the law courts or the assembly, is a rhetoric both of display and self-display, a spectacular speech that we "observe" precisely because its manner calls attention to itself, a pointing "there" that points ego-centrically to "here," an objective "showing" that amounts to a subjective "showing-off." This explains why the epi-deictic is an extraordinary, not an ordinary, language. The point could be put in more contemporary terms by recalling the way Jakobson defines the specifically literary function as that message which stresses itself as merely message. The Renaissance sonnet characteristically amplifies this formal circularity of the language of praise, its recursive reflexivity, through various psychologistic conceits all designed to demonstrate the correlation of admiring subject with admired object. The point to realize is that when Shakespeare gives over the poetry of praise, when he distances himself from a visionary poetics, he not only gives over the themes and imagery of a perennial poetics, but also gives over the semiosis of this profoundly orthodox (and structuralist) literariness.

For the visual imagery employed by Renaissance poetic theory, especially theory of epideixis, see O.B. Hardison, Jr., *The Enduring Monument: A Study of the Idea of Praise in Renaissance Literary Theory and Practice* (Westport, Conn., 1962), 51–67. For general background see R. Tuve, *Elizabethan and Metaphysical Imagery* (Chicago, 1947), chs. 2, 3; R.W. Lee, *"Ut Pictura Poesis:* The Humanistic Theory of Painting," *Art Bulletin* 22 (1940), 197–269; E.H. Gombrich, *"Icones Symbolicae:* The Visual Image in Neo-Platonic Thought," *Journal of the Warburg and Courtauld Institutes* 11 (1948); R.J. Clements, *"Picta Poesis: Literary and Humanistic Theory in Renaissance Emblem Books* (Rome, 1960).

9.   Murray Krieger, "Poetic Presence and Illusion: Renaissance Theory and the Duplicity of Metaphor," *Critical Inquiry* 5:4 (1979), 619.

10.   *Astrophil and Stella*, No. 15.

11.   *Troilus and Cressida*, 5.2.144.

12.   Dante puts homosexuals and usurers in the same circle of hell, on the grounds that they couple, for sterile profit, kind with kind. For a very plausible explanation of why Brunetto Latini is also included here, see Eugene Vance, "Désir, rhétorique et texte," *Poétique* 42 (April, 1980), 137–55.

13.   *Troilus and Cressida*, 4.5.55–57. With regard to the way Shakespeare represents Petrarchism in the plays, compare this with Longaville's sonnet in *Love's Labor's Lost:* "Did not the heavenly rhetoric of thine eye, / 'Gainst whom the world cannot hold argument, / Persuade my heart to this false perjury" (4.3.58–60), or with Romeo's "She speaks, yet she says nothing; what of that? / Her eye discourses, I will answer it," *Romeo and Juliet*, 2.2.12–13.

14.   I develop such an account in *Shakespeare's Perjured Eye: The Invention of Poetic Subjectivity in Shakespeare's Sonnets* (forthcoming, University of California Press); this contains a fuller account of visual metaphors in traditional poetics, especially the way such metaphors are employed in the literature of orthodox and paradoxical praise.

15.   From Aristotle on, rhetoricians regularly identify comparison as the distinctive, characteristic trope of praise, this because comparison allows a speaker to amplify his referent. It is possible to double the two terms of a comparison so that the two terms thus produced stand to each other in a chiasmic relation. This is what happens to eye and heart in sonnet 132. This kind of chiasmic trope is especially characteristic of paradoxical, comic praises of that which is low, this because such par-

adoxical praises present themselves as mimic repetitions of orthodox praise. The technical term for this kind of reduplicating trope—tropes that break, by redoubling, the dual unities of metaphors that "see the same"—is *syneciosis*. Puttenham calls this the "cross-coupler," and associates it with the erotic, unkind mixture of kinds: "Ye have another figure which me thinkes may well be called (not much swerving from his originall in sence) the *Cross-couple,* because it takes me two contrary words, and tieth them as it were in a paire of couples, and so makes them agree like good fellowes, as I saw once in Fraunce a wolfe coupled with a mastiffe, and a foxe with a hounde," in George Puttenham, *The Arte of Englishe Poesie* (1589), facsimile reproduction (Kent, Ohio, 1970), 216.

16.   With their puns on "Will" the dark lady sonnets render explicit a good deal of what is left implicit in the young man sonnets. To begin with, the dark lady sonnets play on the fact that in Elizabethan slang "Will" refers to both the male and female genitals: "Wilt thou, whose will is large and spacious, / Not once vouchsafe to hide my will in thine?" (135). This picks up and extends, by doubling, several *doubles entendres* that run through the sonnets addressed to the young man. In the young man sonnets, for example, Shakespeare develops, in various ways, not only sexual, the image of the "pricked prick"—"But since she prick'd these out for women's pleasure, / Mine be thy love, and thy love's use their treasure" (20)—and uses this to characterize a desire which stands somewhere between the homosexual and the heterosexual. It is the same image, really, as "stell'd" in sonnet 24, or the time-marking "dial hand" of sonnet 104, but Shakespeare clearly enjoys the erotic connotations of the "pricked prick"—consider, for example, the fate of Adonis: "And nousling in his flank, the loving swine/ Sheath'd unaware the tusk in his soft groin" (*Venus and Adonis,* lines 1115–1116), or the bawdy puns of *Love's Labor's Lost,* e.g., "Let the mark have a prick in't" (4.1.132), "The preyful Princess pierc'd and prick'd a pretty pleasing pricket" (4.2.56), or, more elaborately, the way Othello takes as well as "took . . . by the throat the circumcised dog / And smote him—thus" (5.2.355–356). In the dark lady sonnets, however, by virtue of the pun on "Will," the poet becomes not only a "pricked prick," but also, again exploiting Elizabethan slang, the "cut cunt" (compare Malvolio in *Twelfth Night:* "These be her very c's, her u's, and her t's, and thus makes she her great P's" (2.5.86–88). This double doubling, whereby "Will" performs the copulation that the poet speaks about, enables Shakespeare explicitly to develop some of the thematic consequences, not only erotic, that the subject of a verbal name *must* suffer. As a "Will," the poet becomes the chiasmic copula between male and female, presence and absence, inside and outside, waxing and waning, showing and hiding, whole and hole, one and none:

> Among a number one is reckon'd none:
> Then in the number let me pass untold,
> Though in thy store's account I one must be,
> For nothing hold me, so it please thee hold
> That nothing me, a something sweet to thee.
>   Make but my name thy love, and love that still,
>   And then thou lovest me, for my name is Will (136).

Quite apart from the various themes and images that are thus put into crosscoupling play, the "Will" sonnets are significant precisely because they mark the first person of the poet with a name, not a deictic, for this identifies the person of the poet through a system of representational, not presentational, reference. This is quite different from the kind of immediate reference achieved by deictic, I-you, indication, for, as has often been pointed out (e.g., Bertrand Russell on egocentric particulars, Jakobson on shifters, and E. Benveniste on pronouns and relationships of person in the verb), such egocentric reference requires the presence of the speaker to his speech. In contrast, a name retains a stable referent regardless of who speaks it. In ways which I discuss in *Shakespeare's Perjured Eye,* it can be shown, first, that deixis is the mode of first-person speaking required by an epideictic poetics, second, that a post-epideictic poetry, such as Shakespeare experiments with in the dark lady sonnets, acquires its subjective effects from the contest it stages between self-displaying visual deictics and self-belying verbal names, as in sonnet 151, where "flesh . . . rising at thy name doth point out thee / As his triumphant prize," but is also obliged "thy poor drudge to be, / To stand in thy affairs, fall by thy side."

   There is more to say about these disappointing pointers, but I would like to note here that it was Oscar Wilde who first insisted in a strong way on the importance for Shakespeare's sonnets of this quarrel between verbal name and visual deictic. It was Wilde who, reading between the lines, and picking up an old conjecture (going back to Thomas Tyrwhitt in 1766), named the poet's cata-mite "Willie Hughes," doing this in order to draw out the important and pervasive Shakespearean pun on double "hue," "view," "use," and "you"—the same double-U whose present-absent presence distinguishes "whole" from "hole" in sonnet 134. These are the signifiers through which Shake-speare thinks the large narrative of the sonnets. By doubling the dual unity of first and second per-son, Shakespeare introduces, for the very first time, a third person into epideictic lyric. This formally *absent* third person—a "he" or "she" or "it"—who stands in between, as missing connection, the poet's first and second person, is what the poet becomes to himself when he becomes his name. Compare, for example, the progress of Othello from "all in all sufficient" (4.1.265) to "That's he that was Othello; here I am" (5.2.283). Recognizing this, it becomes possible to understand why Wilde's *Portrait of W.H.* is the only genuinely literary criticism that Shakespeare's sonnets have ever yet received. Wilde's novella narrates the argument between the metaphorics of visual presentation, the "Portrait," and the signifiers of linguistic representation, "W.H." In the same way, Wilde's *The Impor-tance of Being Earnest* acts out the question of what is *in* a Shakespearean name, thereby putting an end to a theatrical tradition that begins, at least in English drama, with *The Comedy of Errors*. I discuss the relation of Wilde to Shakespeare more fully in *Shakespeare's Perjured Eye*. I also discuss Wilde's concern with the issue of specifically literary naming in "The Significance of Literature: *The Importance of Being Ernest*," October 15 (1980), 79–90 [reprinted in this volume].

17.   For a discussion of the classical mock encomium, see T.C. Burgess, *Epideictic Literature* (Chi-cago, 1902), 157–66. For discussions of Renaissance praise paradox, see A.E. Mallock, "The Tech-niques and Functions of the Renaissance Paradox," *Studies in Philology* 53 (1956), 191–203; E.N. Thompson, "The Seventeenth Century English Essay," *University of Iowa Humanistic Studies,* 3:3 (1926), 94–105; A.S. Pease, "Things Without Honor," *Classical Philology* 21 (1926), 27–42; H.K. Miler, "The Paradoxical Encomium with Special Reference to its Vogue in England: 1600–1800," *Modern Philology* 53:3 (1956), 145–78; A.H. Stockton, "The Paradoxical Encomium in Elizabethan Drama" *University of Texas Studies in English* 28 (1949), 83–104; R.E. Bennet, "Four Paradoxes by Sir William Cornwallis, the Younger," *Harvard Studies and Notes in Philology and Literature* 13 (1931) 219–40; W.G. Rice, "The *Paradossi* of Ortensio Landi," *University of Michigan Essays and Studies in English and Comparative Literature* 8 (1932), 59–74; "Erasmus and the Tradition of Paradox," *Stud-ies in Philology* 53 (1964), 191–203; W. Kaiser, *Praisers of Folly* (Cambridge, Mass., 1963); B. Vickers, "*King Lear* and Renaissance Paradoxes," *Modern Language Notes* 63:2 (1968), 305–14; R. Colie, *Par-adoxia Epidemica: The Renaissance Tradition of Praise Paradox* (Princeton, N.J., 1966).

18.   At stake here is the difference between a rhetorical paradox and a merely logical paradox, for these are not the same, though in the Renaissance they are, of course, very much related. In con-temporary philosophical terminology, this is something like the distinction between a real logical paradox (which would carry, if such a thing exists, some of the weight of the rhetorical paradox) and a merely semantic paradox (e.g., the Liar's Paradox).

19.   See especially the discussion of *entrelacs* in *Le Visible et l'invisible* (Paris, 1964), ch. 4.

20.   I refer here not only to Lacan's explicit formulations, but also to the development of Lacan's thought, from the early emphasis on visual themes, as in the essay on the "mirror-stage" and accom-panying discussions of aggressivity, to the later emphasis on language, anamorphosis, and accom-panying discussions of (male) desire, to, finally, as a third term added to the opposition of the Imaginary and the Symbolic, Lacan's emphasis on the "Real," the limits of representation, and accompanying discussions of (female) *jouissance*. Lacan's sense of the Renaissance is colored, how-ever, by a very Catholic and Counter-Reformational, a very French, conception of the Baroque: "Le

baroque, c'est la régulation de l'âme par la scopie corporelle," *Encore* (Paris, 1975), 105, which is why Lacan's direct comments on Shakespeare are often disappointing.

21.   Leone Ebreo, *Dialoghi d'amore,* ed. Santino Caramella (Bari, 1929), 5, cited by J.C. Nelson, *Renaissance Theory of Love* (New York, 1958), 86. Ebreo's distinction remains a strong challenge to subsequent writers on the subject. Consider, for example, "Love, universally taken, is defined to be a desire, as a word of more ample signification; and though Leon Hebraeus, the most copious writer of this subject, in his third dialogue makes no difference, yet in his first he distinguisheth them again, and defines love by desire." Robert Burton, *The Anatomy of Melancholy,* ed. A. Shilleto (London, 1903), Part III, sect. 1, mem. 1, subs. 2; vol. III, p. 10.

22.   Ebreo, *Dialoghi,* 207, cited by Nelson, 86–87.

23.   That desire is death is of course a commonplace, e.g., Ronsard's "Car l'Amour et la Mort n'est qu'une mesme chose," *Sonnets Pour Hélène,* II:77, *Oeuvres complètes de Ronsard,* ed. G. Cohen (Paris, 1950). What is important is the specifically double way in which Shakespearean revision revives this dead metaphor.

> Hortensio: *Now go thy ways, thou hast tam'd a curst shrow.*
> Lucentio: *'Tis a wonder, by your leave, she will be tam'd so.*
>
> (5.2.188–9)

In ways which are so traditional that they might be called proverbial, Shakespeare's *Taming of the Shrew* assumes—it turns out to make no difference whether it does so ironically—that the language of woman is at odds with the order and authority of man. At the same time, again in ways which are nothing but traditional, the play self-consciously associates this thematically subversive discourse of woman with its own literariness and theatricality. The result, however, is a play that speaks neither for the language of woman nor against the authority of man. Quite the contrary: at the end of the play things are pretty much the same—which is to say, patriarchally inflected—as they were at or before its beginning, the only difference being that now, because there are more shrews than ever, they are more so. It cannot be surprising that a major and perennially popular play by Shakespeare, which is part of a corpus that, at least in an English literary tradition, is synonymous with what is understood to be canonical, begins and ends as something orthodox. Nevertheless, there is reason to wonder—as my epigraph, the last lines of the play, suggests—how it happens that a discourse of subversion, explicitly presented as such, manages to resecure, equally explicitly, the very order to which it seems, at both first and second sight, to be opposed. This question, raised by the play in a thematic register, and posed practically by the play by virtue of the play's historical success, leads to another: is it possible to voice a language, whether of man or of woman, that does not speak, sooner or later, self-consciously or unconsciously, for the order and authority of man?

Formulated at considerably greater levels of generality, such questions have been advanced by much recent literary, and not only literary, theory, much of which finds it very difficult to sustain in any intelligible fashion an effective critical and adversary distance or difference between itself and any of a variety of master points of view, each of which claims special access to a global, universalizing truth. It is, however, in the debates and polemics growing out of and centering upon the imperial claims of psychoanalysis that such questions have been raised in the very same terms and at precisely the level of generality proposed by *The Taming of the Shrew*—the level of generality measured by the specificity of rubrics as massive and as allegorically suggestive as Man, Woman, and Language—for it is psychoanalysis, especially the psychoanalysis associated with the name of Jacques Lacan, that has most coherently developed an account of human subjectivity which is based upon the fact that human beings speak. Very much taking this speech to heart, psychoanalysis has organized, in much the same ways as does *The Taming of the Shrew,* the relationship of generic Man to generic Woman by reference to the apparently inescapable patriarchalism occasioned by the structuring effects of language—of Language, that is to say, which is also understood in broad genericizing terms. In turn, the most forceful criticisms of psychoanalysis, responding to the psychoanalytic provocation with a proverbial response, have all been obliged, again repeating the thematics of *The Taming of the Shrew,* to speak against this Language for which the psychoanalytic speaks.

Thus it is not surprising, to take the most important and sophisticated example of this debate, that Jacques Derrida's (by comparison) very general critique of logocentric metaphysics, his deconstructive readings of what he calls the ontotheological ideology of presence in the history of the west, turns more specifically into a critique of phallogocentric erotics in the course of a series of rather pointed (and, for Derrida, unusually vociferous) attacks on Lacanian psychoanalysis. Lacan serves Derrida as a kind of limit case of such western "presence," to the extent that Lacan, centering the psychology of the human subject on a lack disclosed by language, deriving human desire out of a linguistic want, is prepared to make a presence even out of absence, and, therefore, as Derrida objects, a God out of a gap. As is well known, Derrida opposes to the determinate and determining logic of the language of Lacan—though with a dialectic that is of course more complicated than that of any simply polar opposition—an alternative logic of *différance* and writing, associating this a-logical logic with a "question of style" whose status as an irreducible question keeps alive, by foreclosing any univocal answer, the deconstructive power of a corresponding "question of woman." Here again, however, it is possible to identify the formulaic ways in which this Derridean alternative to a psychoanalytic logos recapitulates, because it predicates itself as something Supplementary and Other, the general thematics of *The Taming of the Shrew*. And this recapitulation has remained remarkably consistent, we might add, in the more explicitly feminist extensions of the deconstructive line traced out by Derrida, all of which, for all the differences between them, attempt to speak up for, and even to speak, a different kind of language than that of psychoanalytic man (e.g., the preverbal, presymbolic "semiotic" of Julia Kristeva, the *écriture féminine* of Hélène Cixous, the intentionally duplicitous or bilabial eroticism of Luce Irigaray, the Nietzschean narcissism of Sarah Kofman).[1]

This theoretical debate between psychoanalysis and the deconstructive feminisms that can be called, loosely speaking, its most significant other is in principle interminable to the extent that psychoanalysis can see in such resistance to its language, as Freud did with Dora, a symptomatic confirmation of all psychoanalytic thought. In the context of this debate, *The Taming of the Shrew* initially possesses the interest of an exceptionally apt literary example, one to which the different claims of different theories—about language, desire, gender—might be fruitfully applied. On the other hand, to the extent that this debate appears itself to reenact the action that is staged within *The Taming of the Shrew,* there exists the more than merely formal possibility that the play itself defines the context in which such debate about the play will necessarily take place. Understood in this way, the theoretical quarrel that might take place about *The Taming of the Shrew* would then emerge as nothing more than an unwitting reproduction of the thematic quarrel—between Man and Woman or between two different kinds of language—that already finds itself in motion in *The Taming of the Shrew.* If this were the case—and it remains to determine with what kind of language one might even say that this is the case—then the self-conscious literariness of *The Taming of the Shrew,* the reflexively recursive metatheatricality with which the play presents itself as an example of what it represents, would acquire its own explanatory, but not exactly theoretical, value. Glossing its own literariness, the play becomes the story of why it is the way it is, and this in turn becomes a performative account or self-example of the way a theoretical debate centered around the topoi of sexuality, gender, and language appears to do no more than once again repeat, to no apparent end, an old and still ongoing story.

That the story is in fact an old one is initially suggested by the ancient history attaching to the three stories joined within *The Taming of the Shrew*: the Christopher Sly framing plot, where a lord tricks a peasant into thinking himself a lord, which goes back at least as far as a fable in *The Arabian Nights*; the story of Lucentio's wooing of Bianca, which can be traced back, through Gascoigne and Ariosto, to Plautus or Menander; and the taming story proper, Petruchio's domestication of the shrewish

Kate, which is built up out of innumerable literary and folklore analogues, all of which can claim an antique provenance. Correlated with each other by means of verbal, thematic, and structural cross-references, these three independent stories become in *The Taming of the Shrew* a single narrative of a kind whose twists and turns would seem familiar even on first hearing. Indeed, the only thing that is really novel about the plotting of *The Taming of the Shrew* is the way the play concatenates these three quite different stories so as to make it seem as though each one of them depends upon and is a necessary version of the other two.

Moreover, the play itself insists upon the fact that it retells a master plot of western literary history. By alluding to previous dramatic, literary, and biblical texts, by quoting and misquoting familiar tags and phrases, by parodically citing or miming more serious literary modes (e.g., Ovidian narrative and Petrarchan lyric), the play situates itself within a literary tradition to which even its mockery remains both faithful and respectful. This is especially the case with regard to the taming subplot that gives the play its name. Soon after he enters, for example, Petruchio cites proverbial precursors for the cursing Kate, in one brief passage linking her not only to the alter ego of the Wife of Bath but also to the Cumaean Sibyl and Socrates' Xantippe (1.2.69–71) (these references later to be counterbalanced by Kate's translation to "a second Grissel, and Roman Lucrece" (2.1.295–6).[2] Such women are all touchstones of misogynistic gynecology. The commonplace way in which Petruchio evokes them here, drawing from a thesaurus of women whose voices will systematically contradict the dictates of male diction, is characteristic of the way, from beginning to end, the play works to give archetypal resonance and mythological significance to Kate's specifically female speech, locating it in the context of a perennial iconography for which the language of woman—prophetic and erotic, enigmatic and scolding, excessive and incessant—stands as continually nagging interference with, or as seductive and violent interruption of, or, finally, as loyally complicitous opposition to, the language of man.

What kind of language is it, therefore, that woman speaks, and in what way does it differ, always and forever, from the language of man? The first answer given by *The Taming of the Shrew* is that it is the kind of language Petruchio speaks when he sets out to teach to Kate the folly of her ways. "He is more shrew than she" (4.1.85) summarizes the homeopathic logic of the taming strategy in accord with which Petruchio, assimilating to himself the attributes of Kate, will hold his own lunatic self up as mirror of Kate's unnatural nature. As perfect instance and reproving object lesson of his wife's excess, Petruchio thus finds "a way to kill a wife with kindness" (4.1.208). As an example which is simultaneously a counterexample, "He kills her in her own humour" (4.1.180). All Petruchio's odd behavior—his paradoxical and contradictory assertions, his peremptory capriciousness, his "lunacy," to use a word and image that is central to *The Taming of the Shrew*—presupposes this systematic and admonitory program of an eye for an eye, or, as the play defines the principle: "being mad herself, she's madly mated. / I warrant him, Petruchio is Kated" (3.2.244–5; "mated" here meaning "amazed" as well as "matched"). Moreover, all this madness bespeaks the language of woman, for Petruchio's lunatic behavior, even when it is itself nonverbal, is understood to be a corollary function, a derivative example, of the shrewish voice of Kate, as when Petruchio's horrific marriage costume, a demonstrative insult to appropriate decorum—"A monster, a very monster in apparel" (3.2.69–70)—is taken as a statement filled with a didactic sense: "He hath some meaning in his mad attire" (3.2.124).

In Act I, Scene ii, which is the first scene of the taming subplot, Grumio, Petruchio's servant, explains the meaning as well as the method of Petruchio's madness. At the same time, he suggests how this is to be related to all the action, especially the verbal action, of the play:

> A' my word, and she knew him as well as I do, she would think scolding would do little good upon him. She may perhaps call him half a score knaves or so. Why, that's nothing; and he begin once, he'll rail in his rope-tricks. I'll tell you what, sir, and she stand him but a little, he will throw a figure in her face, and so disfigure her with it that she shall have no more eyes to see withal than a cat.
>
> (1.2.108–15)

This is an obscure passage, perhaps intentionally so, but "the general sense," as the editor of the Oxford edition says, "must be that Petruchio's railing will be more violent than Katherine's."[3] Even so, it is the manner of the passage, more than its somewhat bewildering matter, that best conveys "the general sense" of Petruchio's project, a point brought out by the apparently unanswerable puzzle posed by "rope-tricks." On "rope-tricks" the Oxford editor says: "If emendation is thought necessary, 'rhetricks' is the best yet offered; but 'rope-tricks' may well be correct and may mean tricks that can be punished adequately only by hanging." The *Riverside* edition offers a similar answer to the "rope-tricks" question, but does so with even more uncertainty, as evidenced by the parenthetical question-marks that interrupt the gloss: "*rope-tricks*: blunder for *rhetoric* (an interpretation supported by *figure* in line 114(?) or tricks that deserve hanging(?)."

On the face of it, neither of these edgily tentative editorial comments is especially helpful in determining, one way or the other, whether Petruchio, when he "rails in his rope-tricks," will be doing something with language or, instead, performing tricks for which he should be hanged. The "interpretation," as the *Riverside* edition calls it, remains indeterminate. But such determination is of course not the point. The editors recognize—and so too, presumably, does an audience—that it is for what he does with language that Petruchio runs any risk with (bawdy) rope. Hence the special suitability of "rope-tricks" as a term to describe the way in which Petruchio will respond to Kate in verbal kind. Playing on "rhetoric" and on "rope," but being neither, "rope-tricks" simultaneously advances, one way *and* the other, both the crime (rape) and the punishment (rope) attaching to the extraordinary speech the play associates with Kate (rhetoric). "Rope-tricks," moreover, is a uniquely performative word for rhetoric, since "rope-tricks" *is* rhetoric precisely because it is not "rhetoric," and thus discloses, by pointing to itself, a kind of necessary disjunction between itself as a verbal signifier and what, as a signifier, it means to signify. In this way, as a kind of self-remarking case of rhetoric in action, "rope-tricks" becomes the general name not only for all the figurative language in the play but, also, for all the action in the play which seems literally to mean one thing but in fact means another: for prime example, the way in which Petruchio will speak the language of woman in order to silence Kate.

The point to notice about this is that, as far as the play is concerned, the "interpretation" of "rope-tricks," its meaning, is not altogether indeterminate or, rather, if it is indeterminate, this indeterminacy is itself very strictly determined. "Rope-tricks" is a word that univocally insists upon its own equivocation, and this definitive indeterminacy is what defines its "general sense." In a way that is not at all paradoxical, and in terms which are in no sense uncertain, the question posed by "rope-tricks" has as its answer the question of rhetoric, and the play uses this circularity—the circularity that makes the rhetoricity of a rhetorical question itself the answer to the question that it poses—as a paradigmatic model for the way in which, throughout the play, Petruchio will obsessively answer Kate with hysterical tit for hysterical tat.

Understood in this way, as "rope-tricks," we can say that the words and actions of *The Taming of the Shrew* rehearse a familiar antagonism, not simply the battle between the sexes but, more specifically, though still rather generally, the battle between the determinate, literal language traditionally spoken by man and the figurative, indeterminate language traditionally spoken by woman. But by saying this we are only returned, once again, to the question with which we began, for if such indeterminacy is what rhetoric always means to say, if this is the literal significance of its "general sense," why is it that this indeterminacy seems in *The Taming of the Shrew* so definitively to entail the domestication of Kate? Petruchio is never so patriarchal as when he speaks the language of woman—"He is more shrew than she"—just as Kate's capitulation occurs at the moment when she obediently takes her husband at his lunatic, female, figurative word. This happens first when Petruchio forces Kate to call the sun the moon, and then when Petruchio forces Kate to address a reverend father as "young budding virgin," a purely verbal mix-up of the sexes that leads an onlooker to remark: "A will make the man mad, to make a woman of him" (4.5.35–6). In accord with what asymmetrical *quid pro quo* does Petruchio propose to silence Kate by speaking the language she speaks, and why does the play assume that the orthodox order of the sexes for which it is the spokesman is reconfirmed when, madly translating a man into a mad woman, it gives explicit voice to such erotic paradox? Why, we can ask, do things not happen the other way around?

These are questions that bear on current theory. The editorial question-marks that punctuate the gloss on "rope-tricks" mark the same site of rhetorico-sexual inde-terminacy on which Derrida, for example, will hinge his correlation of "the question of style" with "the question of woman" (this is the same disruptive question-mark, we can note, that Dora dreams of when she dreams about her father's death).[4] But again, such questions are foregrounded *as* questions in *The Taming of the Shrew,* and in a far from naive manner. We learn, for example, in the very first lines of the play performed for Christopher Sly that Lucentio has come "to see fair Padua, the nursery of arts" (1.1.2), having left his father's "Pisa, renowned for grave citizens" (1.1.10). Lucentio's purpose, he says, is to "study / Virtue and that part of philosophy / . . . that treats of happiness" (1.1.17–19). This purpose stated, and the crazy psy-chogeography of Padua thus established by its opposition to sober Pisa, Tranio, Lucentio's servant, then rushes to caution his master against too singleminded a "resolve / To suck the sweets of sweet philosophy" (27–8): "Let's be no Stoics nor no stocks," says Tranio, "Or so devote to Aristotle's checks / As Ovid be an outcast quite abjur'd" (31–2). Instead, Tranio advises his master to pursue his studies with a certain moderation. On the one hand, says Tranio, Lucentio should "Balk logic with acquain-tance that you have," but, on the other, he should also "practice rhetoric in your com-mon talk" (34–5). This is the initial distinction to which all the subsequent action of the play consistently and quite explicitly refers, a distinction that starts out as the dif-ference between logic and rhetoric, or between philosophy and poetry, or between Aristotle and Ovid, but which then becomes, through the rhetorical question raised by "rope-tricks," the generalized and—for this is the point—quite *obviously* problematic difference between literal and figurative language on which the sexual difference between man and woman is seen to depend.

Tranio's pun on "Stoics"/"stocks," a pun which is a tired commonplace in Elizabethan comic literature, suggests both the nature of the problem and the way in which the play thematically exploits it. The pun puts the verbal difference between its two terms into question, into specifically rhetorical question, and so it happens that each term is sounded as the mimic simulation of the other. If language can do this to the difference between "Stoics" and "stocks," what can it do to the difference between "man" and "woman"? Is the one the mimic simulation of the other? This is a practical, as well as a rhetorical, question raised by the play, because the play gives countless demonstrations of the way in which the operation of stressedly rhetorical language puts into question the possibility of distinguishing between itself and the literal language it tropes. Petruchio, for example, when we first meet him, even before he hears of Kate, tells Grumio, his servant, to "knock me at the gate" (1.2.11). The predictable misunderstanding that thereupon ensues is then compounded further when a helpful intermediary offers to "compound this quarrel" (27). These are trivial puns, the play on "knock" and the play on "compound," but their very triviality suggests the troubling way in which the problematic question raised by one word may eventually spread to, and be raised by, all. "Knock at the gate," asks Grumio, "O heavens! Spake you not these words plain?" (39–40).

Given the apparently unavoidable ambiguity of language or, at least, the ever-present possibility of such ambiguity, it is precisely the question, the rhetorical question, of speaking plainly that Grumio raises, as though one cannot help but "practice rhetoric" in one's "common talk." Moreover, as the play develops it, this argument between the master and his servant, an argument spawned by the rhetoricity of language, is made to seem the explanation of Kate's ongoing quarrel with the men who are her master. For example, the same kind of "knocking" violence that leads Petruchio and Grumio to act out the rhetorical question that divides them is what later leads Kate to break her lute upon her music-master's head: "I did but tell her she mistook her frets . . . And with that word she strook me on the head" (2.1.149–53).

Such "fretful" verbal confusions occur very frequently in the play, and every instance of them points up the way in which any given statement, however intended, can always mean something other than what its speaker means to say. For this reason, it is significant that, in almost the first lines of the play, Christopher Sly, after being threatened with "a pair of stocks" (Ind.1.2), explains not only why this is possibly the case but, really, why this is necessarily the case, formulating, in a "rope-trick" way, a general principle that accounts for the inevitability of such linguistic indeterminacy. *"Paucas pallabris,"* says Christopher Sly, "let the world slide" (Ind.1.5). The bad Spanish here is a misquotation from *The Spanish Tragedy,* Hieronimo's famous call for silence. An Elizabethan audience would have heard Sly's *"paucas pallabris"* as the comic application of an otherwise serious cliché, i.e., as an amusing deformation of a formulaic tag (analogous to Holofernes' *"pauca verba"* in *Love's Labour's Lost* (4.2.165)), whose "disfiguring" corresponds to the troping way in which Sly mistakenly recalls Hieronimo by swearing by "Saint Jeronimy" (Ind.1.9). So too with Sly's "let the world slide," which is equally proverbial, and which is here invoked as something comically and ostentatiously familiar, as something novel just *because* it sounds passé, being half of a proverb whose other half Sly pronounces at the end of the frame, in the last line of the Induction, which serves as introduction to the play within the play: "Come madam wife, sit by my side, and let the world slip, we shall ne'er be younger" (Ind.2.142–3).

Taken together, and recognizing the register of self-parody on which, without Sly's knowing it, they seem to insist, the two phrases make a point about language that can serve as a motto for the rest of the play. There are always fewer words than there are meanings, because a multiplicity of meanings not only can but always will attach to any single utterance. Every word bears the burden of its hermeneutic history—the extended scope of its past, present, and future meanings—and for this reason every word carries with it a kind of surplus semiotic baggage, an excess of significance, whose looming, even if unspoken, presence cannot be kept quiet. Through inadvertent cognate homophonies, through uncontrollable etymological resonance, through unconscious allusions and citations, through unanticipatable effects of translation (*translatio* being the technical term for metaphor), through syntactic slips of the tongue, through unpredictable contextual transformations—in short, through the operation of "rope-tricks," the Word (for example, Sly's "world") will "slide" over a plurality of significances, to no single one of which can it be unambiguously tied down. Sly's self-belying cry for silence is itself an instance of a speech which is confounded by its excess meaning, of literal speech which is beggared, despite its literal intention, by an embarrassment of unintended semiotic riches. But the play performed before Sly—with its many malapropisms, its comic language lesson, its mangled Latin and Italian, its dramatic vivifications of figurative play, as when Petruchio bandies puns with Kate—demonstrates repeatedly and almost heavyhandedly that the rhetorical question raised by Grumio is always in the polysemic air: "Spake you not these words plain?"

It would be easy enough to relate the principle of *"paucas pallabris"* to Derrida's many characterizations of the way the everpresent possibility of self-citation—not necessarily parodic citation—codes every utterance with an irreducible indeterminacy, leaving every utterance undecidably suspended, at least in principle, between its literal and figurative senses. Even more specifically, it would be possible to relate the many proverbial ways in which the "wor(l)d" "slides" in *The Taming of the Shrew*—"'He that is giddy thinks the world goes round'" (5.2.26), a proverb that can lead, as Kate remarks, to "A very mean meaning" (31)—to Lacan's various discussions of the not so freely floating signifier.[5] But, even if it is granted, on just these theoretical grounds, that the rhetoricity of language enforces this kind of general question about the possibility of a speaker's ever really being able to mean exactly what he means to say, and even if it is further granted that the "practice" of "rhetoric" in "common talk" is a self-conscious issue in *The Taming of the Shrew*, still, several other, perhaps more pressing, questions still remain. Why, for example, does the indeterminate question of rhetoric call forth the very determinate patriarchal narrative enacted in *The Taming of the Shrew*? Putting the same question in a theoretical register, we can ask why the question of rhetoric evokes from psychoanalysis the patriarchalism for which Lacan appears to be the most explicit mouthpiece, just as the same question provokes, instead, the antipatriarchal gender deconstructions—the chiasmically invaginated differences, the differentiated differences, between male and female—for which we might take Derrida to be the most outspoken spokesman.

To begin to think about these questions, it is necessary first to recognize that *The Taming of the Shrew* is somewhat more specific in its account of female language than I have so far been suggesting. For there is of course another woman in the play whose voice is strictly counterposed to the "scolding tongue" (1.1.252) of Kate, and if Kate, as shrew, is shown to speak a misanthropic, "fretful" language, her sister, the ideal Bianca of the wooing story, quite clearly speaks, and sometimes even sings, another and, at least at first, a more inviting tune. There are, that is to say, at least two kinds of language that the play associates with women—one good, one bad—and the play invents two antithetical stereotypes of woman—again, one good, one bad—to be the voice of these two different kinds of female speech.

This is a distinction or an opposition whose specific content is often overlooked, perhaps because Bianca's voice, since it is initially identified with silence, seems to speak a language about which there is not that much to say. Nevertheless, this silence of Bianca has its own substantial nature, and it points up what is wrong with what, in contrast, is Kate's vocal or vociferating speech. In the first scene of the play within the play, which is where we first meet these two women, Lucentio is made to be a witness to the shrewish voice of Kate—"That wench is stark mad or wonderful froward" (1.1.69)—and this loquacity of Kate is placed in pointed contrast to Bianca's virgin muteness: "But in the other's silence do I see / Maid's mild behavior and sobriety" (70–1). This opposition, speech versus silence, is important, but even more important is the fact that it is developed in the play through the more inclusive opposition here suggested by the metaphorical way in which Lucentio "sees" Bianca's "silence." For Bianca does in fact speak quite often in the play—she is not literally mute—but the play describes this speech, as it does Bianca, with a set of images and motifs, figures of speech, that give both to Bianca and to her speaking a specific phenomenality which is understood to be *equivalent* to silence. This quality, almost a physical materiality, can be generally summarized—indeed, generically summarized—in terms of an essential visibility: that is to say, Bianca and her language both are silent because the two of them are something to be *seen*.

One way to illustrate this is to recall how the first scene repeatedly emphasizes the fact that Lucentio falls in love with Bianca at first sight: "let me be a slave, t'achieve that maid / Whose sudden sight hath thrall'd my wounded eye" (1.1.219–20). A good deal of Petrarchan imagery underlies the visuality of Lucentio's erotic vision: "But see, while idly I stood looking on, / I found the effect of love in idleness" (1.1.150–1). More specifically, however, this modality of vision, this generic specularity, is made to seem the central point of difference between two different kinds of female language whose different natures then elicit in response two different kinds of male desire. There is, that is to say, a polar contrast, erotically inflected, between, on the one hand, the admirably dumb visual language of Bianca and, on the other, the objectionably noisy "tongue" (1.1.89) of Kate:

Tranio: Master, you look'd so longly on the maid . . .
Lucentio: O yes, I saw sweet beauty in her face . . .
Tranio: Saw you no more? Mark'd you not how her sister
             Began to scold, and raise up such a storm
             That mortal ears might hardly endure the din?
Lucentio: Tranio, I saw her mortal lips to move,
             And with her breath she did perfume the air.
             Sacred and sweet was all I saw in her.

                                                      (165–76)

In *The Taming of the Shrew* this opposition between vision and language—rather, between a language which is visual, of the eye, and therefore silent, and language which is vocal, of the tongue, and therefore heard—is very strong. Moreover, as the play develops it, this is a dynamic and a violent, not a static, opposition, for it is just such vision that the vocal or linguistic language of Kate is shown repeatedly to speak against. In the first scene this happens quite explicitly, when Kate says of Bianca, in what are almost the first words out of Kate's mouth, "A pretty peat! It is best / Put a finger in the eye, and she knew why" (1.1.78–9). But this opposition runs throughout the play, governing its largest dramatic as well as its thematic movements. To take an example which is especially significant in the light of what has so far been said, we can recall that the "rope-tricks" passage concludes when it prophetically imagines Kate's ultimate-capitulation in terms of a blinding cognate with the name of Kate: "She shall have no more eyes to see withal than a cat." Again, it is in terms of just such (figurative) blindness that Kate will later act out her ultimate subjection, not only to man but to the language of man: "Pardon old father, my mistaking eyes, / That have been so bedazzled with the sun ... Now I perceive thou art a reverent father. / Pardon, I pray thee, for my mad mistaking" (4.5.45–9).

I have argued elsewhere that this conflict between visionary and verbal language is not only a very traditional one but one to which Shakespeare in his sonnets gives a new subjective twist when he assimilates it to the psychology, and not only to the erotic psychology, of his first-person lyric voice.[6] In addition, I have also argued that Shakespeare's different manipulations of this vision/language opposition produce generically different characterological or subjectivity effects in Shakespearean comedy, tragedy, and romance. It is far from the case, however, that Shakespeare invents this conflict between visual and verbal speech, for it is also possible to demonstrate that the terms of this opposition very much inform the metaphorical language through which language is imagined and described in the philosophico-literary tradition that begins in antiquity and extends at least up through the Renaissance, if not farther. While it is not possible to develop in a brief essay such as this the detailed and coherent ways in which this visual/verbal conflict operates in traditionary texts, it is possible to indicate, very schematically, the general logic of this perennial opposition by looking at two rather well-known illustrations. These pictures are by Robert Fludd, the seventeenth-century hermeticist, and they employ a thoroughly conventional iconography.[7] A brief review of the two pictures will be worthwhile, for this will allow us to understand how it happens that a traditional question about rhetoric amounts to an answer to an equally traditional question about gender. This in turn will allow us to return not only to *The Taming of the Shrew* but also to the larger theoretical question with which we began, namely, whether it is possible to speak a Language, whether of Man or of Woman, that does not speak for the Language of Man.

The first picture is Fludd's illustration of the seventh verse of Psalm 63 (misnumbered in the picture as verse 8). *"In alarum tuarum umbra canam,"* says or sings King David, and the picture shows precisely this. King David kneels in prayer beneath an eyeball sun, while from out of his mouth, in line with the rays of theophanic light which stream down on him, a verse of psalm ascends up to a brightness which is supported, shaded, and revealed by its extended wings. Because King David is the master psalmist, and because the picture employs perennial motifs, it would be fair to say that Fludd's picture is an illustration of psalmic speech *per se.* In the picture we see traditional figurations of the way a special kind of anagogic language does homage to an elevated referent. This referent, moreover, represented as an eye which is both seeing and seen, is itself a figure of a special kind of speech, as is indicated by the Hebrew letters inscribed upon its iris. These letters—*yod, he, vau, he*— spell out the name of God, *"Jehova,"* which is the "Name" in which, according to the fourth verse in the psalm, King David lifts up his hands: "Thus wil I magnifie thee all my life, and lift up mine hands in the Name."[8] However, though these letters spell out this holy name, nevertheless, in principle they do not sound it out, for these are letters whose literality, when combined in this famous Tetragrammaton, must never be pronounced. Instead, in accord with both orthodox and heterodox mystical prohibitions, this written name of god, which is the only proper name of God, will be properly articulated only through attributive periphrasis, with the letters vocalized either as *Adonai,* "the Lord," or as *Ha Shem,* "the Name" or even "the Word."

In Fludd's picture, where the verse of psalm and *"Jehova"* lie at oblique angles to each other, it is clearly the case that King David does not literally voice the name of God. It is possible, however, reading either up or down, to take inscribed *"Jehova"* as an unspoken part of David's praising speech, either as its apostrophized addressee or as the direct object of its *"canam."* This syntactic, but still silent, link between the Latin and the Hebrew is significant, for unspeakable *"Jehova"* thus becomes the predicated precondition through which or across which what the psalmist says is translated into what the psalmist sees. The picture is concerned to illustrate the effect of this translation, showing David's verse to be the medium of his immediate vision of the sun, drawing David's verse as though it were itself a beam of holy light. In this way, because the verse is pictured as the very brightness that it promises to sing or speak about, Fludd's picture manages to motivate its portrait of a genuinely visionary

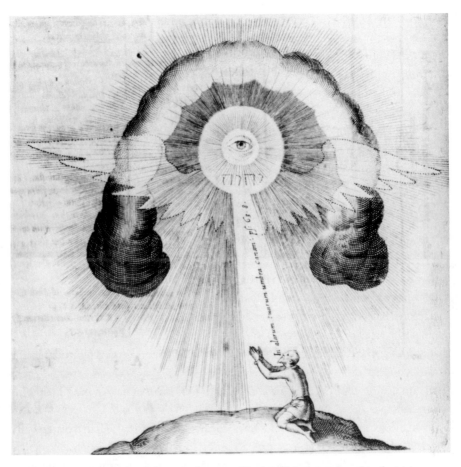

Robert Fludd, illustration of the seventh verse of Psalm 63 (misnumbered in the picture as verse 8). First published in 1621.

speech. In the psalm, the reason why the psalmist praises is the very substance of his praise: "For thy loving kindnes is better then life: therefore my lippes shal praise thee." The same thing happens in the picture, where we see the future tense of *"canam"* rendered present, and where the promise of praise amounts to the ful-fillment of the promise. But again, all this visionary predication depends upon the odd graphesis of unspeakable *"Jehova,"* which is the signifier of all signifiers that even King David cannot bring himself to utter, just as it is the writing of his iris that even Jehova cannot read.

In an elementary etymological sense—remembering that "ideal" comes from Greek *"idein,"* "to see"—Fludd's picture is a portrait of ideal language, of language that is at once ideal and idealizing. As the picture shows it, King David speaks a visual speech, a language *of* vision that promotes a vision *of* language, a language which is of the mouth only in so far as it is for the eye. This visual and visionary logos is noth-ing but familiar. Psalmic speech in particular and the language of praise in general (and it should be recalled that up through the Renaissance *all* poetry is understood to be a poetry of praise) are regularly imagined through such visual imagery, just as the referential object of such reverential praise is regularly conceived of as both agent and patient of sight. (Dante's vision of *luce etterna* at the end of the *Paradiso* would be a good example, though here again the height of vision is figured through a transcendental darkness, when power fails the poet's *"alta fantasia,"* and the poet's "will and desire" then "turn" (*"volgeva"*) with "the love that moves the sun and the other stars.")

In the second picture, which is by no means a strictly Elizabethan world picture (since its details go back at least to Macrobius and, therefore, through Plotinus, to Plato) we see the idealist aesthetics, metaphysics, and cosmology traditionally unpacked from and attaching to this visual idealism or visual idealization of the Word. As the title indicates, all arts are images of the specularity of integrated nature because both art and nature reciprocally will simulate the *eidola* or likenesses of beatific light. This commonplace eidetic reduction, which, by commutation, enables representation iconically to replicate whatever it presents, is what makes both art and nature into psalmic panegyric. Art becomes an art of nature just as nature is itself a kind of art, because they both reflect, but do not speak, the holy name which is the signifier and the signified of art and nature both. From this phenomenologically mutual admiration, which makes of art and nature each other's *special* (from *specere,* "to look at") likeness, it is easy to derive the ontotheological imperatives that inform all visionary art, for example, the poetics of *ut pictura poesis* and "speaking picture." Suspended from the hand of God, the great chain of mimetic being (which Macro-

Robert Fludd, Integrae Naturae Speculum, Artisque Imago. *First published in 1617.*

bius describes as a series of successive and declensive mirrors) reaches down to nature, and through her to man, the ape of nature, whose artful calibration of a represented little world produces a demiurgic *mise en abyme* that in no way disturbs—indeed, one whose recursive reflections do nothing but confirm—the stability of the material world on which the ape of nature squats.

Not surprisingly, Fludd's encyclopedic picture of the hierarchic cosmos also includes a representation of a corresponding gender hierarchy. We can see this by looking at the circle of animals where, on the left, the picture illustrates generic man or *Homo* with his arms unfolded towards the sun, in complementary contrast to the way that woman or *Mulier,* at the right of the circle of animals, looks instead up to the moon which is the pale reflection of the sun that shines above it. It is fair to say that this opposition, which makes woman the mimetic simulacrum of man, sketches out the horizontal gender opposition on which the vertical, metaphysical hierarchy of the cosmos perpendicularly depends. For this reason, however, it is important to notice that, as the picture shows it, this is not a simple or a simply polar contrast. Man is figured by the sun which is always the same as itself, whereas woman is figured by a waxing-waning-changing moon which is always other than itself, because its mimic light of likeness is what illuminates its difference from the sameness of the sun. Perhaps this constitutes a paradox, this lunar light which folds up likeness into difference. But if so, it is a paradox that stands in service of an orthodox erotics for which woman is the other to man, the hetero- to *Homo,* precisely because her essence is *to be* this lunatic difference between sameness and difference. In the same conventional way (conventional, certainly, at least up through Milton) that the difference between the sun and the moon *is* the moon, so too, and equally traditionally, the difference between man and woman is woman herself.[9] This is a piety, moreover, that we see fleshed out in the ornaments of nature, who sports, with all decorum, a sun on one breast, a moon on the other, and, as the castrated and castrating difference between them, a second fetishistic moon upon her beatific crotch. Such is the erotics that is called for by traditional metaphysics. The word whose solar brightness is revealed by that which clouds it bespeaks a female darkness which is veiled by lunar brightness. The sickle-crescent moon of nature, which is cut and cutting both at once, indicates a mystery beyond it which is complementary to the way the odd graphesis of *"Jehova"* is constitutively eccentric to the centered wholeness of the world.

I have put this point in this way so as to point up the fact that there is really only one way to read Fludd's picture, and this precisely because there are two ways to read it. As with "rope-tricks," indeterminacy here again determines a specific story. On the one hand, given a set of assumptions about mimesis that go back at least to Plato, woman is the subordinate sub-version of originary man, in the same way that the moon is nothing more than an inferior reflection of the sun. In this sense, woman is nothing other than the likeness of a likeness. On the other hand, woman is equally the radical subversion of man, an insubordinate sub-version, because this system of mimesis inexorably calls forth a principle of difference which, as difference, is intrinsically excessive to such hierarchic likeness. In this sense, as the embodiment of difference—as, specifically, the difference *of* likeness—woman is nothing other than the other itself. The point to recognize, however, is not simply that these two hands go happily together—the logic of sub-version logically entailing its own sub-version, the "Mirror of Nature" already displaying what Luce Irigaray will call the *speculum de l'autre femme*—but, more important, that the necessity of this double reading is no esoteric piece of wisdom. Quite the contrary; what we see in Fludd's picture is that this is a profoundly orthodox paradox, one whose formal heterogeneity, whose essential duplicity, is regularly figured and expressed by commonplace placeholders of the difference between sameness and difference, as, for example, unspeakable *"Jehova,"* whose circumlocutory logos tangentially straddles the inside and the outside of the universal wholeness, or the titillating hole between the legs of nature whose absent presence is highlighted by discretionary light.

What Fludd's picture shows us, therefore, is that traditional iconography regularly assumes, as though it goes necessarily without saying, that there cannot be a picture of visionary language which is not at the same time an emblem of the limits of vision. This limit, however, as a limit, is built into Fludd's Wittgensteinian picture theory of language, within it as precisely that which such a theory is without. *"Jehova,"* for example, is part of *because* it is apart from the ideal specularity of the praising integrated world, and so too with the secret private parts of nature, whose hole we here see integrated into the deep recesses of nature's integrated whole. Out of this internal contradiction, figured through such motivating motifs, there derives, therefore, a very traditional story about the way the language of ideal desire is correlated with a desire for an ideal language. We see this story outlined in the circle of minerals, where man is associated with *Plumbum,* lead, and where woman is associated with *Cuprum,* named for the copper mines in Cyprus, birthplace of Venus, the goddess of love. Here we are to assume an alchemical reaction whereby Venus, the "Cyprian Queen," at once the object and the motive of desire, as a kind of catalytic converter, translates lead into gold, thereby supernaturally changing sub-nature into super-nature. And we can put this point more strongly by asserting that what Fludd's picture depicts is the thoroughly conventional way in which a universe of logical sameness is built up *on* its logical contra-diction (or, as it is sometimes written nowa-days, as though this were a feminist gesture, its "cuntra-diction," i.e., the language of woman) because it is the very lunacy of discourse that returns both man and woman to the golden, solar order of the patriarchal Word.

At this level of allegorical generality, we can very quickly turn back to *The Taming of the Shrew* and understand how it happens that Petruchio reestablishes the difference between the sexes by speaking the lunatic language of woman. The language of woman *is* the difference between the sexes, a difference Petruchio becomes when, speaking "rope-tricks," he is "Kated." And this translation is dramatically persuasive because the play fleshes it out by invoking the sub-versive, subversive terms and logic of traditional iconography. In the taming story, the first moment of Kate's capitulation occurs when Petruchio, changing his mind, forces Kate first to call the sun the moon and then again the sun: "Then God be blest, it is the blessed sun, / But sun it is not, when you say it is not; / And the moon changes even as your mind. / What you will have it nam'd, even that it is, / And so it shall be so for Katherine" (4.5.18–22). We can call Kate's articulation of "change" the naming of the shrew which is the instrument of her taming, for it is this transcendentalizing, heliotropic, ontotheological paradox of "change"—"Then God be blest"—that leads Kate then to beg a patriarchal pardon for her blind confusion of the sexes: "Pardon, old father, my mistaking eyes, / That have been so bedazzled with the sun." And the same thing happens at the climax of the wooing story, when Lucentio, until then disguised as Cambio, kneels down before his father and reveals his proper self. "Cambio is chang'd into Lucentio" (5.1.123) is the line with which this revelation is theatrically announced. This formula serves to return the father and his son, along with the master and his servant, back to their proper order. But it also offers us an economical example of the way in which the very operation of rhetorical translation serves to change "change" into light.

To say that this paradox is orthodox is not to say that it describes a complete logical circle. Quite the contrary, as is indicated by the aporetic structure of Fludd's pictures, it is *as* a logical problem for logic, as an everpresent, irreducible, and ongoing question raised by self-reflection, that the paradox acquires its effective power. This is the question consistently raised by the insistent question of rhetoric, which is why, when Kate is tamed and order restored, the heretofore silent and good women of the play immediately turn into shrews. The subversive language of woman with which the play begins, and in resistance to which the movement of the play is predicated, reappears at the end of the play so that its very sounding predicts the future as a repetition of the same old story. This is the final moral of *The Taming of the Shrew*: that it is not possible to close the story of closure, for the very idea and idealization of closure, like the wholeness of Fludd's comprehensive cosmos, is thought through a logic and a logos whose internal disruption forever defers, even as this deferment elicits a desire for, a summary conclusion.

Hence, we can add, the function of the larger frame. Speaking very generally—and recalling, on the one hand, the Petrarchan idealism of the wooing story and, on the other, the parodic Petrarchanism, the Petruchioism, of the taming story—we can say that the two subplots of *The Taming of the Shrew* together present what in the western literary tradition is the master plot of the relation between language and desire. Sly, however, to whom this story is presented, wishes that his entertainment soon were over, for only when the play is over will Sly get to go to bed with new-found wife. "Would 'twere done!" (1.1.254), says Sly (these being the last words we hear from him), of a play which, as far as Sly is concerned, is nothing but foreplay. The joke here is surely on Sly, for the audience knows full well that the consummation Sly so devoutly desires will never be achieved; if ever it happens that Sly sleeps with his wife, he will soon enough discover that she is a he in drag disguise. This defines, perhaps, the ultimate perversity of the kinky lord who "long[s] to hear" his pageboy "call the drunkard husband" (Ind.1.133), and who arranges for Sly to be subjected in this tantalizing way to what for Sly is nothing but the tedious unfolding of the play within the play. But it is not only Sly's desire that is thus seductively frustrated; and this suggests the presence, behind the play, of an even kinkier lord. I refer here to the ongoing editorial question regarding the absence of a final frame; for this response to the play's apparent omission of a formal conclusion to the Sly story is evidence enough that the audience for the entirety of the play is left at its conclusion with a desire for closure that the play calls forth *in order* to postpone. To say that this is a desire that leaves something to be desired—a desire, therefore, that will go on and on forever—goes a good way towards explaining the abiding popularity of *The Taming of the Shrew*.[10]

Perhaps this also explains why, at first glance, it looks as though the current theoretical controversy to which I have referred presents us with a lovers' quarrel in which psychoanalysis plays Petruchio to its critics' Kate. It is tempting to see in the debate between Lacan and Derrida, for example, a domestic and domesticating quarrel that reenacts in an increasingly more sophisticated but, for this reason, an increasingly more hapless fashion a proverbial literary predicament. However, this is not the conclusion that I would like to draw from the fact that current theoretical polemic so faithfully shapes itself to traditional literary contours and so voraciously stuffs itself with traditional literary topoi. Again it would be possible to relate the logic of subversive subversion, as it appears in Fludd and Shakespeare, to Derrida's gnostic, a-logical logic of the copulating supplement. And again, and again even more specifically, it would be possible to relate all this to Lacan's account of "The Function and Field of Speech and Language in Psychoanalysis." Lacan's characterization of the relation of the Imaginary to the Symbolic very straightforwardly repeats the motifs of a traditional verbal/visual conflict, and it does so in a way that fully incorporates into itself its equally traditional intrinsic deconstruction, e.g., when Lacan says that the Real is that which cannot be represented. When Lacan says, to take just a few examples, that the being of the woman is that she does not exist, or that the function of the universal quantifier, by means of which man becomes the all, is thought through its negation in woman's not-all, when he says that there is no sexual relation, or when he says that castration, the $-\phi$, is what allows us to count from 0 to 1, he is not only evoking the elementary paradox displayed in Fludd's picture—the class of all classes that do not classify themselves—he is also ornamenting this familiar paradox with its traditional figurative clothing.[11] Thus it is that Lacan, like Derrida, is a master of the commonplace, as when he says that there is no such thing as metalanguage, or that *"La femme n'ex-siste pas,"* or that *"Si j'ai dit que le langage est ce comme quoi l'inconscient est structuré, c'est bien parce que le langage, d'abord, ça n'existe pas. Le langage est ce qu'on essaye de savoir concernant la fonction de la langue."*[12]

To recognize the fact that all of this is commonplace is to see that the argument between Lacan and Derrida, between psychoanalysis and its other (an argument that already takes place within Lacan and within psychoanalysis), repeats, not only in its structure but also in its thematic and illustrative details, a master plot of literature. To see this is also to recognize that coarse generic terms of a magnitude corresponding to that of man, woman, language historically carry with them an internal narrative logic which works to motivate a story in which every rubric gets to play and to explain its integrated role. At this level of generality it goes without saying that the language of woman inexorably speaks for the language of man, and it is therefore not surprising that a feminist critique of psychoanalysis which is conducted at this level of generality will necessarily recathect the story that is fleshed out in *The Taming of the Shrew*. If "Cambio is chang'd into Lucentio," so too, for example, is "Cambio" changed into Luce Irigaray.

It is, however, the great and exemplary value of both Lacan and Derrida that in their quarrel with each other they do more than scrupulously restrict their readings of the central topoi of western self-reflexive language to the level of generality appropriate to the register of allegorical abstraction called for by such massive metaphoremes and motifs. In addition, they recognize this level of generality for what it is:

the logic of the literary word in the west. Doing so, they open up the possibility of an extraliterary reading of literature. In a specifically literary context, Shakespeare is interesting because in Shakespeare's texts (from Freud's reading of which, we should recall, psychoanalysis originally derives) we see how, at a certain point in literary history, allegorical abstractions such as man, woman, language—formerly related to each other in accord with the psychomachian dynamics which are sketched out in Fludd's pictures—are introduced into a psychologistic literature, thereby initiating a recognizably modern literature of individuated, motivated character. But the relation to literature is not itself a literary relation, and there is no compelling reason, therefore, especially with the examples of Lacan and Derrida before them, why readers or critics of master literary texts should in their theory or their practice act out what they read.

Notes

Reprinted from *Shakespeare and the Question of Theory,* ed. Patricia Parker and Geoffrey Hartman (New York: Methuen, 1985), 138–159.

1.   Derrida's most explicit criticisms of Lacan can be found in "The Purveyor of Truth" (*Yale French Studies,* 52 (1975)); and in *Positions,* tr. Alan Bass (Chicago, 1981). See also *Spurs: Nietzsche's Styles,* tr. Barbara Harlow (Chicago, 1979); *La Carte postale* (Paris, 1980), which republishes and expands upon "The Purveyor of Truth"; Julia Kristeva, *Desire in Language: A Semiotic Approach to Literature and Art* (New York, 1980); Hélène Cixous, *La Jeune Née* (with Catherine Clément) (Paris, 1975); "The Laugh of the Medusa," K. Cohen and P. Cohen (*Signs,* I (Summer 1976), 875–99); Luce Irigaray, *Speculum de l'autre femme* (Paris, 1974); *Ce sexe qui n'est pas un* (Paris, 1977); Sarah Kofman, "The Narcissistic Woman: Freud and Girard" (*Diacritics* (Fall 1980), 36–45); *Nietzsche et la scène philosophique* (Paris, 1979).

2.   All Shakespeare references are to *The Riverside Shakespeare,* ed. G. B. Evans (Boston, 1974).

3.   *The Taming of the Shrew,* ed. H. J. Oliver (Oxford, 1982), 124.

4.   "It was at this point that the addendum of there having been a question-mark after the word 'like' occurred to Dora, and she then recognized these words as a quotation out of a letter from Frau K. which had contained the invitation to L ____, the place by the lake. In that letter there had been a question mark placed, in a most unusual fashion, in the very middle of a sentence, after the intercalated words 'if you would like to come'" (Sigmund Freud, *Dora: An Analysis of a Case of Hysteria* (1905), tr. J. Strachey (New York, 1963), 118). Dora dreams here, quite literally, of *écriture féminine,* but Frau K.'s peculiar question mark, even if its interruption is taken as a signal of the lesbianism Freud insists on in the story, still marks the specifically Freudian question of female desire: "What does woman want?" This question—not simply "if you would like to come" but, instead, "if you would like to come," i.e., do you desire desire?—remains a question at the end of the Dora case; and it seems clear enough that this enigma not only stimulates Freud's countertransference to Dora's transference (Freud introduces the concept of transference in the Dora case), but also accounts for Freud's failure to analyze, on the one hand, his patient's relation to him and, on the other, his relation to his patient. This double failure explains why the Dora case, like *The Taming of the Shrew,* concludes inconclusively. As Freud reports it, the analysis of Dora amounts to a battle between doctor and patient wherein, in response to Freud's demand that Dora admit her desire for Herr K.—i.e., that she avow her Freudian desire—Dora refuses to say what she wants. This is a characteristic Freudian frustration. As in Freud's dream of Irma's injection, where Freud looks into

Irma's mouth for evidence of a specifically psychoanalytic sexuality that would prove Freud's psychoanalytic theory true, so Freud wants Dora to speak her desire so as thereby to satisfy Freud's desire for a confirmation of his theory of desire. In the Irma dream, Freud receives as enigmatic answer to this question the uncanny image of "Trimethylamin"—not only a picture of a word, but a picture of the very word that formulates female sexuality—whereas in the Dora case the question is answered with the re-marked question mark. In both cases, however, it is the question of female desire, staged as an essential and essentializing question, that leads Freud on in a seductive way. When Dora, manhandling Freud, breaks off her analysis, she leaves Freud with the question of woman, the answer to which Freud will pursue for the rest of his life, up through the late, again inconclusive, essays on gender, in all of which Freud argues for a determinate indeterminacy, a teleological interminability.

5.   For example, "The Function and Field of Speech and Language in Psychoanalysis," in Jacques Lacan, *Ecrits,* tr. Alan Sheridan (New York, 1977), 30–113.

6.   Joel Fineman, *Shakespeare's Perjured Eye: The Invention of Poetic Subjectivity in the Sonnets* (Berkeley, 1985).

7.   Figure 6 comes from Fludd's *Tomi Secundi Tractatus Secundus; De Prœternaturali Utriusque Cosmi Majoris . . .* (Oppenheim, 1621); Figure 7 comes from *Utriusque Cosmi Majoris . . .* (Oppenheim, 1617). There is a convenient collection of Fludd's illustrations in Joscelyn Godwin's *Robert Fludd* (London, 1979).

8.   All quotations from the psalm are from the Geneva translation.

9.   See Milton, *Paradise Lost,* III, 722–32.

10.   It is here that the affinities of *The Taming of the Shrew* with Henry James's *The Turn of the Screw,* to which I am of course alluding in my title, are most apparent. In both texts a specifically rhetorical "turning," "troping," "versing," understood on the model of "rope-tricks," generates an interpretive mystery which is then correlated with a sexual tropism towards, or an apotropaic aversion from, an uncanny, true-false, *female* admixture of male and female. In *The Taming of the Shrew* Sly's framing desire for the pageboy disguised as a woman is a metatheatrical filter that puts into question any univocal understanding of the coupling of Petruchio and Kate. Hence the continuing critical question as to whether the Pauline patriarchalism of Kate's final speech should be understood ironically, i.e., whether she is most a shrew when she is most submissive. This hermeneutic question with regard to Kate corresponds to the traditional duplicity of woman: Sly's metatheatrical desire for the pageboy defines the essence of femininity as masquerade. So too with *The Turn of the Screw,* which shares with *The Taming of the Shrew* the same heavy-handed, play-within-play, *mise en abyme* structure, and which uses this reflexive literariness to invite and to excite a series of relevant but irresolvable, and therefore continuing, critical questions, for example, is the governess's story true or false? is the governess crazy or sane? In *The Turn of the Screw* such interpretive questions find their objectification, their objectification *as* questions, in "Peter Quint," a kind of verbal pageboy whose nominality evokes the primal scene—half-real, half-fantasy—that motivates the governess's hysterico-obsessive desire for Miles and Flora. Again the point to notice is the way in which rhetorical indeterminacy generates a determinate erotics. The name that couples male and female genitals, "Peter" and "Quint," produces a specifically *female* uncanny: the name is quaint—indeed, "cunt"—because both "Peter" and "Quint." So too, a master text such as *The Turn of the Screw* uses precisely this indeterminacy to rescure the place of the "Master" in relation to his servants.

11.   See, especially, Jacques Lacan, *Encore* (Paris, 1975), 49–94.

12.   For Lacan's remarks on "metalanguage," see, in *Ecrits,* "On a Question Preliminary to Any Possible Treatment of Psychosis." The concluding two quotations come, respectively, from *Télévision* (Paris, 1974), 60, and *Encore,* 126.

The Sound of *O* in *Othello:*
The Real of the Tragedy of Desire

Thus it follows that in love, it is not the meaning that counts, but rather the sign, as in everything else. In fact, therein lies the whole catastrophe.

—Jacques Lacan, *Television*

The sexual impasse exudes the fictions that rationalize the impossible within which it originates. I don't say they are imagined; like Freud, I read in them the invitation to the Real that underwrites them.

—Jacques Lacan, *Television*

Iago: *I must show out a flag and sign of love, Which is indeed but sign.*

Othello, 1.1.156–157

Othello: *O, Desdemon dead, Desdemon dead, O, O!*

Othello, 5.2.282

I have two preliminary remarks.[1] First, this paper adapts material from a chapter on *Othello* in a book I am writing called *Shakespeare's Will.*[2] This book builds upon an argument I develop elsewhere, in a different book on Shakespeare's sonnets, whose claim is that in his sonnets Shakespeare introduces into literature an altogether novel, lyric, first-person poetic subject or subjectivity effect, which subsequently becomes, for more or less formal, even formalist, reasons having to do with the history of literary history, the governing and paradigmatic model of subjectivity in literature successive to Shakespeare.[3] In the book I am writing now, I am initially concerned, as a matter of practical literary criticism, with understanding how the lyric, first-person poetic subject of Shakespeare's sonnets informs both the authorial third person of Shakespeare's narrative poems and the formally zero-authorial person immanent in Shakespeare's plays. I am also concerned, however, in this new book, with understanding why the literary formalism to which I have referred possesses its historically documentable power. In my current project, therefore, I am concerned, on the one hand, with formal constraints governing the formation and reception of Shakespearean literary characterology, on the other, with the connection of the historical, singular, authorial Shakespeare—the one who writes "by me, *William Shakespeare*" when he signs his will—to these more general formal literary exigencies. In short, I am concerned with what relates Shakespeare, the person, a particular and idiosyncratic historical subject, to the literary invention of Shakespearean subjectivity effects; in particular, with how the contingency of the former informs and is informed by what I understand to be the necessity of the latter. This accounts for my interest in what I call, very literally, Shakespeare's "Will," or what I will be calling "The Real of the Tragedy of Desire."

Because this discussion is set within the context of a colloquium on the psychoanalytic work and thought of Jacques Lacan, I will be concerned here mostly with the way language, as theme and performed action, generates in *Othello,* the play, a specifically Shakespearean psychologistic formation marked by what I want to identify as a characteristically Shakespearean signature. I must say in advance, however, that, given the constraints of the context, I will be obliged to do this only perfunctorily and to presuppose almost completely the full-scale reading of *Othello* on which much of my argument depends. Perfunctory, therefore, as my account will be, I nevertheless think it is relevant to the concerns of this colloquium because, insofar as it suggests an explanation for the way, at the level of subjectivity, the particularity of Shakespeare's person is related to Shakespeare's literary personae, it also helps to explain how the uniquely individual and individuated Shakespeare speaks to and founds an institution, the Shakespearean in general. In several respects this is relevant to a colloquium on Lacan, not only because, as I will try to show, there are striking thematic homologies between, on the one hand, the psychoanalytic subject as described by Lacan and, on the other, the characteristically Shakespearean (most especially with regard to a Real that can be neither specularized nor represented),

but also because these homologies raise the historical question of the relation of psychoanalysis to the institution of literature as such. This allows us to ask whether we
should understand Shakespeare as corroborating evidence of Lacanian psychoanalysis or, instead, whether we should understand Lacanian psychoanalysis as epiphenomenal, institutional, and literary consequence of what is characteristically
Shakespearean.

Second, still preliminary, I want, before beginning, to note that it was Angus
Fletcher who first drew my attention to the sound of O in *Othello,* in a graduate seminar in which he remarked the haunting quality of the sound in the play. While it is
altogether likely Angus Fletcher will not be altogether persuaded by the explanation
I propose to offer of the force of the sound of O in *Othello,* I want to acknowledge
this particular debt, and, more generally, a larger debt, since the work of Angus
Fletcher has very much influenced my thinking about psychoanalysis, literature, and
the relation of each of these to the other.

If Shakespeare knew even a little of the little Greek Ben Jonson begrudgingly
allowed him ("small Latine & lesse Greeke," says Johnson in his prefatory verse to
the *First Folio*), he would most likely have known the Greek verb *ethelō,* which
means "wish," "want," "will," "desire," though Shakespeare would more probably
have known the word in its *New Testament* form, *thelō,* where the initial epsilon has
dropped out.[4] Since Shakespeare appears to have chosen or invented Othello as
proper or appropriate proper name for the more or less anonymous "The Moor,"
whom he reads about in Cinthio's source-story, we are actively entitled to think the
semantic field attaching to *ethelō*—"wish," "want," "will," "desire"—identifies the
specifically Greek resonance—appropriate to Cyprus, birthplace of Aphrodite, and
also the locus of the central action of the play—that *The Tragedy of Othello* calls forth
for or from Shakespeare, a nominal speculation further warranted by the fact that
Cinthio, at the end of his version of the story, explictly explains the destiny of Desdemona by reference to the meaning of her name in Greek: *dusdaimon,* "the unfor-
tunate."[5] Accordingly, assuming Shakespeare read a little Greek and also read a little
Cinthio—and scholarship speaks for both assumptions—we can say *The Tragedy of
Othello,* as it is called in both the Quarto and Folio versions of the play, would have
been for Shakespeare, at least in one summary, etymological register, a tragedy of
wishing and wanting or, quite literally, *The Tragedy of Will* or *The Tragedy of Desire.*[6]
Yet more precisely, if we hear the first O of O-thello as some reflection of the Greek
augmenting and inflecting prefix, either aorist or imperfect—again assuming Shakespeare would have known the *New Testament,* not the classical, form of the word,

i.e., *thelō,* not *ethelō*—we can still translate *The Tragedy of Othello* as *The Tragedy of Will* or *The Tragedy of Desire,* but with the understanding now that both *Will* and *Desire* are here denominated as something in or of the past, "I wish" or "I desire" becoming "I wished" or "I desired" when one adds to its beginning the e (ε) or $\bar{e}$ (η) to *thelō.*[7]

Taking, therefore, this name, Othello, as it is given, at its word, a series of inter-related questions almost immediately arises. First, why is this, for Shakespeare, the proper proper name for the unhappy Moor? Initially, this is a question about Shake-speare, the person, not about the Moor, the tragic hero of the play, and so, para-phrasing Juliet's famous question to Romeo—"What's in a name?" (*RJ,* 2.2.43)—we can ask what is it about *Othello,* the name, or in it, that makes it what we can call, using a technical term, Shakespearean? Second, if it is right to hear a specific semantic field resonating out of or around the name *Othello*—again, "wish," "want," "will," "desire"; and, however playfully he may have done so, Shakespeare certainly elsewhere liked thus to derive connotation out of designation, or perhaps the other way around: e.g., Bottom is an ass in *A Midsummer Night's Dream,* Perdita is lost in *The Winter's Tale,* to take some obvious examples; or, to take some yet more pertinent examples, the ways in which in several sexy sonnets Shakespeare plays upon his own name, Will—why is this semantic field called up by Shakespeare as something in the past?[8] Why, for Shakespeare, is it O-thello and not *thelō,* i.e., why is it *I wished* or *I desired,* and not *I wish* or *I desire,* that is thus sounded out by the temporally inflecting O in this Shakespearean name? Finally, or third, both more generally and more particularly, if, for Shakespeare, *Othello* is at once the personal and personalizing name of desire, why is this generically determined as something tragic, as, specifically, *The* Tragedy *of Othello*? Why, that is, for Shakespeare, is the story of the man named desire a story that is tragic and not, for example, something pastoral, or comic, or romantic?

Phrased this way, all these questions address themselves to Shakespeare, the person, and to his quite literal and personal relation to the name and naming of desire. Yet the same questions may also be raised, and in straightforwardly thematic ways, in relation to Othello—not himself a person, but the literary representation thereof—since Othello seems to act out his love story—a characteristically Shake-spearean love story of delusional, paranoid, and mortifying jealousy—as though it were effectively determined by his registration of his name. If so, what is the relation between these two distinct relations, that of Shakespeare, the person, and that of the Moor, the literary figuration of a person, to the same name, *Othello*? To begin an answer to this question, which is a question about the relation of an author to an authorized persona—the relation, therefore, between a historical subject, whom we call Shakespeare, and, equally historical, one of Shakespeare's strongest literary sub-jectivity effects, whom Shakespeare called Othello—I want to suggest that the lexical issues I have so far mentioned in connection with *ethelō* are relevant in more than simply thematic ways to two questions of motivation regularly raised by or addressed to the play: on the one hand, why is Othello so gullible; on the other, why does Iago do what he does to Othello?

Since we know Iago is the motivator of Othello, Othello's first cause, we know also that an answer to the second of these questions is effectively an answer to the first. But this is precisely why Iago's motivation—the motive for his actions which are in turn the motive for all other actions in the play—has always seemed a central prob-lem, one foregrounded by the play insofar as all Iago's explanations of the reasons for his actions either seem inadequate as motives or, instead, to contradict or under-cut each other—e.g., Iago's resentful disappointment at Cassio's military promotion over himself, or Iago's expressed suspicions, which he himself suspects, that both Othello and Cassio have cuckolded him, or Iago's stressedly homosexual envy of the "daily beauty" (5.1.18) in Cassio's life. This enigma attaching to the motives of Iago was the cue for Coleridge's famous characterization of Iago's diverse and conflicting rationalizations as "the motive hunting of motiveless malignity." The phrasing points to the fact that the question of Iago's motivation has regularly been posed in moral terms, which is why, as developed Vice-figure, the particular motive for Iago's par-ticular evil is so readily assimilated to the general motive of generic evil as such. In either case, however, particular or general, the question of Iago's motivation pre-sents itself as a familiar question about the motive at the origin of evil, a question about the origin of the energy for originary sin, and the reason why this question is familiar is that traditional psychology can only understand desire, that is, that which motivates an action, as an impulse or a pulsion toward the good.[9] Speaking very broadly, we can say that, for the tradition of philosophical and faculty psychology that extends from Plato to the Renaissance, it is relatively easy to explain the motive for an action by reference to an ultimately instrumental reason that conduces toward the satisfaction of a rational desire. In this tradition there is, therefore, necessarily, a good reason for doing something good, since Reason is the reason for doing anything whatsoever, and, moreover, Reason is, by definition, something good. For this very Reason, however, there can, in principle, be no good reason, and therefore no rea-son whatsoever, for doing something bad, which is why, for all intents and purposes, that is, as a matter of intentional or purposeful action, we can say that in this tradition there is no such thing as evil. Hence, for example, the familiar ontological definition of evil as the absence or privation of the good, and the corresponding psychological explanation of an agent's evil motivation in terms of either his mistaken or his thwarted movement toward the good.

If we take this tradition seriously, and if we agree Iago is the motivator of Othello's actions in the play, we can begin to understand how and why Othello acquires both his large and at the same time empty grandeur. At the very beginning of the play, Iago explains himself to Roderigo, and does so in terms of his relation to Othello: "I follow him to serve my turn upon him" (1.1.43), "It is as sure as you are Roderigo, / Were I the Moor, I would not be Iago" (1.1.56–57), and finally, a pregnant phrase, the opposite of Yahweh's self-denomination, "I am not what I am" (1.1.65). Thus defined, Iago presents himself as a being whose being consists in being that which is not what it is, an entity—here we can think either of Jacques-Alain Miller's discussion of the Lacanian zero in Frege or of Shakespeare's arithmetic of *Will* in sonnet 136: "Among a number one is counted none"—that is nonidentical to itself.[10] And it is this principle—"I am not what I am"—a principle of seeming-being—to be *as* not to be—that, we can say, Iago, as complementary opposite of a less complicated Othello, introduces to or into Othello in the course of the play. Given the tight economy of their stipulated relation—"I follow him to serve my turn upon him," "Were I the Moor, I would not be Iago"—we can think of Iago, precisely because he is the motivator of Othello, as the inside of Othello, as a principle of disjunct being—"I am not what I am"—introduced into the smooth and simple existence of an Othello who, at least at the beginning, is, whatever else he is, surely what he is.

It is in this way, through the idea of a "one" inhabited by "none," that we can understand *The Tragedy of Othello* as, specifically, *The Tragedy of Desire,* and at the same time understand how a specifically Shakespearean conception of tragic motivation conduces towards a specific subjectivity effect. The play unfolds so as to show the passage of Othello from being, as Lodovico describes him, and as we see him at the start, "all in all sufficient" (4.1.265)—"Is this the noble Moor whom our full senate/Call all in all sufficient?" (4.1.264–265)—to being, instead, eventually, the empty shell of a hero self-proclaimed by Othello at the end as "That's he that was Othello, here I am" (5.2.284). This evacuating clarification of Othello, most fully realized at this moment when the hero names his name, is what gives Othello his heroic, tragic stature, at the same time, however, as it specifies the way in which Othello, as a tragic hero, is inflated with his loss of self. This subject who speaks, in the third person and in the past tense, of "he that was Othello," is at the same time present, deictic referent of the *I* who tells us "here I am." And yet this *I* who stands and speaks before us can only speak about himself in terms of how he now survives as retrospective aftermath of what was once the "all in all sufficient," as though the name *Othello* only served to warrant or to measure how Othello, now, as speaking I, is absent to the self that bears his name. Speaking, therefore, of himself as *he,* because his *I*—what Roman Jakobson would call a shifter, what Bertrand Russell would call an egocentric particular—is thus subjectively discrepant to the "Othello" *I* recalls, Othello thus assumes his name only through his registration of his distance from its designated reference. And if it is Iago's *I* to which the play initially accords the paradoxical condition of an entity unequal to itself—"I am not what I am"—then we can see the way in which it is Iago—whom I will now define as *ego*—who leads Othello thus explicitly to speak about—indeed, to name—his structured difference from his own denomination: "That's he that was Othello, here I am not what I am." The image from *The Voyages and Travels of Sir John Mandeville,* a picture of what Othello describes to Desdemona, when he woos her, as "the Cannibals that each other eat, / The Anthropophagi, and men whose heads / Do grow beneath their shoulders" (1.3.143–144),

From The Voyages and Travels of Sir John Mandeville.

is an illustration of the way this kind of materialized absence of self to itself might be imagined to inhabit or to inhere in the experience of self, thereby generating the substantialized emptiness that motivates and corroborates precisely that psychologistic interiority for which and by means of which Shakespeare's major characters are often singled out. The picture schematically illustrates an anorectic, homophagic economy of subjectifying self-cannibalization, "feed[ing] thy light's flame with self-substantial fuel, / Making a famine where abundance lies," to use the carefully considered language of Shakespeare's very first sonnet.[11]

I have elsewhere argued that Shakespeare is not only responsible for first introducing this kind of literary subject, compact of its own loss, into literary history, but that the literary features through which this Shakespearean subject is constructed and imagined are, for more or less formal reasons, strictly circumscribed.[12] Summarizing that claim very briefly, I have argued that Shakespeare writes at the end of a tradition that identifies the literary, and therefore literary language, with idealizing, visionary praise, a tradition in which there is, at least figuratively speaking, an ideal Cratylitic correspondence, usually figured through motifs of visual or visionary language, between that which is spoken and that which is spoken about. Registering the conclusion of this tradition of the poetry of praise, a tradition that reaches back to the invention of the "literary" as a coherent theoretical category, Shakespeare, *to be* literary, is obliged to recharacterize language as something duplicitously and equivocally verbal rather than something truthfully and univocally visual, and, as a consequence, Shakespeare is both enabled and constrained to develop novel literary subjects of verbal representation for whom the very speaking of language is what serves to cut them off from their ideal and visionary presence to themselves. More clearly and starkly than any other Shakespearean tragedy, *Othello,* the play, is organized or thought through precisely such a large disrupting and disjunctive thematic opposition between visionary presence and verbal representation, not only when Iago determines, as he puts it, "to abuse Othello's ear" (2.1.385), or to "pour this pestilence into his ear" (2.3.356)—and such poisoning through the ear is of course a Shakespearean commonplace; think of Hamlet's father—but, more generally, in Iago's plot to substitute for the "ocular proof" (3.33.360) Othello demands—"I'll see before I doubt" (3.3.190)—the indicators or the signifiers whose "imputation and strong circumstances ... lead," Iago falsely says, "directly to the door of truth" (3.3.406–407).[13] Because, as Iago explains to Othello, there are things, especially sexual things, "It is impossible you should see" (3.3.403), Othello will receive instead the signs—like the misplaced, fetishistic handkerchief, ornamented with aphrodisiacal strawberries—which, conceived and conceited as something verbal, "speak against her with the other proofs" (3.3.441). We can say, speaking very abstractly, that this arrival of the specifically and corruptingly linguistic—through the instrument of Iago—is what determines the details of Othello's destiny as well as the two morals of the play, summarized at the end, after Othello's suicide, as, on the one hand, "All that is spoke is marr'd" (5.2.357), and, on the other, "The object poisons sight, / Let it be hid" (5.2.364–365). So too, we can also say, speaking formally, that it is only to the extent the play manages to make its own language perform, as does the Liar's Paradox, the truth of its own falseness, that Othello, as the representation of a person, exudes a powerfully psychologistic subjectivity effect.

This performative aspect of the play's language accounts for my concern with the sound of O in *Othello,* for I understand the sound of O in *Othello* both to occasion and to objectify in language Othello's hollow self. Thus it is that the line I took as one of my epigraphs—Othello's "O, Desdemon dead, Desdemon dead,/O,O!" (5.2.282)—is not only the conclusion of Othello's discovery of Iago's plot, but is also immediate preface to the line in which Othello names his absence to himself "That's he that was Othello, here I am" (5.2.284). In some respects, my insistence on the importance and significance of this sound is not a novel claim. Frank Kermode, for example, in his introduction to the *Riverside* edition of the play, makes something like, or almost like, this point when he says: "*Othello* no less than the other great tragedies invents its own idiom. The voice of the Moor has its own orotundity, verging, as some infer, on hollowness."[14] Yet if we initially agree that what Kermode calls Othello's "hollowness" is materialized in the sound of O, it is important also to realize that this peculiar voicing is sounded out throughout the entirety of the play, that is, that *Othello's* O is by no means restricted to Othello's mouth. We hear it, for example, in almost all the names of the characters—Brabantio, Gratiano, Lodovico, Othello, Cassio, Iago, Roderigo, Montano, Desdemona; again, most of these so-called by Shakespeare—and so, too, is it evoked or invoked as a continual refrain, often metrically stressed, throughout the dialogue, for example, these lines from Act 5, Scene 1:

> *Iago:*   *O* treacherous villains! What are you there? Come in and give
>   some help.
> *Roderigo:* *O* help me there!
> *Cassio:*   That's one of them.
> *Iago:*   *O* murd'rous slave! *O* villain!
> *Roderigo:* *O* dam'd Iago! *O* inhuman dog! (5.1.57–63)

or, a few lines later:

Bianca:	What is the matter ho? . . .
	O my dear Cassio, my sweet Cassio!
	O Cassio, Cassio, Cassio!
Iago:	*O* notable strumpet! Cassio, May you suspect
	Who they should be that have thus mangled you?
Cassio:	No.
Gratiano:	I am sorry to find you thus; I have been to seek you.
Iago:	Lend me a garter. So.—O for a chair
	To bear him easily hence!
Bianca:	Alas he faints! *O* Cassio, Cassio, Cassio! (5.1.74–84)

These are representative examples, which could be multiplied, of the way the sound of *O* is sounded out throughout the entirety of the play, and not just by Othello.

Why is it, then, that this sound—these abject *O*s, which I will soon want to associate with Lacan's *objet a,* that is, what for Lacan is the occasion of desire and the mark of the Real—is, both for Shakespeare and for Othello, constitutive of Othello's self? This is a more precise way of asking the questions I asked earlier as to why, for either Shakespeare or Othello, Othello's tragic passage into empty, retrospective self occurs at the climactic moment when the hero names his name? In search of an answer, I want now to turn to some of Lacan's remarks concerning proper names, beginning with what is perhaps the most well known of these, the passage in "The Subversion of the Subject and the Dialectic of Desire in the Freudian Unconscious," where Lacan explains the relation of a subject to a signifier:

> My definition of signifier (there is no other) is as follows: a signifier is that which represents the subject for another signifier. This signifier will therefore be the signifier for which all the other signifiers represent the subject: that is to say, in the absence of this signifier, all the other signifiers represent nothing, since nothing is represented only *for* something else.[15]

Lacan speaks here, more or less straightforwardly, of the way, as he understands it, the speaking subject is constitutively precipitated, as ruptured or as broken subject, as an effect of the language in which he finds himself bespoken—and no more so self-evidently than when this subject speaks explicitly about himself. For Lacan, as he explains in this section of "The Subversion of the Subject," the subject comes to be a subject through his dialectical relation to a generalized Other conceived to contain or to comprise, like a thesaurus or treasury, the entirety of signifiers that for one single and particular signifier represent the subject. This unique and distinct signifier—distinct because within the treasury of signifiers in the locus of the Other, it represents the subject for another signifier, indeed, for *any* and for *every* other signifier—is at once the mark of the totality of language for the speaking subject and of the totality of the subject thus bespoken. In either case, however, speaking either of the subject or of the Other, the entirety thus marked as something total is for that very reason lacking that which marks it as complete. Lacan explains:

> Since the battery of signifiers, as such, is by that very fact complete [what Shakespeare would call "all in all sufficient"], this signifier [i.e., that which represents the subject for another signifier] can only be a line (*trait*) that is drawn from its circle without being able to be counted part of it. It can be symbolized by the inherence of a (-1) in the whole set of signifiers. As such it is inexpressible, but its operation is not inexpressible, for it is that which is produced whenever a proper name (*nom propre*) is spoken (*prononcé*). Its statement (*énoncé*) equals its signification ("Subversion of the Subject," 316–317).

It may seem odd, a kind of vestigial Cratylism, for Lacan to say of the operation of the proper name that its statement equals its signification, but this is because, for the subject, the paradoxical statement of the proper name, like the Liar's Paradox, is that its statement is *not* equal to its signification. We can say that this is the *only* statement language can speak truly to and for a subject. Hence the precision, which is only slightly comic, of Lacan's algebraic formulation of the signification, for the subject, of the signifier that represents him for another signifier:

$$\frac{S(\text{signifier})}{s(\text{signified})} = s \text{ (the statement), with } S = (-1), \text{ produces } s = \sqrt{-1}$$

where the signifier, understood as minus one, is to be divided by the signified it equals, which is therefore also understood as minus one, yielding as the product of division the imaginary but still useful number we have learned to call the square root of minus one ("Subversion of the Subject," 317). Lacan immediately explains what this means for the subject: "This [i.e., the $\sqrt{-1}$] is what the subject lacks in order to think himself exhausted by his *cogito,* namely, that which is unthinkable for him" ("Subversion of the Subject," 317).

This lack in the subject—on the one hand, unthinkable for the subject; on the other, responsible for His (his/her) constitution *as* subject, specifically, as a desiring subject—is, at least in this formulation, occasioned by the subject's registration of His

(his/her) proper name, the *trait unaire,* as Lacan explains in "The Subversion of the Subject," "which, by filling in the invisible mark that the subject derives from the signifier, alienates this subject in the primary identification that forms the ego ideal" (p. 306). This alienation is a function, Lacan says, of "the relation of the subject to the signifier—a relation that is embodied in an enunciation whose being trembles with the vacillation that comes back to it from its own statement" (p. 300); "An enunciation that denounces itself, a statement that renounces itself, ignorance that dissipates itself, an opportunity that loses itself, the trace of what *must* be in order to fall from being?" (p. 300). And this fall therefore determines, Lacan says, the being of the subject, determines it as "Being of non-being, that is how *I* as subject comes on the scene, conjugated with the double aporia of a true survival that is abolished by knowledge of itself, and but a discourse in which it is death that sustains existence" (p. 300). Or, to cite one of Lacan's many glosses of Freud's "*Wo es war, soll Ich werden,*" but which might equally well serve to gloss the temporal structuration of "That's he that was Othello, here I am," *not* what *The Standard Edition* translates as "where id was there shall ego be," but, instead, and more Shakespearean, "There where it was just now, there where it was for awhile, between an extinction that is still glowing and a birth that is retarded, 'I' can come into being and disappear from what I say" (p. 300).

Lacan always, by no means only in "The Subversion of the Subject," returns to this necessary lack, gap, absence, disjunction, hole, determined for the subject by the very registration or denomination of the all, the complete, the total, the one, the whole, in which the subject finds himself, and therefore finds himself as lost. Elsewhere, in the *Seminar on Identification* (1961–62), Lacan develops the same point, again in connection with proper names and the unitary trait, in terms of the paradox of classes with which Russell confounded Frege.[16] Lacan uses the diagram of an inverted figure-eight to illustrate the paradox that results when one asks, as inevitably one must, whether the class of classes that do not contain themselves is itself contained in the class of classes that do not contain themselves.[17] If so, then it is con-

E^B ᴊ ensemblesqui ᴊe comprennent eux-mêmes
ʃ^B ᴊensemblesqui ne se comprennent pas
eux-mêmes

schéma

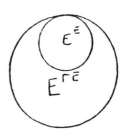

tained in the class of classes that do not contain themselves, which is paradoxical, and, if not, then we come upon an analogous impasse. We can note the way Lacan's inverted figure-eight reproduces the structure of subjective inversion imaged by the Mandeville drawing of "the men whose heads do grow beneath their shoulders"— the circle within and without that which it circles—an inversion Lacan explains in terms of a redoubling, or turn, or return, by means of which, in Russell's paradox, the interiority of the inside is rendered homogeneous with the exteriority of the out-side in a systematically aporetic way.[18] Between the one and the other, between, that is, an inside and an outside that are both turned inside out, stands the tangential, placeless, autodifferential mark that is neither the one nor the other, but, instead, the lack in both that derives from their disjunctive conjunction, the same lack that is dis-closed, Lacan says in the *Seminar on Identification,* by the fact that "a signifier, inso-far as it might serve to signify itself, is obliged to pose itself as different from itself."[19]

This determination of the autodifferential mark—which Lacan alternately develops in terms of the post-Cartesian difference between the subject who speaks and the subject who is bespoken, or in terms of the difference between the subject of the signifier and the subject of the signified, or in terms of the desire precipitated by the infinite discrepancy between finite need and infinite demand, or in terms of the fading of the subject in the intersubjective dialectic between the intersaid (*inter-dit*) and the intra-said (*intradit*), or in terms of the disjunctive intersection of the Imag-inary and the Symbolic (I say in passing that all this can be directly related to the by now familiar quarrel in Anglo-American philosophy between descriptivist and causal-chain theorists of proper names)—is for Lacan the mark of the Real: "the cut in discourse, the strongest being that which acts as a bar between the signifier and the signified" ("Subversion of the Subject," 299). As Lacan puts it in "The Subversion of the Subject": "This cut in the signifying chain alone verifies the structure of the subject as discontinuity in the Real" (p. 299). And it is around this cut, experienced *as* cut, that the subject finds the motivating lack around which his desire circulates in a structurally asymptotic and vain effort to plug up the hole within the w-hole that is its ongoing, constituting cause, as does Othello, when, entering the bedroom to strangle Desdemona, he explains: "It is the cause, it is the cause, my soul; / Let me not name it to you, you chaste stars, / It is the cause. Yet I'll not shed her blood, / Nor scar that whiter skin of hers than snow, / And smooth as monumental alabaster" (5.1.1–3). On the one hand, the mark of this cut determines what is erotic in the so-called "erogenous zone": "the result of a cut (*coupure*) expressed in the antomical mark (*trait*) of a margin or border—lips, 'the enclosure of the teeth,' the rim of the anus, the tip of the penis, the vagina, the slit formed by the eyelids, even the horn-shaped aperture of the ear" ("Subversion of the Subject," 314–315); on the other, "this mark of the cut is present in the object described by analytic theory: the mamilla, faeces, the phallus ([as] imaginary object), the urinary flow" (an unthinkable list, if one adds, as I do, the phoneme, the gaze, the voice, the nothing) ("Subversion of the Subject," 315). And so, too, says Lacan, is this the "'stuff,' or rather the lining . . . of the very subject that one takes to be the subject of consciousness. For this subject, who thinks he can accede to himself by designating himself in the statement, is no more than such an object" ("Subversion of the Subject," 315). It is for this reason, also, that I associate the sound of *O* in *Othello,* insofar as this is sounded out as mark of a subjectifying name, with the mark of the Real, the *objet a,* that occasions desire in the first place, as well as its subjective temporality as aftermath, also in the first place.

But what kind of desire is this, really? Lacan, though he says it elsewhere, offers an answer in *Television* when he says, stressing the banality of the observation that "there is no sexual relation," that is, that there is no sexual rapport, by which he means, at the very least, that the ideal unity of two is precisely that which forecloses the possibility of union, thereby provoking a desire for precisely that which it prevents.[20] The topos brings us back to Othello, the representation of a person, and through him back to Shakespeare, the person.

It is often remarked that Othello's jealousy is necessarily delusional, for, given the compressed and double time-scheme of the play, there is literally no time for Cassio to have cuckolded Othello. It is not so often noticed, however, that, for the same reason, there is no time in the play for Othello ever to have consummated his marriage to Desdemona.[21] What should have been the lovers' first married night together, in Venice—in Venus—is interrupted by the announcement of the Turkish threat, whereupon Othello and Desdemona both set out for Cyprus in separate ships. In Cyprus, the postponed honeymoon night is once again delayed and interrupted by Cassio's noisy, drunken riot, and the interruption occurs at precisely that moment when Iago says, "the General hath not yet made wanton the night with" Desdemona (2.3.16). Affectively, that is to say, Othello never consummates his marriage until the climactic moment in which he strangles Desdemona, when the marriage bed, in characteristically Shakespearean fashion, becomes the death bed. This consistent instantiation of Othello's *coitus interruptus,* an interruption specifically signalled by noise, is emblematized in a small scene, often cut in production, in which some wind musicians, at Cassio's behest, come on stage to serenade Othello and Desdemona from beneath their bedroom window. No sooner do they start to play, however, than

Othello's clown comes out to tell them to be silent: "The General so likes your music, that he desires you for love's sake to make no more noise with it" (3.1.11–12). Instead, says the Clown, "If you have any music that may not be heard, to't again," but, if not, "Go, vanish into air, away!" (3.1.15–16).[22]

I stress the emblematic significance of this scene because I take its evoked "music without sound" to be a definition, "for love's sake," of the sound of O in *Othello.* And the reason why this seems important is that this "music without sound" returns again to the play, and does so in a passage that, for purely vocal reasons, has always seemed, to critics and to audiences, profoundly strange and haunting. I refer to Desdemona's "Willow Song," which she sings just prior to her murder and where even the "wind" of the wind musicians reenters the diegesis of the play, and reenters it again *as* interruption:

> *Desdemona.* "The poor fool sat sighing by a sycamore tree,
> Sing all a green willow;
> Her hand on her bosom, her head on her knee,
> Sing willow, willow, willow.
> The fresh streams ran by her, and murmur'd her moans,
> Sing willow, willow, willow;
> Her salt tears fell from her, and soft'ned the stones,
> Sing willow"—
> Lay by these—
> [Singing.] "—willow, willow"—
> Prithee hie thee; he'll come anon—
> [Singing.]
> "Sing all a green willow must be my garland.
> Let nobody blame him, his scorn I approve"—
> Nay, that's not next. Hark, who is't that knocks?
> *Emilia.* It's the wind.
> *Desdemona.* [Singing]
> "I call'd my love false love; but what said he then?
> Sing willow, willow, willow;
> If I court moe women, you'll couch with moe men."—
> So get thee gone, good night. Mine eyes do itch;
> Doth that bode weeping?
> *Emilia.* 'Tis neither here nor there.
> *Desdemona.* I have heard it said so. (4.3.40–60)

The central, we can say the most Shakespearean, fact about this "Willow song" is that it is *not* by Shakespeare, and would have been recognized as such, i.e., as non-Shakespearean, by the original audience for the play.[23] What is called Desdemona's "Willow song" is, in fact, a traditional ballad, reproduced in miscellanies, that appears to have captured Shakespeare's aural imagination—inspired him, we can say, thinking of the wind—and which he here introduces into the play as though to sound out something that comes from a literary place outside the literariness of the play. Recognizing this, my claim is a simple one, but one with several consequences: namely, that the "willow" of Desdemona's "Willow song" amounts to Shakespeare's literal and personal translation of the Greek verb *ethelō,* and that this is a significant translation because Desdemona's "Willow song," understood in this way, therefore marks the place where Shakespeare's own name, Will, is itself marked off by the invoked, cited sound of the sound of *O* in *Othello*—"Sing will-ow, will-ow, will-ow." If this is the case, then we can say, at least in this case, precisely what there is in a Shakespearean name that makes it Shakespearean. It is specifically the *O,* calling to us from an elsewhere that is other, that determines the Shakespearean subject as the difference between the subject of a name and the subject of full being, or, even more precisely, as the subject who exists as the difference between the *Will* at the beginning of Will-iam and the *I* of Williams's *I am: Will-O-I am.*[24]

In Desdemona's "Willow song," therefore, we can say the Real of the subject of Shakespeare enters the play, informing with the force of its contingency the otherwise merely formal literary exigencies with which and through which the subjectivity effect of the hero is constructed. And this is important because we can thereby account for the powerful investment, specifically at the level of subjectivity, of both author and audience in the character of Othello, for in both cases what is necessarily and structurally at stake in the representation of a persona whose subjective evacuation is substantiated by the sound of *O* in *Othello* is the way in which, in the words of Lacan that I took as epigraph, "The sexual impasse exudes the fictions that rationalize the impossible within which it originates." For both author and audience these fictions—what I will elsewhere call the "alibi" (*alius abi,* i.e., the elsewhere) of subjectivity—really are "the invitation to the Real that underwrites them," but of a specifically Shakespearean Real, the willful legacy of which continues to determine, as the example of Lacan makes evident, not only the erotic contents but also the tragic contours of the literature of person. Hence the concluding answer I propose to the question I raised earlier as to whether we should see in Othello and Shakespeare the corroborating proof or evidence of Lacan's theorizations about subjectivity or, instead, whether we should see in Lacan's theorizations an epiphenomenal consequence of the powerful literary subjectivity effect Shakespeare invents toward the end of the English Renaissance: given the historical force of the sound of O in *Othello,* I say the latter and call him, Lacan, Shakespearean.

Notes

Reprinted from *October,* no. 45 (Summer 1988), 76–96.

1.   This paper was originally delivered at a colloquium on Lacan's *Television* (Paris, Editions du Seuil, 1974), sponsored by *October/Ornicar?,* April 9–10, 1987. The two epigraphs from *Television* appear in the translation published in *October,* no. 40, trans. Denis Hollier, Rosalind Krauss, and Annette Michelson (Spring 1987), 45 and 34, respectively. All Shakespeare references are to *The Riverside Shakespeare,* ed. G. B. Evans et al. (Boston: Houghton Mifflin, 1974).

2.   Forthcoming, University of California Press.

3.   Joel Fineman, *Shakespeare's Perjured Eye: The Invention of Poetic Subjectivity in Shakespeare's Sonnets* (Berkeley: University of California Press, 1986).

4.   For Shakespeare's probable Greek education, see T. W. Baldwin, *Shakspere's Small Latine and Lesse Greek,* 2 vols. (Urbana: University of Illinois Press, 1944). According to F. W. Gingrich's *Shorter Lexicon of the Greek New Testament,* rev. F. W. Danker (Chicago: University of Chicago Press, 1983), *thelō* means primarily "wish," "will," "desire," but, also, "resolve" and "purpose"; as with French *vouloir, thelō* also carries the sense of want as lack, for example, a *want* "to mean" or "to be," e.g., *Ac.* 2:12, *"ti thelei touto einai,"* "what does this mean?"

5.   Of the many plausible Greek etymologies to associate with the name Desdemona, Cinthio, in conclusion, stresses: "It appeared marvelous to everybody that such malignity could have been discovered in a human heart [here speaking of the Iago prototype]; and the fate of the unhappy Lady was lamented, with some blame for her father, who had given her a name of unlucky augury" (excerpt from *Gli Hecatommithi* [1566 edition], trans. and ed. Geoffrey Bullough, *Narrative and Dramatic Sources of Shakespeare* (New York: Columbia University Press, 1973), vol. 7, 250. There are alternate speculations regarding Shakespeare's source for the name Othello, e.g., Thorello, in Ben Jonson's *Everyman in His Humour* (1598). Shakespeare often associates Venus, or Aphrodite, with Cyprus, referring directly to her mythological birthplace, e.g., the final couplet of *Venus and Adonis*: "holding their course to Paphos, where their queen / Means to immure herself, and not be seen" (1193–1194). The *Revels Accounts* records the first performance of *Othello*—before the king, on November 1, 1604—as "The Moor of Venis" by "Shaxberd" (Bullough, *Sources,* 193).

6.   In his Introduction, Bullough reviews arguments for and against Shakespeare's knowledge of Cinthio's text (*Sources,* 193–238). Cinthio's text was first published in 1565, and Shakespeare may have read this; there is also a French translation, dated 1584, by Gabriel Chappuys, which Shakespeare may also have read. The first English translation appears in 1753.

7.   The prefix-marker in Greek for aorist or imperfect tenses is *e* (ε) or, under certain circumstances *ē* (η). The first-person imperfect for *thelō* is thus *ēthelōn,* with the final *ōn* marking the first person. Hence my remarks above. Various Greek scholars with whom I have conferred are willing to hear a collation between the sound of O in *Othello* and the initial prefix—*ē*—but they also insist they do not hear a convincing collation between the sound of O and the final *ōn* of the first-person imperfect. Despite such philological objections, I continue to think Shakespeare—who had very little Greek indeed, and who regularly makes greater and far freer auditory free-associations in English—would have heard a connection between the sound of O and the final *ōn* of the first-person imperfect of *thelō*. However, if one does not grant this final association, then my argument above about the subjective force of the sound of O in *Othello* loses only one half of its two markers of the first-person imperfect, and, in either case, the argument retains its validity with regard to the subjective apprehension of the present. However, in the context of what I say later about Lacan's account of the constitution of the subject, it is significant that the two markers of the ongoing first-person past (*ē* at the beginning and *ōn* at the end) are bound up together in the sound of O in *Othello,* for,

thus conjoined, they register the durative experience of the (insistently repeated) moment of the constitution of the subject as the sustained and immediate *passing* of the present, as in my discussion above of "That's he that was Othello, here I am" (5.2.284).

8.   The most immediately relevant Shakespeare Sonnets are 135 and 136. I quote them here so as to recall, first, the performative way Shakespeare exploits the fact that his name designates both male and female genitals, second, the "overplus" arithmetics of *Will* (for discussions of these sonnets, see *Shakespeare's Perjured Eye,* ch. 5):

135
Whoever hath her wish, though hast thy *Will,*
And *Will* to boot, and *Will* in overplus;
More than enough am I that vex thee still,
To thy sweet will making addition thus.
Wilt thou, whose will is large and spacious,
Not once vouchsafe to hide my will in thine?
Shall will in others seem right gracious,
And in my will no fair acceptance shine?
The sea, all water, yet receives rain still,
And in abundance addeth to his store,
So thou being rich in *Will* add to thy *Will,*
One will of mine to make the large *Will* more.
Let no unkind, no fair beseechers kill;
Think all but one, and me in that one *Will.*

136
If thy soul check thee that I come so near,
Swear to thy blind soul that I was thy *Will,*
And will, thy soul knows, is admitted there;
Thus far for love my love suit, sweet, fulfil.
Will will fulfill the treasure of thy love,
Ay fill it full with wills, and my will one.
In things of great receipt with ease we prove
Among a number one is reckon'd none:
Then in the number let me pass untold,
Though in thy store's account I one must be,
For nothing hold me, so it please thee hold
That nothing me, a something sweet to thee.
Make but my name thy love, and love that still,
And then thou lovest me, for my name is *Will.*

9.   Lacan accounts for the subjective experience of original sin by reference to the lack imported into the subject through His (his/her), subjectively constitutive, accession to a name through the discourse of the Other: "'I' am in the place from which a voice is heard clamoring 'the universe is a defect in the purity of Non-Being.' And not without reason, for by protecting itself this place makes Being itself languish. This place is called *Jouissance,* and it is the absence of this that makes the universe vain. Am I responsible for it, then? Yes, probably. Is this *Jouissance,* the lack of which makes the Other insubstantial, mine, then? Experience proves that it is usually forbidden me, not only, as certain fools believe, because of a bad arrangement of society, but rather because of the fault [*faute*] of the Other if he existed: and since the Other does not exist, all that remains to me is to assume the fault upon 'I,' that is to say, to believe in that to which experience leads us all, Freud in the vanguard, namely, to original sin" ("The Subversion of the Subject and the Dialectic of Desire in the Freudian Unconscious," *Ecrits: A Selection,* trans. Alan Sheridan (New York: W. W. Norton, 1977), 317.

10.   Jacques-Alain Miller, "'La suture': Eléments de la logique du signifiant," *Cahiers pour l'ana-lyse,* no. 1/2 (1966), 37–49; e.g., "C'est l'énoncé décisif que *le concept de la non-identité-à-soi est assigné par le nombre zéro* qui suture le discours logique," 46.

11.   Shakespeare probably took the anthropophagi topos from Philemon Holland's 1601 trans-lation of Pliny's *Natural History.* Shakespeare regularly conceives eating in terms of self-consum-mation, as in the opening procreation sonnets to the young man or, for another example, as in *Troilus and Cressida,* "He that is proud eats up himself. Pride is his own glass, his own trumpet, his own chronicle, and whatever praises itself but in the deed, devours the deed in the praise" (2.3.154–157). Lacan remarks, apropos Freud's dream of Irma's injection, "If there is an image that might rep-resent for us the Freudian notion of the unconscious, it is exactly that of a headless subject, of a sub-ject who has no more ego, who is beyond the ego, decentered in relation to the ego, who is not of the ego" ("S'il y a une image qui pourrait nous représenter la notion freudienne de l'inconscient, c'est bien celle d'un sujet acéphale, d'un sujet qui n'a plus d' *ego,* qui est extrême à l' *ego,* dé-centré par rapport à l'*ego,* qui n'est pas de l' *ego*"). *Le moi dans la théorie de Freud et dans la technique de la psychanalyse* (Paris: Editions du Seuil, 1978), 200.

12.   See *Shakespeare's Perjured Eye.*

13.   The relation of vision to speaking, mediated by the motif of writing—a writing which is nei-ther the former nor the latter and yet, nevertheless, a little of both—is how the play, quite apart from its critics, explains the original motivation of Iago; this is specified quite clearly in the opening lines of the play, when Iago complains about

> One Michael Cassio, a Florentine
> (A fellow almost damn'd in a fair wife),
> That never set a squadron in the field,
> Nor the division of a battle knows
> More than a spinster—unless the bookish theoric,
> Wherein the toged consuls can propose
> As masterly as he. Mere prattle, without practice,
> Is all his soldiership.
> But he, sir, had th' election;
> And I, of whom his eyes had seen the proof
> At Rhodes, at Cyprus, and on other grounds
> Christen'd and heathen, must be belee'd and calm'd
> By debitor and creditor—this counter-caster,
> He (in good time!) must his lieutenant be,
> And I (God bless the mark!) his Moorship's ancient. (1.1.20–33)

What Iago here calls "bookish theoric," the preference for which explains why, according to Iago, "Preferment goes by letter and affection,/And not by old gradation, where each second/Stood heir to th' first" (1.1.36–38), can serve as both the motto and the explanation of *The Tragedy of Othello,* if we remember the etymology of "theoric," from Greek *theorein, to see,* and if we appreciate the way this "bookish theoric" stands at odds with the immediate vision of an "I" "of whom his eyes had seen the proof." This is related to the military, erotic, and semiotic issues at stake in the matter of Iago's promotion, his rise from the rank of "Ancient," or ensign—the man who bears before the troops the flag or insignia of their collective power—to the rank of "Lieutenant," the man who, behind the troops, stands as executive *place-holder* of a power that is thus represented rather than seen; hence my first epigraph from *Othello:* Iago's "I must show out a flag and sign of love, / Which is indeed but sign" (1.1.156–157). Very roughly, I am here connecting Lacan's three knotted reg-isters, the Imaginary, the Symbolic, and the Real, to, respectively, Shakespeare's equally knotted con-catenation of the visual, the verbal, and the written; see note 24, below.

14.   Frank Kermode, Introduction to *Othello, The Riverside Shakespeare,* 1198.

15.   Lacan, "The Subversion of the Subject," 316; subsequent references to this essay will be noted in the text within parentheses.

16.   I thank Helena Schulz-Keil, first, for many helpful and instructive conversations about the work of Lacan, second, for bringing to my attention both the existence of this unpublished typescript redaction of the *Seminar on Identification* and its discussion of the *trait unaire*; on the unitary trait, see also Helene Muller, "Another Genesis of the Unconscious," *Lacan Study Notes,* 5 (Summer 1985), 1–22. I will be referring to the eighteenth meeting of Lacan's Seminar, May 2, 1962; page numbers refer to the typescript's numeration.

17.   *Seminar on Identification,* 9. I discuss this paradox in relation to proper names and Lacan in "The Significance of Literature, *The Importance of Being Earnest,*" *October,* no. 15 (Winter 1980), 79–90 [reprinted in this volume].

18.   *Seminar on Identification,* 9. For the Shakespearean resonations—especially the materialized liquidity of ejaculate suspense: "the phenomenology of the spurt"—attaching to this image of a space both within and without itself, see my illustration and discussion of the death of Lucrece in "Shakespeare's *Will*: The Temporality of Rape," *Representations,* no. 20 (Fall 1987), 25–76 [reprinted in this volume].

19.   "En fait c'est une chose excessivement bête et simple ce point très essentiel que le signifiant en tant qu'il peut servir à se signifier lui-même doit se poser comme différent de lui-même" (*Seminar on Identification,* 10).

20.   *Television, October,* 45 ("'Il n'y a pas de rapport sexuel': Il est frappant que ce sens réduise au non-sens: au non-sens du rapport sexuel, lequel est patent depuis toujours dans les dits de l'amour," *Television,* 18).

21.   Exceptionally and suggestively, Stanley Cavell stresses the interruption of Othello's honeymoon night (*The Claim of Reason* (New York: Oxford University Press, 1979), 487).

22.   The anal and syphilitic reverberations of the "wind" in this scene are significant:

> *Clown:* Why, masters, have your instruments been in Naples, that they speak i' the nose thus?
> *Musician:* How, sir, how?
> *Clown:* Are these, I pray you, wind instruments?
> *Musician:* Ay, marry, are they sir.
> *Clown:* O, thereby hangs a tail.
> *Musician:* Whereby hangs a tale, sir?
> *Clown:* Marry, sir, by many a wind instrument that I know. But, masters, here's money for you; and the general so likes your music, that he desires you for love's sake to make no more noise with it.
> *Musician:* Well, sir, we will not.
> *Clown:* If you have any music that may not be heard, to't again; but (as they say) to hear music the general does not greatly care.
> *Musician:* We have none such, sir.
> *Clown:* Then put up your pipes in your bag, for I'll away. Go, vanish into air, away!
> *Exeunt Musicians* (3.1.1.20)

23.   Norman Sanders, editor of *The New Cambridge Othello,* notes: "This is a version of a song well-known before Shakespeare used it and often quoted in earlier plays and poems. The fullest texts of the original can be found in Percy's *Reliques of Ancient English Poetry,* 1765, 1, 199–203, and *The Roxburghe Ballads,* ed. W. Chappell, 1888, 1, 171. For his version Shakespeare changed the sex of the singer and drew mainly on stanzas 1, 2, 5, 6, 7, and 11 of the original. There are three contemporary musical settings of the song in British Library Add MS 15117 (1616 or earlier), The Lodge Book, Folger Library (early 1570s) and the Dallis Book, Trinity College, Dublin (c. 1583)" (Cambridge: Cambridge University Press, 1974), 190.

24.   I have argued elsewhere in "Shakespeare's *Will*: The Temporality of Rape," that Shakespearean signature effects are regularly related not only to Shakespeare's registration of his name

but also to the orthographic staging of the writing of this name through the chiastic coordination of the letters *WM,* the first and last letters of Shakespeare's first name, and also Shakespeare's abbreviation of his name, at least as he signs it to the mortgage deed of Blackfriar's House, "W^M Shakspē"; this happens here, again, with the O of Desdemona's "Willow Song," for example, "The fresh streams ran by her, and *m*urmur'd her *m*oans, / Sing *w*il-low, *w*illow, *w*illow," or "Sing *w*illow, *w*illow, *w*il-low; / If I court *m*oe wo*m*en you'll couch with *m*oe *m*en"—lines, by the way, Freud cites to exemplify the logic of projective jealousy; see Sigmund Freud, "Certain Neurotic Mechanisms in Jealousy, Paranoia, and Homosexuality" (1922), in *Sexuality and the Psychology of Love,* ed. Philip Rieff (New York: Collier Books, 1970), 162.

It can not only be shown that this *WM* formation is related to Greek omega—written as ω, but sounded as O—but in addition that there is a longstanding tradition that interprets the orthography of Greek omega in thematic terms that correspond to those I am arguing are associated with the subjectivity effect of the "characteristically Shakespearean." I refer here, too briefly, to the opening of the treatise "On Apparatus and Furnaces: Authentic Commentaries on the Letter Omega," by the third-century hermetical alchemist known as Zosimos:

> Round Omega is the bipartite letter, the one that in terms of material language belongs to the seventh planetary zone, that of Kronos. For in terms of the immaterial it is something else altogether, something inexplicable, which only Nokotheos the hidden knows. In material terms Omega is what he calls "Ocean, it says, 'the birth and seed of all gods,'" as he says, "the governing principles of material language" (*Zosimos of Panopolis On the Letter Omega,* ed. and trans. Howard M. Jackson (Missoula, Mo.: University of Montana Press, 1978), 17.

Zosimos, though obscure, is important because he contributes to an influential tradition of hermetic and alchemical iconography that survives up through and beyond the Renaissance; there are many manuscript versions of his commentary scattered through the libraries of Europe. (There is also reason to suppose that Lacan would have been familiar with the document, either from the partial version printed in the *Corpus Hermeticum,* ed. Arthur Nock and André-Jean Festugière, vol. 4 (Paris: Société d'éditions "les Belles Lettres," 1954), 117–121, or the full version printed in Carl Jung's *Psychologie und Alchemie* (Zurich: Rascher Verlag, 1952) 360–368.)

The significance of this text, in this context, is that for someone like Shakespeare, who has only a little Greek, the Greek alphabet would not have been a transparent medium of signification; on the contrary, the graphic inscription of the Greek alphabet would have been for Shakespeare something whose typographic materiality would be literally visualizable. This suggests that when Shakespeare had Greek in his mind, or when he thought the letter omega—again, written as ω, but sounded as O—he would have *seen w* but would have *heard O*. Accordingly, it is through this slippage between the visual and the spoken, mediated by the unrepresentable phenomenality of writing, that the sound of O in *Othello* acquires its *characteristically* Shakespearean subjective properties.

What is thus *idiosyncratically* Shakespearean, however, also corresponds with what is a general, even a generic, tradition assembled around omega. Consider, in this context, the editor's note on the passage from Zosimos cited above: "The shape of the Greek letter omega (ω) suggests the descriptions of 'round' and 'bipartite.' The reason for their inclusion is not so obvious, but it is probably in anticipation of correlating the letter omega with Ocean. Ocean was conceived to be a river that encircled the world; Homer describes the shield of Hephaistos for Achilles as depicting Ocean flowing around its outer rim (*Iliad,* 18.607; cf. also Herodotus 4.8) [cf. the Mandeville or Lacan illustrations above; also the circular river of blood that surrounds the dying Lucrece]. This fact accounts for omega's being called *stroggulōn* [round]. The explanation for *dimerēs* [bipartite] is perhaps that Zosimos held ocean to be a hermaphrodite being. The alchemist Olympiodoros (who just may be identical with the Neo-Platonic commentator of Plato) cites Zosimos as saying that the sea is *arreno-thēlus* [bisexual] (Berthelot II, iv, 32, texte grec 89.19). The background for this odd, un-Greek conception is supplied by a statement in Diodorus of Sicily (actually his source Hekataios of Abdera): the Egyptians say that 'the ancients named the moist element "Okeane," which means "Sustenance

Mother"; but by some of the Greeks it is held to be "Okeanos" (i.e., masculine)' (1.12.5). In classical Egyptian cosmogonies the primeval waters of chaos are a divine syzygy, Nwn and Nwnt. Furthermore, Diodorus (1.12.6) goes on to say that the Egyptians consider Ocean to be the Nile, and the ancient Egyptians often depicted the god Nile as a man with pendulous breasts" (p. 39).

The central practical literary question raised by the regular occurrence of the Shakespearean signature is to determine what topoi control the relation of the speaking to the writing of a name. In *Othello,* writing calls up a particularly coded erotic name, which is why Othello would rather not write: "Was this fair paper, this most goodly book, / Made to write 'whore' upon?" (4.2.71–72). Accordingly, Othello strangles Desdemona rather than scar her, for reasons Lacan articulates in the conclusion of the quotation from "The Subversion of the Subject" cited above: "For this subject who thinks he can accede to himself by designating himself in the statement, is no more than such an object. Ask the writer about the anxiety that he experiences when faced by the blank sheet of paper, and he will tell you who is the turd (*l'étron*) of his phantasy," 315. In Shakespeare's tragedies *l'étron,* like the "letter," always returns to its sender in inverted form:

> *Othello:* I took by th' throat the circumcised dog,—and smote him—thus.
> *Lodovico:* O bloody period! (5.2.355–357)

Shakespeare's *Will:* The Temporality of Rape

There is a great difference, whether any Booke choose his Patrones, or finde them. This hath done both.

—Editors' Dedication to *The Shakespeare First Folio*[1]

The loue I dedicate to your Lordship is without end: wherof this Pamphlet without beginning is but a superfluous Moity.

—Shakespeare's Dedication to "The Rape of Lucrece"[2]

Lucius Tarquinius (for his excessive pride surnamed Superbus), after he had caused his own father-in-law Servius Tullius to be cruelly murd'red, and contrary to the Roman laws and customs, not requiring or staying for the people's suffrages, had possessed himself of the kingdom, went, accompanied with his sons and other noblemen of Rome, to besiege Ardea; during which siege, the principal men of the army meeting one evening at the tent of Sextus Tarquinius, the King's son, in their discourses after supper every one commended the virtues

*of his own wife; among whom Colla-
tinus extolled the incomparable chastity
of his wife Lucretia. In that pleasant
humor they all posted to Rome, and
intending by their secret and sudden
arrival to make trial of that which every
one had before avouched, only Collatinus finds his wife (though it were late in
the night) spinning amongest her maids;
the other ladies were all found dancing
and revelling, or in several disports;
whereupon the noblemen yielded Collatinus the victory, and his wife the fame.
At that time Sextus Tarquinius being
inflamed with Lucrece' beauty, yet
smothering his passions for the present,
departed with the rest back to the camp;
from whence he shortly after privily with-
drew himself, and was (according to his
estate) royally entertained and lodged
by Lucrece at Collatium. The same night
he treacherously stealeth into her chamber, violently ravish'd her, and early in
the morning speedeth away. Lucrece, in
this lamentable plight, hastily dispatcheth
messengers, one to Rome for her father,
another to the camp for Collatine. They
came, the one accompanied with Junius
Brutus, the other with Publius Valerius;
and finding Lucrece attired in mourning habit, demanded the cause for her
sorrow. She, first taking an oath of them
for her revenge, revealed the actor, and
whole manner of his dealing, and withal
suddenly stabbed herself. Which done,
with one consent they all vowed to root
out the whole hated family of the Tar-*

> *quins; and bearing the dead body to*
> *Rome, Brutus acquainted the people*
> *with the doer and the manner of the vile*
> *deed; with a bitter invective against the*
> *tyranny of the King, wherewith the people*
> *were so moved, that with one consent*
> *and a general acclamation the Tarquins*
> *were all exiled, and the state government*
> *changed from kings to consuls.*
>
> —The Argument, "The Rape of Lucrece"

I

Because the first sentence of Shakespeare's Dedication to Southampton speaks of "this Pamphlet without beginning," it is not altogether certain Shakespeare wrote "The Argument" that precedes the text of "The Rape of Lucrece": "without beginning" very likely refers to the fact that "the poem begins," as the glossing apparatus of the *Riverside* edition puts it, "in the middle of the action," but it might just as well refer to the absence of a conventional, prefatory, narrative summary.[3] In neither case, however, is there anything especially peculiar about the way the poem or, more precisely, "this Pamphlet," is lacking something from the start. With or without an Argument, no surprise attaches to the way the poem opens *in media res,* with Tarquin rushing "From the besieged Ardea all in post" (1), this being a conventional way to initiate the narration of such well-known epically contexted stories as that of the rape of Lucrece. So too, again because the rape story and its epic frame (the formation of the Roman republic) are both so famous and familiar, there is nothing very strange about Shakespeare having chosen to omit, if he did, what was a customary, but by no means an obligatory, introductory recapitulation. For this reason, however—because a shared literary history presumptively resumes the story before a reader reads it, because both within and without the poem a general literary context supplies the pretext of an Argument—it is striking that Shakespeare, looking back at "The Rape of Lucrece" from the distance of the Dedication, remarks the way "this Pamphlet" begins "without beginning," all of the more so since, as it is written, "this Pamphlet without beginning" stands in complementary contrast to a dedicatory love "without end."

The absolute formality of this abstract opposition, plus the intricacy of the logical and syntactic hinge through which the opposition is coordinated—"wherof"—

establishes a field or spectrum that at first appears to be exhaustive: a systematic completeness in between two interminable extremes, an enormity of everything extending forward, to begin with, to beyond the end, reaching backward, to conclude with, to before the beginning. And yet, at least in this first sentence of the Dedication of "The Rape of Lucrece," the entirety thus so blankly and encyclopedically imagined, specified neither in terms of space nor time, contains within it only that which is excessive to the wholeness it comprises: namely, the "superfluous Moity" Shakespeare advances as his judgment on or of his text's relation to his "love." "Moiety" is a word that for Shakespeare most often connotes a conflicted and contested, usually binary, portion of a larger whole—as at the opening of *King Lear* where "in the division of the kingdom, it appears not which of the Dukes he values most, for equalities are so weigh'd, that curiosity in neither can make choice of either's moi'ty" (1.1.4–7)—but here, because the dedicated "Moity" is "superfluous," it becomes a portion that exists as something surplus to the whole of which it is a part. And this is not altogether an abstraction. Precipitated out of the conjunction of an inconclusive "loue . . . without end" and a headless "Pamphlet without beginning," there emerges a poem that is "but a superfluous Moity." But Shakespeare knew enough Latin that we can be certain this textual superfluity contains for him a very vivid image: a liquid portion that runs over, a fluidity that overflows.

As it happens, this image is quite central to "The Rape of Lucrece," figuring not only the rape but also its motivation and consequences, so it is significant that Shakespeare, speaking in the authorial first-person of the patronizing Dedication, in this way associates his poem with the phenomenology of the spurt, with both the energy and the materiality of a liquified ejection, as though his text itself, as "superfluous Moity," were the objectification of an ejaculate suspense. It remains to determine why, here and elsewhere, the "superfluous Moity," both in its material fluidity and in its constrained directionality—thrusting outward from the aftermath of the pre-beginning toward the unreachable horizon of an ultimate inconclusivity; a movement, frozen in a static motility, between a departure always initiated *après coup* and an arrival prospectively postponed in anticipation of a forever deferred and receding destination: "Before, a joy propos'd, behind, a dream," to use the language of sonnet 129—so readily, frequently, and circumscribingly informs Shakespeare's imagination of what comes to pass when the erotic ("The loue I dedicate") and the poetic ("this Pamphlet") go together. That this happens here, in the first-person address to Southampton, suggests that this is partially a biographical question, a matter of what Shakespeare found convenient when he represents himself as speaking in his own subjective voice. That this happens elsewhere, however—in Shakespeare's poems, even when they are not in the first-person, as well as in the plays—suggests that this is not simply a personal but also a more general literary matter, having to do with the way Shakespeare imagines the literary presentation of subjective character as such, the way he constructs or achieves the literary effect of psychologistic, characterological subjectivity.

In what follows I want to show that the individually inflected cast of Shakespeare's character, on the one hand, and the varied cast of Shakespearean literary characterology, on the other—together, the personal and the personalizing Shakespeare, i.e., the person who creates literary personae—are related to each other in ways quite literally prescribed by the contours of the "superfluous Moity." More precisely, in what follows I want not only to show that there is something characteristically Shakespearean about the way Shakespeare summons up the figure of an interposed or intervening excess when he locates the endlessness of the sexual and the beginninglessness of the textual in relation to each other but that, *because* this is so, this determines the formation and reception of the Shakespearean subject. Accordingly, because the large question I am concerned with is how the singularity of a contingent personality—the idiosyncratic Shakespeare—corresponds with, informs, motivates and is motivated by, a generic and highly determined subjective literary phenomenon—Shakespearean characterology—it is necessary to say clearly, before beginning, that the terms of my argument are at once more particular and more general than might at first appear: by "characteristically Shakespearean" I refer to that which literally marks out Shakespeare, Shakespeare's *"Will,"* not his name but its signature; by "the Shakespearean subject" I refer both to Shakespeare's biographical first-person—the one who writes "By me *William Shakespeare*" when he signs his will—and also to the subjectivity effect sometimes evinced by Shakespeare's literary representations of human character, where there are lyric and narrative as well as dramatic examples.[4] This is why "The Rape of Lucrece," though it is not usually recognized as a major work by Shakespeare, and though the subjectivity effect it generates is relatively feeble, is worth considering in considerable detail, for it provides a clear-cut illustration of the way the impression of psychologistic person in Shakespeare's texts characteristically effects and is effected by the mark of Shakespeare's person. Given the institutional force of Shakespearean characterology, given what goes on in Shakespeare's name, this is an important and not only literary issue.

I have elsewhere argued that in his sonnets Shakespeare invented a genuinely novel poetic first-person, one that comes to possess enormous power and authority in post-Shakespearean literature because, in a uniquely literary way, it reflects and responds to the conclusion or waning of the poetics and poetry of praise.[5] From antiquity to the Renaissance, in both literary theory and practice, the poetics of praise—i.e., epideictic or demonstrative oratory—defines the rhetorical mode not just associated with but, more strongly, identified with the literary per se; accordingly, Shakespeare's registration or production of a difference in this longstanding tradition represents an important event in literary history, for it speaks to a significant rethinking of the means and meaning of literature as such. One necessary consequence of this rethinking or mutation of the literary, I have argued, is the arrival of specifically psychologistic literary subjectivity effects.

According to this argument, three large and related literary features mark the way Shakespeare's sonnets revise what until Shakespeare is taken to be an orthodox literariness. First, at the level of theme, Shakespeare's sonnets, situating themselves posterior to the poetry of praise, forswear the idealization of poetic language formally and historically endemic to the language of poetic idealization. Second, corresponding, at the level of motif, to this thematic recharacterization of the nature of poetic language, Shakespeare's sonnets give over a general imagery of vision, the homogeneous phenomenality of which traditionally materializes the ideality not only of the object of praise but also of the poet's epideictic language and desire, and, instead, develop an imagery of phenomenal heterogeneity the conflicted physicality of which embodies an interruption in or wrinkling of familiar imagery of visionary sameness, identity, reflection, likeness. Third, a change of poetic manner corresponding to these changes in poetic matter, Shakespeare's sonnets regularly develop a four-term tropic structure of cross-coupling chiasmus the complicated figurality of which works not only to redouble but thereby to introduce disjunction into typically two-term comparisons and metaphorical identities developed in the poetry of praise.

Considered independently, any of these innovations—thematic, material, tropic—amounts to an important rewriting of orthodox epideictic literariness; taken together, however, these three features reciprocally corroborate each other in a decisive way, for the chiastic rhetoricity of Shakespeare's sonnets serves to foreground a specifically verbal duplicity that confirms the way poetic language, heard as language and invoked as such, is essentially discrepant to idealizing, unitary, visionary speech. In this way, the very languageness of language in Shakespeare's sonnets, sounded out, becomes both witness and performance of the belation and belying of linguistic idealization, with the result that poetic voice in Shakespeare's sonnets, to the extent it is registered as voice, not vision, establishes the first-person speaker of the sonnets, whom the sonnets will sometimes call "Will," as the internally divided, post-idealist subject of a "perjur'd eye" (sonnet 152). It can be shown that this subject, "Will," again for purely formal reasons, possesses a specific characterological profile; e.g., he—for this subject is conceived as male—experiences his own phenomenal substantiality as a materialized heterogeneity; he is subject of an unprecedentedly heterosexual, and therefore misogynist, desire for an object that is not admired; he speaks a language that effectively speaks against itself and derives from the experience of such speaking a specific sense of space and time.

I summarize this argument regarding Shakespeare's sonneteering first-person not because in what follows I want to presuppose either its assumptions or its conclusions but because I want to bear its terms in mind as part, though only part, of my claim that what happens in "The Rape of Lucrece" is characteristically Shakespearean. Accordingly, it seems significant, in the light of Shakespeare's "perjur'd eye," that "The Rape of Lucrece" organizes at its beginning the very same literary features— again, thematic, material, tropic—as those that condition the formation of Shakespeare's lyric self, and does so so as to tell a story about what happens after praise. These are the opening stanzas of "The Rape of Lucrece":

> From the besieged Ardea all in post,
> Borne by the trustless wings of false desire,
> Lust-breathed Tarquin leaves the Roman host,
> And to Collatium bears the lightless fire,
> Which in pale embers hid, lurks to aspire,
> > And girdle with embracing flames the waist
> > Of Collatine's fair love, Lucrece the chaste.
>
> Happ'ly that name of "chaste" unhapp'ly set
> This bateless edge on his keen appetite;
> When Collatine unwisely did not let
> To praise the clear unmatched red and white
> Which triumph'd in the sky of his delight;
> > Where mortal stars as bright as heaven's beauties,
> > With pure aspects did him peculiar duties.

                                                        (1–14)

As the first two stanzas introduce the story, there was a time, before the beginning of the poem, when things were as they should be, an originary time of ideal and specifically visual "delight," when "mortal stars as bright as heaven's beauties, / With pure aspects did him peculiar duties." This is how the poem initially images or imagines Collatine's initial happiness—what the third stanza of the poem will call "the treasure of his happy state"—as a primal shining moment in the past to which the poem's present-tense narrative now remembers back as absolute beginning of the diegetic story. At the same time, however, at least in opening narrative retrospect, this is a strange beginning in the sense that, as beginning, it may never have begun, as the fourth stanza explains:

> O happiness enjoy'd but of a few,
> And if possess'd, as soon decay'd and done
> As is the morning's silver melting dew
> Against the golden splendor of the sun!
> An expir'd date, cancell'd ere well begun.
>
>   (22–26)

What puts a more or less immediate end to this ideal beginning, the reason why "the morning's silver dew" melts "against the golden splendor of the sun," or the reason why this happy beginning—and here we can think of "this Pamphlet without beginning"—is "cancell'd ere well begun," is the fact that, as the second stanza recalls, "Collatine unwisely did not let / To praise the clear unmatched red and white." This is a very precise and repeatedly emphasized narrative stipulation. The poem understands Collatine's praise of Lucrece, his "boast of Lucrece' sov'reignty" (29), as fundamental cause of Tarquin's rape of Lucrece; pointedly, it is not Lucrece's chastity but "that name of 'chaste'" that "set / This bateless edge on his keen appetite." And if it is Collatine's praise that motivates Tarquin's movement, at the opening of the poem, "From the besieged Ardea all in post" "to Collatium," the poem from its beginning consistently develops this movement as an oxymoronic clouding, a systematic complication, of the simple, lucid visuality of Collatine's praiseworthy past, so that, in contrast to "the clear unmatched red and white" and the "pure aspects" of "mortal stars as bright as heaven's beauties" that we hear about in the second stanza, "lust-breathed Tarquin," instead, in the first stanza, while he is "all in post," "bears the lightless fire, / Which in pale embers hid, lurks to aspire."

Reversing the narrative order in which the first two stanzas of the poem present this information, we can therefore reconstruct a serial chronology for the story as a whole: first there is or was an original moment of visual ideality that elicits Collatine's praise (this is "that sky of his delight," which, given the conventions of Renaissance poetry and the "clear unmatched red and white," we can provisionally take to be Lucrece's cheeks); in turn, Collatine's boasting leads on to Tarquin's posting, which in turn leads on to the rape of Lucrece. Generalizing, we can say that, according to

the poem, in the beginning or, rather, in immediate response to the beginning—
even more precisely, before or "ere" the beginning was "well begun"—was the
word, specifically, Collatine's provocative epideictic word, "that name of 'chaste,'"
that, when spoken, spelled an end not only to the beginning but also to the pure,
clear vision in terms of which this beginning is now retrospectively conceived. Moreover, as the poem presents it, this focus on a fall, conceived or conceited as a corruption of vision, that follows from and after epideictic speaking is more than a
merely thematic matter, since the poem itself performs or activates this same praising
word of which it speaks when it speaks about the way "that name of 'chaste' unhapp'ly
set / This bateless edge on his keen appetite."[6] Here, in the first line of the second
stanza, the poem makes a point of mentioning its use of "chaste" in the last line of
the first, but this remarking or citation of its own language, when the poem for the
first time recalls its own speaking, is how the poem manages to raise a merely ordinary adjective into something extraordinary, effectively translating "chaste" into
"'chaste'" within implicitly remarked quotation marks, or what the poem here
properly calls a "name," as though the poem intended by such self-quotation to
repeat or to reenact at its beginning the original event of epideictic designation it
recalls.

Naming, we will see, is a central theme of "The Rape of Lucrece"—also the narrative climax of the poem, much more so than the rape itself—so it is significant that
the first line of the second stanza, where the poem both blames and names "that
name of 'chaste,'" is also where the poem first establishes for itself a rhetorically self-
conscious narrative persona. By means of the poem's editorializing conjecture with
regard to Tarquin's motive, and by quoting its own prior speaking, the poem
acquires an immanent authorial agency appropriate to its own intentionality, a distinct poetic voice expressing the poem's or, rather, its narrator's point of view. For
this reason, however, it should also be noted that the first line of the second stanza
is also where the poem first introduces what we will learn to recognize as its most
distinctive rhetorical trope: namely, the chiasmus of "Happ'ly that name of 'chaste'
unhapp'ly set." This is an almost textbook illustration of the figure of speech that
George Puttenham, the sixteenth-century theoretician of poetic rhetoric and ornament, called the "cross-coupler," which is the syneciostic trope that "takes me two
contrary words, and tieth them as it were in a paire of couples, and so makes them
agree like good fellowes."[7] Reading "hap'ly," on the one hand, as "perhaps," "by
chance," on the other, as "in a happy manner," "gladly" (the two alternatives are, of
course, already compact in each other, e.g., "fortune"-"fortunate"), the initially oxymoronic "Happ'ly"-"unhapp'ly" combination is transformed into chiasmus by the

double correlation of two bivalent terms. The wordplay here is obvious, even, as is typical of "The Rape of Lucrece," ostentatious, which is why critics so frequently notice, even when they do not complain about, the poem's extravagant rhetorical manner, the brittle artificiality of the diction, its over-conceited style. But, even if they do so in a hyperrhetorical way, the four permuted propositions opened up by the line's positive and negative cross-coupling of two equivocations—blending happiness with sadness ("happily"-"unhappily") and the contingency of chance with the destiny of the determinate ("haply"-"unhaply")—together formulate the poem's official and explicit account of just why Tarquin is "all in post" to begin with. Putting a very fine point on it, this is precisely what "set / This bateless edge on his keen appetite."

The point is significant because, as when it names "that name of 'chaste,'" the stressed rhetoricity of the first line of the second stanza again enforces a strangely performative correspondence between the poem's matter and its manner. The heavy-handedly chiastic rhetoricity of "Happ'ly"-"unhapp'ly," to which the poem seems deliberately to draw attention, offers the motivation for Tarquin's movement "From the besieged Ardea" "to Collatium," i.e., the reason for his "posting." But if this describes the origin and constitution of Tarquin's rapacious desire, it is at the same time an origin mimicked, *ex post facto,* at the beginning of the poem precisely to the extent that the poem begins with Tarquin "all in post." Again, the poem starts off, very straightforwardly, with Tarquin rushing, "all in post," "From the besieged Ardea" "to Collatium." Moving in this way, in the first stanza, from one place to another, Tarquin, from the beginning, is geographically and thematically, as well as diegetically, *in media res*; specifically he is in between and in transit between a siege and rape. But this straightforward progress, though it goes in only one direction, becomes, as we hear more about it, to some considerable extent refractive, for not only is it defined as a movement from the public and foreign outside of Rome (Ardea) to Rome's private and familiar inside (Collatium) but, more precisely, as a movement from, on the one hand, an outside Rome surrounds for the purpose of violent entry to, on the other, an inside Tarquin enters so as therein to surround what turns out to be another or a second inside there within. Tarquin therefore, *in media res* at the beginning, as he follows out the path of "false desire," thus withdraws from the outside of the outside to an inside on the inside, but the imagery of encirclement with which this intrusion is initially imagined—"girdle with embracing flames the waist / Of Collatine's fair love, Lucrece the chaste"—makes his penetrating movement to and into the recesses of a deep internality inversely complementary to the way in which, when he "leaves the Roman host," he departs from and without the enveloped externality of the "besieged Ardea."

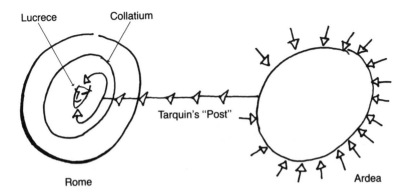

This is how the poem first figures Tarquin on the road to rape, moving toward a conclusion that, as final destination, is nothing more than the Beginning in inverted form. And it is in the context of the more or less chiastic formation of this initial "bifold" posting journey—the vector of two reciprocally complicating movements, each conceived as the other inside out (a first movement of "from," defined as the extracurricular evasion of an external invasion; a second movement of "to," defined as an invasive and internal but yet circumferential and encapsulating penetration)—that the ostentatiously chiastic rhetoricity of "happ'ly"-"unhapp'ly" seems not only to explain but also to example both the motivation and the movement that leads Tarquin on to the rape of Lucrece.[8] Just as Tarquin, when he is "all in post," is in between an inside and an outside that are both turned inside out, so too "that name of 'chaste,'" which is the cause of Tarquin's desire, is located at the disjunct intersection formed by the cross-coupling of "happ'ly" with "unhapp'ly." And this becomes a more directed displaced place of in-betweenness when we discover later on that the very same inside-outside imagery of "post," as well as this chiastic formulation and formation, is also used to illustrate and explicate the rape toward which this "name" and posting lead. Summarizing, therefore, we can say that the end of Tarquin's desire (the rape), and the motivation of Tarquin's desire ("that name of 'chaste'"), and also the movement of Tarquin toward the satisfaction of his desire (Tarquin's "posting"), are all located in the same expulsive *in extremis* in-betweenness as is the Dedication's "superfluous moity"; they are all intrinsically excessive to the boundaries that chiastically enclose them, boundaries folded over on each other in a way that leads what lies between them into an open-ended *cul de sac*.

I am looking so carefully at the way the poem thinks its way into the beginning of its story so as to guard against a variety of naturalistic or naturalizing accounts that

might be advanced to explain both the causes and the consequences of Shakespeare's version of the rape of Lucrece. Given the boasting contest conducted by the
Roman men around the military camp at Ardea, one might want to see the rape as
Tarquin's deflected response to his implicitly homosexual relation to Lucrece's husband Collatine, as a version, therefore, of the kind of jealously paranoiac defense
against homosexuality whose root propositional attitude Freud formulated, in a
famous formula, as "I do not love him, she loves him."[9] There are surely many features of the poem that might support such a reading, as when Tarquin, for example,
later on, trying to talk himself out of the rape, imagines Collatine repeating Tarquin's
"post":

> "If Collatinus dream of my intent,
> Will he not wake, and in a desp'rate rage
> Post hither, this vile purpose to prevent?
> This siege that hath engirt his marriage."
>
>   (218–21)

So too, less psychoanalytically, more anthropologically, but following out pretty
much the same kind of reasoning, the story might be understood to exemplify René
Girard's account both of the operation of mimetically mediated desire and of the
mythographizing scapegoat mechanisms through which, according to Girard, soci-
eties formulate instances of effective difference with which to organize and to sustain
culturally significant structures of hierarchical order; from the point of view of such
a reading the achievement of just such grounding and orientating Difference would
be the function both of the initial heroicizing boasting contest, where, as the Argument puts it, "the noblemen yielded Collatinus the victory, and his wife the fame,"
and also of its vilifying and victimizing outcome, on the one hand, the chastening and
mortifying rape, on the other, the scapegoating expulsion of Tarquin from Rome to
which the poem refers in its final couplet: "The Romans plausibly did give consent
/ To Tarquin's everlasting banishment" (1855–56).[10] In a similar mythographic vein,
the story could be understood, in the manner of Lévi-Strauss, to package strong cultural oppositions in a reconciliatory, pacifying way—e.g., the way the martial violence of the siege at Ardea and the erotic intimacy of a domestic Collatium are
married to each other in the principle of rape, where the desire for violence and the
violence of desire each become, quite traditionally, expressions of the other; it
would not be difficult to show how such representations work to resecure the force
of larger social interdictions and demands, e.g., the operation of kinship laws, the
exchange of women, etc.[11] All such accounts, which no doubt could be developed

more elaborately, especially if eked out by relevant feminist or Marxist commentary (e.g., Eve Sedgwick's inflection of Girard's ungendered triangles in terms of more and less Freudian homophobic social patterns, or Pierre Macherey's Marxist analysis of ideology in terms of what is essentially Lévi-Straussian reflection theory), speak to various aspects of the poem, and it is also fair to say that the general story of "The Rape of Lucrece," the one Shakespeare inherits, in many respects invites such readings and responses, as could be seen by comparing in detail the terms and assumptions of such readings with traditional commentary and critical controversies attaching to the story, from St. Augustine on, e.g., whether Collatine has only himself to blame for the rape of his wife, or whether Lucrece is morally right or wrong to kill herself, or whether rape is a form of suicide or suicide a form of rape, etc.[12]

Shakespeare's poem, however, as distinct from the myth or story he inherits, is, as we have already seen, considerably more specific in its account of the motive of the rape, stipulating as its effective cause the fact that Collatine spoke his words of praise, as though it were this speaking that the poem holds responsible for the story it recounts. Again, it is because "Collatine unwisely did not let / To praise the clear unmatched red and white" that "that sky of his delight" will soon be clouded over, just as it is as a consequence of "that name of 'chaste'" that Tarquin is "all in post." And this is an explicit thematic claim of the poem as we discover soon enough, in the fifth stanza, when the narrator asks, in his own voice, the poem's first rhetorical question, to which he then responds with an equally and specifically rhetorical answer:

> Beauty itself doth of itself persuade
> The eyes of men without an orator;
> What needeth then apology be made
> To set forth that which is so singular?
> Or why is Collatine the publisher
> > Of that rich jewel he should keep unknown
> > From thievish ears because it is his own?
>
> Perchance his boast of Lucrece' sov'reignty
> Suggested this proud issue of a king;
> For by our ears our hearts oft tainted be.
>
> (29–38)

The ideal visuality of "that sky of his delight" is here presented as a "beauty" that "persuade[s] / The eyes of men without an orator," just as desire is here said to be corrupted, as well as occasioned, by the language that it hears: "For by our ears our hearts oft tainted be." And, again, precisely because the poem thus makes thematic and incriminating issue out of "oratory," the poem's own rhetoricity is once again performatively implicated in the rape that it reports, as though the poem itself, *because* it speaks rhetorically, were speaking to its reader's "ear" so as to "taint" its reader's "heart."

All three features, therefore, that I previously characterized as characteristically Shakespearean—1) the evocation of a fallen language opposed to a clear vision, 2) a stressedly chiastic figurality, 3) the imagination of a material phenomenality folded over on itself—are not only present at the beginning of "The Rape of Lucrece" but they are also all operatively assimilated to the poem's own status as a verbal artifact, so that, in principle, from the very first oratorical word of the poem, from "From," we are situated in a present both successive to or "post" an ideal past at the same time as this present is directed toward a future that will end in rape. Moreover, the poem quite frankly adopts the rapacious point of view of this both retrospective and ten-dentious present, so that, in contrast to the way that Collatine, in the past, looked at Lucrece and praised "the clear unmatched red and white," both Tarquin and the nar-rator, in the poem's narrative present, instead regard her in an altogether different light, as when, a few stanzas later, we see what Tarquin and the narrator together see when they look at Lucrece:

> This heraldry in Lucrece' face was seen,
> Argued by beauty's red and virtue's white;
> Of either's color was the other queen,
> Proving from world's minority their right;
> Yet their ambition makes them still to fight,
>> The sovereignty of either being so great
>> That oft they interchange each other's seat.
>
> This silent war of lilies and of roses,
> Which Tarquin view'd in her fair face's field
> In their pure ranks his traitor eye encloses.
>
>   (64–73)

The "interchange" of red and white is, of course, a commonplace in Petrarchist lyric, but, as "The Rape of Lucrece" develops it, this chiastic color scheme—two col-ors systematically at odds not only with each other but with themselves as well: "Of either's color was the other queen"—specifically defines the point of view of rape, not only implicitly, as in the first stanza, where Tarquin "bears the lightless fire, / Which in pale embers hid, lurks to expire," but explicitly, as when, but this is only one example among many, Lucrece demands of Tarquin "Under what color he commits this ill" (475) and:

> Thus he replies: "The color in thy face,
> That even for anger makes the lily pale,
> And the red rose blush at her own disgrace,
> Shall plead for me and tell my loving tale. . . ."
>
>   (477–80)

We will see later on how emphatically, and, again, heavy-handedly, "The Rape of Lucrece" associates this particular conflict of colors not only with rape and wounding death but also with the way that language, being false, gives a subjectifying lie to the seeming truth of vision: according to the poem's color scheme, red and white, chiastically conjoined, yield a dappled purple that the poem not only imagines as the specific color of rhetoric but with which the poem also thematically colors its own purple rhetorical passages. For the moment, however, the only point important to insist on is that this particular color scheme, though nothing but conventional, is nevertheless something characteristically Shakespearean, at least insofar as Shakespeare organizes his two narrative poems around precisely such erotic war of red and white. Thus, Shakespeare's other and earlier narrative poem, "Venus and Adonis," also dedicated to Southampton, begins with a "purple"—its first line, "Even as the sun with purple-color'd face"—which it immediately presents as compact of the chiastic war between internally conflicted red and white, and then proceeds, as does "The Rape of Lucrece," to develop this "check'red" red-white combination, first, as image of the object of venereal desire—e.g., when Adonis "low'rs and frets, / 'Twixt crimson shame and anger ashy-pale. / Being red, she loves him best, and being white, / Her best is better'd with a more delight" (75–78)—then, as image of the castrating wound that marks the object of desire—the murderous boar "sheath[es]" his "tusk in his soft groin" (1116), thereby forming "the wide wound that the boar had trench'd / In his soft flank, whose wonted lily white / With purple tears, that his wound wept, was drench'd" (1052–54)—and, finally, as image of the conclusion of desire, when the dead Adonis, at the end of the poem, is transformed into "A purple flow'r sprung up, check'red with white / Resembling well his pale cheeks and the blood / Which in round drops upon their whiteness stood" (1168–70). Again, we will see "The Rape of Lucrece" develop, in a focused way, the same color imagery through the same topoi to the same end, but for now the simple point to notice is that this is something characteristically Shakespearean, first, because Shakespeare does the same thing in his two narrative poems, second, because he does it in so fixed and formulaic a fashion that it impresses itself on readers as a kind of identifying trait, as we can confirm from the fact that contemporary references to "Venus and Adonis," whether serious or parodic, fasten on and remark the poem's purple and chiastic red-and-white, as though the poem's first readers recognized in Shakespeare's handling of the motif something characteristically and characterizingly Shakespearean. Here is Gullio, in the third act of *The Return from Parnassus, Part 1,* paraphrasing "Venus and Adonis":

> Thrise fairer than my selfe, thus I began
> the gods faire riches, sweete above compare
> Staine to all Nimphes, [m]ore loueley the[n] a man
> More white and red than doues and roses are
> Nature that made thee wth herself had strife,
> saith that the world hath ending wth thy life
>
> . . . .
>
> Even as the sunn wth purple coloured face
> had tane his laste leaue on the weeping morne. &c.;
>
> (3.1.1006–21)

and here is Ingenioso, one act later, also intending an echo of "Venus and Adonis":

> Faire Venus queene of beutie and of loue
> thy red doth stayne the blushinge of the morn
> thy snowy neck shameth the milke white doue
> thy presence doth this naked world adorne.
>
> (4.1.1189–92)[13]

At the very least, it is fair to say an ethusiastic reader of the first poem, "Venus and Adonis"—the sort who to "worshipp sweet M^r. Shakespeare, and to honoure him will lay his Venus, and Adonis under my pillowe"—who also notes the way "The Rape of Lucrece" begins with "clear unmatched red and white," might plausibly expect the poem to develop this image, as in fact it does, in a coherent and self-conscious way.

So too with the four-term chiastic rhetorical form, as distinct from the chiastic content of the red-white motif, for the structured criss-cross of this tropic feature—to which I have already referred in connection with "Happ'ly that name of 'chaste' unhapp'ly set"—is also equally prominently and stressedly evident in both "Venus and Adonis" and "The Rape of Lucrece." A short example from "The Rape of Lucrece" will serve to illustrate the way Shakespeare conceives the rhetorical structure of the cross-coupler at the level of the signifier, rather than at the level of the signified, at the same time as the example suggests how such a purely formal concatenation nevertheless calls forth from Shakespeare a specific ensemble of semantic, and specifically Shakespearean, associations. Here is Tarquin in his bedroom, a little later in the poem, mulling over whether he should or shouldn't rape Lucrece:

> As one of which doth Tarquin lie revolving
> The sundry dangers of his will's obtaining;
> Yet ever to obtain his will resolving,
> Though weak-built hopes persuade him to abstaining.
>
> (127–30)

The rhetorical wit of these lines derives from the way, through the repetition of "re-"s, "re-volving" and "re-solving" are turned over or "re-turned" over on each other so that each is heard as near anagrammatic replication of the other. With "re-volving" and "re-solving" folded back upon themselves in this literal, and by no means subtle, fashion, the indecisive *volvere* of Tarquin's "revolving" turns out to be, because the sounding of "revolving" is audibly turned inside out, precise prefiguration of Tarquin's decisively rapacious "will resolving." In the same way, the hard rhyme of "ob-taining" and "ab-staining" works to sound out the "stain" that soon becomes the poem's dominant image of Lucrece's rape. Though local, the example possesses general interest because, as we will see, these are not, for Shakespeare, casual configurations. For example, we can think of these lines in the context of *Twelfth Night,* where just these signifiers control the characterological relations of the play, in the often remarked anagrammatic correlation of "Malvolio"–"Viola"–"Olivia," and where what is nominally at stake in the flamboyant, allegoricizing anagrammatics is the pointed pun on *voglio*—"will" or "bad-will" ("Mal-volio"). We can add that in *Twelfth Night* all this is initially thought or presented through the sound associated with the purple flower called up in the opening lines of the play—"the sweet sound / That breathes upon a bank of violets" (1.1.5–6)—a violet, moreover, the play associates not only with "Viola" but also with the violence and violation of her imagined rape (*violare*).[14] I cite the example, and will return to it later, because the repetition of "re-"s in "re-volving" and "re-solving" in these lines from "The Rape of Lucrece" turns on the remarked repetition of "will"—"will's obtaining"-"will resolving"— which "The Rape of Lucrece" will give us good reason to consider a specifically and personal Shakespearean nominal repetition—as, of course, does *Twelfth Night,* if we recall the apposite alternative the play itself entitles: *or What You Will.*[15]

Leaving this Shakespearean "will" to the side, for the moment, the question raised by "The Rape of Lucrece," given the way the poem ostentatiously foregrounds its chiastic matter and manner, is why chiasmus—either the chiastic content of Lucrece's red and white or the chiastic rhetorical form of the cross-coupler—is understood to motivate desire in general and rape in particular. Specifically, why is it that "Happ'ly that name of 'chaste' unhapp'ly set / This bateless edge on his keen appetite," and why is it that Tarquin "posts" to Rome because Collatine "did not let / To praise the clear unmatched red and white?" We get the beginnings of an answer when the poem proceeds to elaborate Tarquin's indecision at the moment he decides upon his rape.[16]

> Away he steals with open list'ning ear,
> Full of foul hope, and full of fond mistrust;
> Both which, as servitors to the unjust,
>   So cross him with their opposite persuasion,
>   That now he vows a league, and now invasion.
>
> (283–87)

The interest of these lines derives from the way Shakespeare here makes a point of showing how a certain kind of tropic figurality is, as such, itself the figure of subjective motivation. We recognize, presumably, since the narrator makes the point explicit, that Tarquin is here "crossed" between two coupled oxymorons. The "foul hope" of his lust is poised off against the moral reservation of his "fond mistrust" in a conjunction that reverses the normal connotations of all four terms. As a result, because the positives become negatives and the negatives become positives, Tarquin is left suspended between a foul fondness and a hopeful mistrust, a rhetorical indeterminacy that serves, at least initially, to illustrate his hesitation between a peaceful "league" and an aggressive "invasion." Again, this is a general formal feature of "The Rape of Lucrece," as when Lucrece, resisting the rape, defensively appeals to Tarquin's better nature and tells him not to let a tiny spot of lust "stain the ocean of thy blood. / If all these petty ills shall change thy good, / Thy sea within a puddle's womb is hearsed, / And not the puddle in thy sea dispersed" (652–58), a conceit that asks us to imagine, as with Tarquin's "posting," the inside on the outside and the outside on the inside, as though the infinitely small were larger than the infinitely large and the "boundless flood" containable "within a puddle's womb"—a conceit whose titillating resonance and contours seem, under the circumstances, uniquely ill designed to accomplish Lucrece's chastening, prophylactic purpose. What the example indicates, however, is that their structure of chiastic indeterminacy, whereby Tarquin alternately "vows a league, and now invasion," itself determines a determinate desire—to rape—as we see if we follow out the movement of Tarquin's indecisive lust.

The poem does not give us a graphic description of Tarquin's rape of Lucrece, at least not of the actual "invasion," this being passed over by the poem in a single discreet line to which we will soon turn. Instead, beginning where the lines on "foul hope" and "fond mistrust" end, the poem projects the details of the rape onto a description of Tarquin's progress toward Lucrece's bedroom, his movement through the passageways of her castle to her "chamber door" (337) being developed as a kind of pornographic *effictio.* In the course of this movement—it is fair to say in the intercourse of this movement—three obstacles bar Tarquin's progress, three hindrances stand, as the narrator puts it, "between her chamber and his will" (302). First, there is a series of locked doors, "each one by him enforc'd retires his ward" (303). Then, "as each unwilling portal yields him way" (309) "the wind wars with his torch to make him stay" (311). Finally, there is "Lucretia's glove, wherein her needle sticks" (317), which, when Tarquin picks it up, "the needle his finger pricks" (319). All three of these items—the doors, the wind, the glove—slow Tarquin down, as though the material world conspired to retard the rape. All three, however, are at the same time, and very obviously so, precisely rendered images *of* the rape, its physical objectification: the doors whose locks are "enforc'd" and which "unwilling" "yields him way"; the wind, which "through little vents and crannies of the place" (310) "wars with his torch . . . And blows the smoke of it into his face" (311–12); the fetishistic glove "wherein her needle sticks." Moreover, not only is each one of these things, in the resistance that it offers, an image of the rape that it repulses, but so too does each one of these bars to Tarquin's desire manage also to spur the rapist on. The "his" of "retires his ward" refers both to Tarquin and the door. The wind that blows out Tarquin's torch also inspires "his hot heart, which fond desire doth scorch, / [To puff] forth another wind that fires the torch" (314–15). So too with the clitoral "prick" of the glove that "pricks" the rapist on: "This glove to wanton tricks / is not inured" (320–21).[17]

All this does not go by unnoticed, either by the narrator or by Tarquin. With regard to the hindrances to Tarquin's desire, the narrator observes:

> He in the worst sense consters their denial:
> The doors, the wind, the glove that did delay him,
> He takes for accidental things of trial;
> Or as those bars which stop the hourly dial,

> Who with a ling'ring stay his course doth let,
> Till every minute pays the hour his debt.
>
> (324–29)

The narrator's image is of a clock whose hour hand, connected to a spring mechanism, builds up potential energy when its movement is restrained by protuberant minute markers. At successive intervals the hour hand bursts past each momentary "let" in an explosive, jerky movement that measures time and brings the marker of the hours to its next repulsing and propulsing impediment. It is an image of inviting resistance, of an impetus derived from its frustration, and as such illustrates not only the way "the doors, the wind, the glove that did delay him" promote what they postpone, but also illustrates the rape itself, the way, that is, that Tarquin "consters" Lucrece's "denial."

It is perhaps an obvious point, for Tarquin draws the same moral for himself, immediately repeating—indeed, sharing—the narrator's image of the temporal "let":

> "So, so," quoth he, "these lets attend the time,
> Like little frosts that sometimes threat the spring,
> To add a more rejoicing to the prime,
> And give the sneaped birds more cause to sing."
>
> (330–33)

However, even if the erotic psychology thus enunciated is proverbial, and its sententious phrasing makes it seem as though it is, it is important to notice that the erotic psychology of the "let," as well as the material phenomenology of the doors, the wind, and the glove, unpacks the cross-coupling formal rhetorical logic of "foul hope" and "fond mistrust."[18] That is to say, when Tarquin was initially indeterminately suspended between oxymorons, when he was "crossed" by "their opposite persuasion," he was already, by virtue of the very structure of this indeterminacy, embarked upon his rape. Speaking thematically we can say that Tarquin's indecision is decisive: its static framing is what thrusts him into the directed duration of erotic time. But this is also a significant point for Shakespearean poetics, because it shows us that the cross-coupler, at least as Shakespeare here employs it, is not a neutral trope; it is instead the trope of a specific desire whose hindrance is what gives it leave to go. Specifically, it is the tropological structure and expression of an eros whose *contrapposto* energy, the resistance to resistance, simulates the action of a rape—and of a rape, moreover, that, rendered genially pastoral by "the little frosts that sometime threat the spring, / To add a more rejoicing to the prime," offers itself as general model for the motivating and consummating *friction* of heterosexual desire per se. This, at any rate, seems to be both the erotic and the rhetorical logic of "let" that links Lucrece to Tarquin and that makes Lucrece responsible for her rape by virtue of the energetic and energizing resistance that she offers to it. Lucrece herself becomes a "let," because, as Tarquin says, in response to her cross-coupling entreaties:

> "Have done," quoth he, "my uncontrolled tide
> Turns not, but swells the higher by this let.
> Small lights are soon blown out, huge fires abide,
> And with the wind in greater fury fret.
> The petty streams that pay a daily debt . . ."
>
> > (645–48)

These lines make swelling, overflowing, or "superfluous" water, along with the already erotically coded imagery of torch and wind, into a metaphor of the results of "let": "my uncontrolled tide / Turns not, but swells the higher by this let." But just a few lines later the metaphor is literalized or activated when Tarquin, for what is the final time—as though his dam had finally broken, or as though the moment for the movement of his hour hand had come round at last—inserts himself into or, rather, inter-rupts Lucrece's spoken "let":

> "So let thy thoughts, low vassals to thy state"—
> "No more," quoth he, "by heaven I will not hear thee."
>
> > (666–67)[19]

This is the last instance of outspoken resistance in the scene of rape, after which there is no turning back. Given the dramatic staging, however, with the two principals acting out the "let" that they engage in, it is fair to say that this is how the poem *accounts* for rape: through this increasingly obtrusive sounding out of "let." Accordingly, we can better understand the constitutive energy built into the rape's initiating moment: "When Collatine unwisely did not let / To praise the clear unmatched red and white." As it echoes through the text of "The Rape of Lucrece," Collatine's original and originating "let," though voiced by the narrator, is heard to contain within itself, as its own provocation, the chiasticized formation and materialization of Tarquin's rapacious desire: "Happ'ly that name of 'chaste' unhapp'ly set / This bateless edge on his keen appetite." And, again, this is something the poem enforces not only thematically but also by means of its elaborated rhetoric, so that both the poem's matter and manner, its cross-coupled signifieds along with its criss-crossing signifiers, work together to establish the initial equi-vocation of Collatine's reverberating "let" as that which pro-vokes the rape of Lucrece. Moreover, we can now add, if this conjoined chiastic form and matter—the literal correspondence of Collatine's "let" with the phenomenology of Shakespearean copulation: the wind, the torch, the glove, the swelling water—thus immanently characterize both the motive of the rape and Tarquin's movement toward the rape—either the obstructed movement of Tarquin's "will" through the passageways of Lucrece's castle to her "chamber door" or the opening rush of Tarquin toward Collatium when he is "all in post"—so too does it describe the very action of the rape, as it occurs, soon after Tarquin's interruption, in one climactically chiastic line:

> This said, he sets his foot upon the light,
> For light and lust are deadly enemies;
> Shame folded up in blind concealing night,
> When most unseen, then most doth tyrannize.
> The wolf hath seiz'd his prey, the poor lamb cries,
>   Till with her own white fleece her voice controll'd
>   *Entombs her outcry in her lips sweet fold.*
>
>   (673–79)

"En-tombs her out-cry" replicates the same reciprocally complicated four-term topography of inside-outside invagination that we have already come upon several times. But if this appears to open up a space that folds the inside and the outside over on each other, the space itself, for all its aporetic complications, is firmly placed within the "in" of "her lips sweet fold."[20]

It is fitting that the rape, when it finally occurs, is figured in and as a simultaneously emergent and recessive in-betweenness forming and informing the "fold" of Lucrece's lips, for the smirky collation of Lucrece's mouth with her vagina supports the formal implication that Lucrece is asking for her rape because her "no," as "no," means "yes." Hence the correspondence of the "sweet fold" of "her lips" with the "Shame" or "pudendum" "folded up in blind concealing night." Beyond that, however, this focus at the climax of the scene of rape on "her voice controll'd"—and the syntax of the line leaves undecided just who the agent of the verb is, Tarquin or Lucrece—brings out the fact that Tarquin and Lucrece both speak the *same* language, a point, already clear enough from the equivalent tonalities and diction, the shared motifs, the stichomythian back-and-forth rhythms, through which the two of them conduct their formal argument, *in utramque partem,* pro and contra rape. Not surprisingly, this is something critics often complain about, on the grounds that the poem, a mere exercise in rhetoric, thus fails to individuate the characters of Tarquin and Lucrece. But such criticism misses a point on which the poem itself insistently insists: that Tarquin and Lucrece are inverse versions of each other, and for this reason *together* make the rape of Lucrece, as is no doubt suggested by the objective and subjective genitive of the poem's title.[21] Hence, too, the disjunctive conjunction of the rape itself, where Tarquin and Lucrece, because the two of them are both chiastically imagined, both come together "in her lips sweet fold."

This elaborated correspondence between Tarquin and Lucrece, which partially accounts for the oddly abstract and near comic inevitability the poem accords Lucrece's violation, is something the poem continues to develop in the aftermath of the rape, when Tarquin exits from the narrative and the poem turns its attention to Lucrece and to her lamentations. Thus, immediately after "Entombs her outcry in her lips sweet fold," the narrator forges a characteristically chiastic link, a "forced league," between the rapist and his victim:

> But she hath lost a dearer thing than life,
> And he hath won what he would lose again;
> This forced league doth force a further strife.
>
> (687–89)

So too, the poem continues to decorate Tarquin and Lucrece with the same motifs, so that, for example, Tarquin, as he steals away, "bear[s] away the wound that nothing healeth, / The scar that will despite of cure remain" (730–32), whereas Lucrece remarks her "unseen shame, invisible disgrace! / O unfelt sore, crest-wounding private scar!" (827–28; in this second section of the poem, which focuses on Lucrece and not on Tarquin, the poem establishes many such metaphoric correlations between Tarquin and Lucrece). So too, Lucrece herself anticipates a future in which, adding rhetorical insult to an already rhetoricized injury, "The orator to deck his oratory / Will couple my reproach to Tarquin's shame" (815–16).[22] Yet more powerful, however, in its effect, than any of these articulated correspondences between Tarquin and Lucrece is the way the outspoken oratory of Lucrece's own formally declaimed complaint reiterates with its chiastic manner the chiastic matter of the rape. Thus, addressing herself to a series of allegorical abstractions—just the sort of abstractions one expects to find in a Complaint poem—first Night, then Opportunity, Lucrece concludes her lamentation with a vilifying apostrophe to personified Time; for it is Time, imagined as a particular kind of person, whom she holds responsible for what has come to pass:

> "Misshapen Time, copesmate of ugly Night,
> Swift, subtle post, carrier of grisly care,
> Eater of youth, false slave to false delight,
> Base watch of foes, sin's pack-horse, virtue's snare!
> Thou nursest all, and murth'rest all that are.
>> O hear me then, injurious shifting Time,
>> Be guilty of my death, since of my crime."
>
> (925–31)

It is difficult to determine whether, as "Swift, subtle post," generic Time here emerges as a version, after the fact, of rapacious Tarquin rushing to Collatium "all in post" or, instead, whether Tarquin, from the beginning, is himself already a proleptic version of "Misshapen Time." In either case, "Misshapen Time" is presented as the initiating cause as well as the condition of the rape: "But some untimely thought did instigate / His all too timeless speed" (43–44). For this very reason, however, remembering that it is through a specific imagery of time—"those bars which stop the hourly dial, / Who with a ling'ring stay his course doth let, / Till every minute pays the hour his debt"—that the poem explicitly presents its logic of "let," and remembering how, according to Tarquin, "'these lets attend the time,'" the peroration of Lucrece's address to Time, with its symphony of reiterated, hortatory "lets," seems intentionally to call forth or to sound out, as much as it regrets and reviles, the same moment and momentum—Collatine's "let"—that potentiates her rape in the first place:

> "Thou ceaseless lackey to eternity,
> With some mischance cross Tarquin in his flight.
> Devise extremes beyond extremity,
> To make him curse this cursed crimeful night.
> *Let* ghastly shadows his lewd eyes afright,
>> And the dire thought of his committed evil
>> Shape every bush a hideous shapeless devil.
>
> "Disturb his hours of rest with restless trances,
> Afflict him in his bed with bedred groans;
> *Let* there bechance him pitiful mischances
> To make him moan, but pity not his moans;
> Stone him with hard'ned hearts harder than stones,

And *let* mild women to him lose their mildness,
Wilder to him than tigers in their wildness.

"*Let* him have time to tear his curled hair,
Let him have time against himself to rave,
Let him have time of Time's help to despair,
Let him have time to live a loathed slave,
Let him have time a beggar's orts to crave,
     And time to see one that by alms doth live
     Disdain to him disdained scraps to give.

"*Let* him have time to see his friends and foes,
And merry fools to mock at him resort;
Let him have time to mark how slow time goes
In time of sorrow and how swift and short
His time of folly and his time of sport;
     And ever *let* his unrecalling crime
     Have time to wail th'abusing of his time."

(967–94)

As with "Happ'ly that name of 'chaste' unhapp'ly set," the central fact about these stanzas is the way their insistently chiastic rhetoricity, drawing attention to itself, appears to determine what they say, as though the entire speech were programmatic explication or duplication of what the poem associates with "let." With chiastic flourishes—"ex-tremes beyond ex-tremity"—Lucrece demands that Time, the "ceaseless lackey to eternity," "with some mischance cross Tarquin in his flight." But the "mischance cross" that Tarquin is supposed to bear is constructed of the same conflicted intersection of contingent destiny and happy sadness as is packed into "Happ'ly"-"unhapp'ly": "Let there bechance him pitiful mischances." In such oblique and yet accented ways, Lucrece's speech, for all its force and fluency, ends up crossing itself, developing the rhetorical "cross" of the cross-coupler in so ostentatious a fashion that the chiastic content of the lines becomes the performative vehicle of their chiastic form, rather than the other way around. Again, for a rhetorically sophisticated Elizabethan reading audience this would define the oratorical "wit" of Lucrece's complaint, a wit that signals a rhetorical self-consciousness thoroughly suffusing and yet still distanced from Lucrece's imprecations. Repeatedly repeating individual words within a syntax that circles round upon itself—"Disdain to him disdained scraps to give," "Let him have time to mark how slow time goes / In time of sorrow and how swift and short / His time of folly and his time of sport," etc.— Lucrece's speech becomes, despite herself or her intentions, the systematic instrument and issue of the chiastic folds on which consistently it turns. Only a reader for whom rhetoric has no force or function could fail to notice this, and it is just such indifference to the effect of the poem's rhetorical effects that regularly produces critical complaints about the poem's declamatory style, its idly extravagant rhetoricity. What we must also note, however, is that such complaints about the poem's excessively rhetorical manner themselves repeat what Tarquin or Lucrece—the rapist and, as we have seen, his rhetorically willing victim—themselves will say about this very topic, as, for example, a few lines later, when Lucrece, tired of her formal railing, proclaims:

> Out, idle words, servants to shallow fools,
> Unprofitable sounds, weak arbitrators!
> Busy yourself in skill-contending schools,
> Debate where leisure serves with dull debaters
>
> (1016–19)

lines that echo the way Tarquin earlier, when he grew tired of his own rhetorical indecision, resolved upon the rape: "'Why hunt I then for color or excuses? / All orators are dumb when beauty pleadeth . . . / Then childish fear avaunt, debating die!'" (267–74).

A long and familiar history of anti-rhetorical sensibility no doubt lies behind Lucrece's pejorative assessment of "unprofitable sounds," or what she calls a few lines later "this helpless smoke of words," so there is nothing in any way novel about either Lucrece's or Tarquin's stated thoughts about the issue of rhetoric. Neither is it surprising, given the structural symmetry the poem establishes between them, that this expressed concern for solid rhetorical matter as opposed to empty rhetorical manner is something that the rapist and his victim share: Tarquin's vice is consistently presented by the poem as reciprocal inversion and occasion of Lucrece's virtue, and vice versa, to the point of view that either one of them adopts on any topic whatsoever will likely be a version of the point of view adopted by the other. But, again, this is *not* the point of view of the poem itself, or at least this characterization of rhetoric as something "idle" or inexigent is not the point of view of the poem's personified narrator, who, from the first moment that a coded narrative voice enters the poem— i.e., from the moment of "Happ'ly that name of 'chaste' unhapp'ly set"—takes quite a different position with regard to the question of rhetorical effect, explicitly blaming the rape of Lucrece on Collatine's "oratory," and saying outright, as clearly and straightforwardly as possible, to ears willing to hear it, that "by our ears our hearts oft tainted be."

The point is worth stressing because it allows us to take the narrator at his own oratorical word and thereby to recapture a specifically Elizabethan reading experience of the poem's rhetoricity, one that is thereby attuned to, or responsive to, the effect of an author induced by the poem's rhetoricity. In ways that go, so to speak, necessarily without saying, "The Rape of Lucrece" calls out for a reading that attends to the different ways in which the poem's signifiers control its signifieds, to the way the poem's manner, *as* manner, determines its matter. This is a literal, *not* a metaphorical, way of putting things. When an Elizabethan reader reads Lucrece's apostrophe to Time and comes upon its reiterated "lets," he will hear them as performative climax of the way, for Tarquin, "these lets attend the time." But this performance, to the extent a reader registers it, is neither Tarquin's nor Lucrece's doing; it is instead a function of the immanent authorial agency governing the poem's rhetorical production, even though this authorial agency is itself an effect of the way the poem rhetorically unfolds. Similarly, when an Elizabethan reader reads Lucrece's apostrophe to Time and comes upon a couplet like:

> And let mild women to him lose their mildness,
> Wilder to him than tigers in their wildness.

the lines carry literary weight for him in good part because the criss-cross structure of "mild"-"mildness"-"wild"-"wildness" invites him to see how the *M* of "mild," thus cross-coupled with the W of "wild," literally enacts the chiastic "fold" of "her lips sweet fold": Ŵ.[23] It is this porno-graphic staging of the literal letters in its lines, the way the chiasmus makes erotic *theater* of the poem's textuality, that gives the couplet its rhetorical spirit, at the same time as this raises such literal inversion to the level of a theme. But neither Tarquin nor Lucrece can ever be the authors of these letters that perform them, and so it is the very crossing of the letters that calls forth the figure of an author who can serve as the inscribing agent of the way the letters cross.

Taken by itself, this last example, the anacreontic *MW,* may at first sight seem a trivial example of what in the poem are more urgent or more telling thematic matters, but I want now to argue that the example does more than simply illustrate or exemplify how, as I said earlier, the characteristically Shakespearean determines the formation, on the one hand, of the subjectivity of the historical Shakespeare—Shakespeare, the person—and, on the other, the formation of Shakespeare's literary subjectivity effects, i.e., the impression of psychologistic person that we associate with some, though by no means all, of Shakespeare's fictional characters. To see why this should be the case, however, it is necessary, first, to understand in what way this chiastically acrostic *MW* collation is, in fact, characteristically Shakespearean, second, how, as such, it relates both to Shakespeare's person and to the subjectivity effects sometimes exerted by Shakespearean literary personae.

To begin with, simply as a matter of statistical frequency, we can again say, as with the red-white-purple motif, that this is something distinctively Shakespearean, for there are six such prominently chiastic typographic configurations of *MW* in "The Rape of Lucrece." Even by the measure of Elizabethan poetry, where such letter play is in fact rather common, this seems a striking, if not inordinate, number. Moreover, all six examples are not only thematically suggestive in themselves, but they also tend to form a coherent ensemble of cross-referencing associations. In the first instance, the narrator explains that Lucrece cannot "read the subtle shining secrecies / Writ in the glassy margents of such books" (i.e., Tarquin's eyes) and, in addition:

> Nor could she *m*oralize his *w*anton sight,
> *M*ore than his eyes *w*ere open'd to the light.
>
> (104–5)

The second example describes what is erotic about Lucrece's hair:

> Her hair like golden thread play'd with her breath—
> O *m*odest *w*antons, *w*anton *m*odesty.
>
> (400–401)

In the third example Tarquin explains to Lucrece that:

> Thy beauty hath ensnared thee to this night,
> Where thou *w*ith patience must my *w*ill abide—
> *M*y *w*ill that *m*arks thee for *m*y earth's delight.
>
> (485–87)

In the fourth example Lucrece explains how she will kill herself to set a good example:

> How Tarquin must be us'd, read it in me:
> *M*yself thy friend *w*ill kill *m*yself thy foe
> And for *m*y sake serve thou false Tarquin so.
>
> This brief abridgement of *m*y *w*ill I make.
>
> (1195–98)

I have already cited the fifth example:

> And let *m*ild *w*omen to him lose their *m*ildness,
> *W*ilder to him than tigers in their *w*ildness.
>
> (978–79)

In the sixth example, the narrator explains the reason for Lucrece's tears, and why she is not "author" of her "ill":

> For *m*en have *m*arble, *w*omen *w*axen *m*inds,
> And therefore are they formed as *m*arble *w*ill,
> The weak oppress'd, th' impression of strange kinds
> Is form'd in them by force, by fraud, or skill,
> Then call them not the authors of their ill.
>
> (1240–44)

Taking these examples, somewhat artificially, together, we can say the criss-cross *MW* inversion, when it appears in "The Rape of Lucrece," seems to collate themes of reading and of marking with images of things that are either violent or erotic (it would be possible to look at these examples in more detail and discuss the way they relate to and support larger themes and images that run throughout the poem). At the same time, however, we can also note—even though it is very unlikely that a reader would in fact notice this as he reads through the poem—that either in or in a field adjacent to almost all the examples, and again in a way that seems statistically significant, there is a remarkably consistent remarking or foregrounding, either through repetition or through wordplay, of the word "will."[24]

Recognizing this, and recognizing also at the same time the bizarre particularity and apparent reductiveness of the claim, I want now to suggest that the chiastic typographic inversion of these letters, *MW,* is for Shakespeare a characteristic—indeed, *the* characteristic—indication of his own name, "Will," i.e., that it is a version, literally at the level of the letter, of the way earlier we saw "will" acquire a peculiar place and charge through its framed repetition in between the chiastic coordination of "will's obtaining" and "will resolving," a repetition or self-citation corresponding to the way that "chaste," in the first and second stanzas of the poem, is raised into "that name of 'chaste'" when it appears within the chiasmus of "happ'ly"-"unhapp'ly." I propose, therefore, that 〽, as formal and performative index of an internal revolving that turns turning or "revolving" inside out, possesses for Shakespeare the same nominalizing function; that it functions as a signature—like the proper-name determinative in Egyptian hieroglyphs—that for Shakespeare, first, raises the ordinary word "will" into the proper name "Will," and, second, thereby "set[s] / This bateless edge on his keen appetite." Consciously or unconsciously, by happenstance chance or by designed destiny, for good or for bad—i.e., "Happ'ly"-"unhapp'ly"—*MW*, when it happens these letters or characters are chiastically staged in Shakespeare's texts, stand out for Shakespeare as sign of his own name, possessing the same kind of self-remarking function as is conveyed or gestured at by Shakespeare when he writes, on the last page of his will, "By me, *William Shakespeare*"—and we can now add that on the second page he shortens this to *"Willm Shakspere,"* and that elsewhere, even shorter, in what we can call, using Lucrece's phrase, a "brief abridgement of my will," he writes yet more simply *"Wm Shakspē."*[25]

This is why I said before that by the "characteristically Shakespearean" I meant to refer to that which literally marks out Shakespeare, not his name but its signature. And I want now to add that this remarking of his own name, as a signature effect, possesses for Shakespeare—for Shakespeare, the person, the historical subject—a strictly circumscribed and circumscribing subjectifying function. Specifically, I propose that the criss-cross conjunction of the two letters that mark the beginning and end of Shakespeare's name—"Willia*M*"—*because* they serve as signature of Shakespeare's name, determine the experience of Shakespearean subjectivity as psychological equivalent of the chiastically extracted "superfluous Moity," i.e., that Shakespeare's sense of his own bio-graphicized person is for him the subjective objectification of what stands between or, rather, ex-ists between the cross-coupling boundaries of a textualized beginning without beginning and an eroticized end without end. Yet more specifically, I propose that the cross-coupling orthographics of *MW*, when these two folded letters are thus folded over on each other, spell out for Shakespeare a structure of subjective constitution organized by the three post-epideictic literary features to which I earlier referred: 1) the evocation of a fallen language opposed to clear vision, 2) a stressedly chiastic tropic figurality, 3) the imagination of a material phenomenality folded over on itself. In turn, I want also to propose that this explains why Shakespeare's literary characters, when it happens they give off a strong subjectivity effect, both evidence and are conditioned by a particular Shakespearean erotics and a particular Shakespearean sense of space and time. For example, I say Shakespeare's person is itself marked out, and thereby subjectively constituted, by the literal chiasmus of *MW*:

"*Will*" ← Ⓜ

and, moreover, that this touch of the personally Shakespearean latently informs the formal disposition of:

> For *m*en have *m*arble, *w*omen *w*axen *m*inds,
> And therefore are they formed as *m*arble *w*ill.

Assuming the *MW* formation, as it is here deployed, effectively evokes the erotic logic of chiastically conjoined man and woman that runs throughout "The Rape of Lucrece"—as when Tarquin and Lucrece come disjunctively and "shamefully" together in "Entombs her outcry in her lips sweet fold"—we can understand how it happens that "The Rape of Lucrece," as do all of Shakespeare's literary writings, recognizes the difference between the two sexes—as this difference emerges in their violent, "bifold," and cross-coupling copulation—at the same time as it attributes subjectivity only to the "will" of man:[26]

$$\text{"}Will\text{"} \leftarrow \text{Ⓜ} \frac{(en)}{(omen)}$$

Is it possible so much can come of the writing of letters? The question returns us to the unfolding action of "The Rape of Lucrece," for, only a few stanzas after the "waxen minds"-"marble will" example, Lucrece herself sits down to write a letter, calling out for "'paper, ink, and pen'":

> "Bid thou be ready, by and by, to bear
> A letter to my lord, my love, my dear.
> Bid him with speed prepare to carry it,
> The cause craves haste, and it will soon be writ."
>
> (1289–95)

The writing of this letter marks the end of Lucrece's formal lamentation, when she stops complaining about the rape and begins to do something about it: namely, informing her husband of what has come to pass. But, though "the cause craves haste, and it will soon be writ," the writing of her letter is immediately postponed, and this because, as she sits down to write, Lucrece's "wit" and "will" engage in a protracted battle:

> Her maid is gone, and she prepares to write,
> First hovering o'er the paper with her quill.
> Conceit and grief an eager combat fight,
> What wit sets down is blotted straight with will;
> This is too curious-good, this blunt and ill:
> > Much like a press of people at a door,
> > Throng her inventions, which shall go before.
>
> (1296–1302)

With the fight they stage between "conceit and grief," these lines more than call up, they also thematize, all the issues of plain matter versus ornate manner, pro and con, that the hyperrhetorical diction of "The Rape of Lucrece" regularly elicits from its critics. But the poem does not evoke what is probably the most tired cliché of Renaissance poetics so as to take a stand, one way or the other, on the matter of matter versus manner but, instead, so as to focus on the way the writing of Lucrece's letter establishes within Lucrece an indecisive, though still "eager," fight between her "wit" and "will": "Hovering o'er the paper with her quill. / Conceit and grief an eager combat fight, / What wit sets down is blotted straight with will." Like the rape that comes of its obstruction, the writing of Lucrece's letter is thus presented as specific issue of Lucrece's writing block; it is a writing "let" that writes her "letter," spotting it with "blots" of "will."[27] If it seems too much to say that Shakespeare's own "Will" here marks his "wit," it remains the case that the poem here describes a scene of writing involving the same kind of heavy-handedly indeterminate, internal, rhetorical quarrel that earlier, just *because* it was something indeterminate, determined Tarquin, when he was "crossed" between "foul hope" and "fond despair," to embark upon the rape: Lucrece's "will," if not Shakespeare's, is figured through the same, specifically rhetorical, figure of ongoing indeterminacy that earlier prefigured Tarquin's "will," as well as its rapacity, in terms of a chiastic excess in "between her chamber and his will." So too, the liquid blot that now spills out of Lucrece's "will"—in the course of "eager combat," crossing out her "wit"—is no less undetermined than was the "superfluous Moity" of the Dedication or than was the little drop of Tarquin's lust that sought "to stain the ocean of thy blood"; it marks Lucrece's "wit" just as Tarquin put his willful mark upon Lucrece: "'Where thou with patience must my will abide— / My will that marks thee for my earth's delight.'" And so too does Lucrece's letter, as a whole, bear the same distinctive willful mark. Because Lucrece now writes her letter to Collatine in the same chiastic way that Tarquin earlier raped Lucrece, because the writing of the letter is materially precipitated by the "let" that is its motive, her letter too turns out to bear the characteristic wrinkle of "her lips sweet fold":

> Here folds she up the tenure of her woe,
> Her certain sorrow writ uncertainty.
> By this short schedule Collatine may know
> Her grief, but not her grief's true quality.
> She dares not thereof make discovery,
>> Lest he should hold it her own gross abuse,
>> Ere she with blood had stain'd her stain'd excuse.
>>> (1310–16)

For the moment, it is true, folding up the letter, "her certain sorrow writ uncertainly," Lucrece postpones a full report; she keeps her secret to herself, choosing not to put her rape directly into words until her suicide will vouchsafe the truth of what she has to say. Her blood itself must "stain her stain'd excuse," and so, pending the final staining of her stain or the final blotting of her blot, we await the moment when Lucrece's bloody, visible matter will confirm her merely verbal manner:

> To shun this blot, she would not blot the letter
> With words till action might become them better.
>
> To see sad sights moves more than hear them told,
> For then the eye interprets to the ear
> The heavy motion that it doth behold,
> When every part a part of woe doth bear.
> 'Tis but a part of sorrow that we hear.
>> Deep sounds make lesser noise than shallow fords,
>> And sorrow ebbs, being blown with the wind of words.
>>> (1322–30)

But this postponement—lest "sorrow ebb, being blown with the wind of words"—itself repeats the poem's already fully elaborated structure of rapacious delay, i.e., the way the poem turns watery and windy deferral into the experience of rape, as when Tarquin's "uncontrolled tide / Turns not, but swells the higher by this let," or as when "The doors, the wind, the glove that did delay him, / He takes for accidental things of trial; / Or as those bars which stop the hourly dial, / Who with a ling'ring stay his course doth let" (323–28). Accordingly, and not only etymologically (*post-ponere*), it seems to be precisely this temporal postponement—while the poem looks forward to a future when "the eye interprets to the ear"—that puts Lucrece's letter in the "post":

> Her letter now is seal'd, and on it writ,
> "At Ardea to my lord with more than haste."
> The post attends and she delivers it.
>
> (1331–33)

As conclusion to Lucrece's static, even tedious, lamentations, the dispatching of this letter amounts to a dramatic and decisive gesture. However "uncertainly" Lucrece now writes her "certain sorrow," however delayed her will to write the letter—"it will soon be writ"—the delivery of her letter to the "post" marks a turning point in the unfolding action of the poem: once posted, her letter bears the promise of her rape's eventual revenge. For this very reason, however, *as* a turning point, the posting of Lucrece's letter also returns us to the beginning of the poem and thereby to the way what I have called the characteristically Shakespearean determines the formation of a specifically Shakespearean subjectivity effect. We have seen that "The Rape of Lucrece" begins with Tarquin rushing "From the besieged Ardea all in post," and we have also seen that the poem makes elaborate issue of the fact that Tarquin sets out on this journey because "Collatine unwisely did not let / To praise the clear unmatched red and white." Quite literally—we can say, quite "characteristically"—according to the first two stanzas of the poem, it is Collatine's "let" that puts Tarquin "all in post," this "posting" being the unintended consequence of Collatine having praised Lucrece's "chastity." Given the postal or epistolic motif the poem now introduces, as well as the variety of heavy-handed correspondences the poem has hitherto established between the "let" and rape, we can say "The Rape of Lucrece," as it now rhetorically unfolds, here retroactively directs its reader to conceive of Tarquin, in his first "posting" movement, as a letter initially dispatched by Collatine—more precisely, by Collatine's "let"—to his own address: "From the besieged Ardea all in post" "to Collatium." Correspondingly, when Lucrece now explicitly addresses her letter to Collatine—"'At Ardea to my lord with more than haste.' / The post attends and she delivers it"—the poem seems to make a point of relaying Collatine's letter back to where it came from, back to Collatine, by return "post." Taking these two movements together—Tarquin's "post" and its reversed repetition by Lucrece's "post"—we can say the poem looks forward to a moment in which Collatine will eventually receive a version of the very letter he himself initially had posted. But our reading of the poem already tells us in advance that the meaning of this letter is inverted, not repeated nor reversed, in the course of its transmission, since the letter that Lucrece now writes will once again assert Lucrece's "chastity" but in the unexpected, inverse form of rape.

This complicating structure of repetition, reversal, and inversion—which works to add a new corroborating wrinkle to Collatine's original praise of Lucrece's "clear unmatched red and white"—explains why the "posting" of Lucrece's letter not only marks a turning point in the poem but one that will turn out, as such, to be conclusive. As repetition of Tarquin's "post," Lucrece's epistolic gesture first serves to reverse the directed movement of the poem, returning Collatine's "let" and letter to their original author. But this reversal thereby serves to complete, *by* inflectively inverting, the poem's directed movement, folding Tarquin's "post" back upon itself so that Collatine's first "let" and "letter," in this way ex-plicated and re-turned to sender, concludes a comprehensive circuit "From the besieged Ardea" "to Collatium," and then back again, "'At Ardea to my lord with more than haste.'"

It is, of course, a merely formal circuit—first one "post," Tarquin's, and then, now, with Lucrece's letter, another—thus traced out by "a certain sorrow writ uncertainly." But the complete trajectory of the letter—a narrative trajectory composed, like the literal formation of chiastic *MW,* of two folded letters folded over on each other—turns out in "The Rape of Lucrece" to enforce a precise literary consequence. For the only anthropomorphic figure in the poem who possesses, at least a little, some of the characteristic density, textured internality, and affective pathos we associate with Shakespeare's fully developed psychologized characters is neither Tarquin nor Lucrece—both of whom seem, throughout the poem, both tonally and struc-

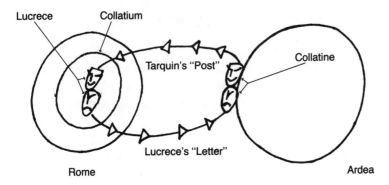

turally, like abstract, allegorical versions of each other—but, instead, Lucrece's husband, Collatine, whom the poem at its beginning describes as author of the rape—because he is the "orator" and "publisher / of that rich jewel" (30–34)—and to whom at its conclusion the poem will turn its full attention when Collatine at last receives his "let" and "letter" back by postponed "post." Anticipating this conclusion, as well as the way in which Collatine is transformed into a recognizably Shakespearean literary character when his letter finally arrives at what is both its first and final destination, I propose that the constellation of the "let," the "letter," and the "post," as this is developed in "The Rape of Lucrece," shows us in simple, reductive, skeletal form how Shakespeare conceives the formation of literary subjectivity in general, so that the poem's particular elaboration of a postal circuit whereby Collatine becomes a sender who receives his message back in an inverted form (inverted by the movement of re-turning or re-versing repetition) describes the way in which *all* Shakespeare's strong literary characters acquire their specifically psychologistic literary power.

It takes time, however, for a letter, even one transmitted "with more than haste," to reach its destination, and so, before turning to the end of the poem and to a discussion of Collatine, it is necessary to pause, as does "The Rape of Lucrece," to consider what takes place within the temporal interval separating the letter's dispatch and its delivery. This brings us, following the poem's expository development, to the long section the poem now devotes to a description of a "skillful painting" that depicts illustrative scenes from the *Iliad.* This ekphrastic digression, which is of course a convention of Complaint poems, is explicitly presented as that which passes "time" while Lucrece's messenger and message enact a movement of "return":

> But long she thinks 'til he return again,
> And yet the duteous vassal scarce is gone;
> The weary time she cannot entertain.

> (1359–61)

At the same "weary time," however, while her letter follows out the circle of its circuit, it is as something understood as novel that Lucrece, "Pausing for means to mourn some newer way" (1365), turns to examine the visual image of her own complaint:

> At last she calls to mind where hangs a piece
> Of skillful painting made for Priam's Troy,

> Before the which is drawn the power of Greece,
> For Helen's rape the city to destroy.
>
> (1366–69)

In some obvious ways, the Homeric story, because it collates the military siege of Troy with the rape of Helen, fits Lucrece's situation to a T. In other ways, equally obvious, the Homeric story is to some extent ill chosen, since for Shakespeare, if not for Homer, it is the rape of "strumpet" Helen—as Lucrece soon calls her: "show me the strumpet that began this stir" (1471)—that occasions the siege, rather than, as happens with the chaste Lucrece, the other way around.[28] In either case, however, appropriate or not, the poem's citation of the Homeric story gives an exemplary dimension to Lucrece's situation, making it another instance of the primal "rape" (or cuckolding) with which our literary tradition historically begins, another version of the same old story. So too, because "Beauty itself doth of itself persuade / The eyes of men without an orator," or because "to see sad sights moves more than hear them told," the "skillful painting" promises to function as powerful eye-witness to Lucrece's plight. And indeed, it is for just this reason, because "the eye interprets to the ear," that the poem now thematically emphasizes the specifically visual modality of the "skillful painting," not just because the painting, as a painting, is something to be seen, but because, for the most part, what the "skillful painting" movingly depicts is eyes, and looks, and gazes, as though the painting were primarily concerned, by focusing on such images *of* vision, to illustrate the visual itself. Consider, to take just a few examples, the painted details mentioned in the first two stanzas of the narrator's description:

> A thousand lamentable objects there,
> In scorn of nature, art gave liveless life:
> Many a dry drop seem'd a weeping tear,
> Shed for the slaught'red husband by the wife;
> The red blood reek'd, to show the painter's strife
>   And dying eyes gleam'd forth their ashy lights,
>   Like dying coals burnt out in tedious nights.
>
> There might you see the laboring pioner
> Begrim'd with sweat, and smeared all with dust,
> And from the tow'rs of Troy there would appear
> The very eyes of men through loop-holes thrust,

> Gazing upon the Greeks with little lust.
>> Such sweet observance in this work was had,
>> That one might see those far-off eyes look sad.
>>> (1373–86)

Perhaps yet more emphatic, we are told a stanza later that:

> In Ajax and Ulysses, O what art
> Of physiognomy might one behold!
> The face of either cipher'd either's heart,
> Their face their manners most expressly told:
> In Ajax's eyes blunt rage and rigor roll'd,
>> But the mild glance that sly Ulysses lent
>> Showed deep regard and smiling government.
>>> (1394–1400)

Moreover, even when the painting paints the act of speaking, it does so by making language into something visual, into something more or less directed to the eye, as when, a stanza later, it illustrates "Nestor's golden words" (1420):

> There might you see grave Nestor stand,
> As 'twere encouraging the Greeks to fight,
> Making such sober action with his hand,
> That it beguil'd attention, charm'd the sight.
>> (1401–4)

At stake in all this, of course, or what is being presupposed throughout, is the perennial aesthetic of the "speaking picture," the idea, as well as the ideal, of a visual verisimilitude, a specular mimetics, so effective and affective as to erase the difference between representation and that which representation represents. And this familiar visionary aesthetic, an aesthetic of transparent imitation, of presentational representation—which is traditionally applied to all the referential arts, not just to painting, as in the doctrine of *ut pictura poesis*—in turn entails or presupposes, as the narrator now points out, an equally perennial and equally visionary semiotics, one whereby a signifier, conceived as something visually iconic, is so fixedly and unequivocally related to its signified that by itself it can present its meaning or its referent to the "eye of mind":

> For much imaginary work was there,
> Conceit deceitful, so compact, so kind,
> That for Achilles' image stood his spear,
> Grip'd in an armed hand, himself behind
> Was left unseen, save to the eye of mind:
> > A hand a foot, a face, a leg, a head
> > Stood for the whole to be imagined.
>
> (1422–28)[29]

This eloquent language of the "speaking picture," because it can "persuade / The eyes of men without an orator," is what powers Lucrece's empathetic response to the "skillful painting," whether that response is sympathetic, as when with pity she beholds the look of Hecuba "Staring on Priam's wounds with her eyes" (1448), or antipathetic, as when she looks disdainfully at Helen's lascivious eye: "Thy eye kindled the fire that burneth here, / And here in Troy, for trespass of thine eye, / The sire, the son, the dame, and daughter die" (1475–77). And the same essentially visionary motives and motifs also govern Lucrece's mouth, such that even what Lucrece will say about the painting is but the evoked image of the way the painting looks: "Here feelingly she weeps Troy's painted woes . . . / To pencill'd pensiveness and color'd sorrow; / She lends them words, and she their looks doth borrow" (1492–98).

And yet, despite the way the poem here presupposes and calls forth the entire system of specular ideality as this is conventionally deployed in the Renaissance, despite the power of the painting to address itself directly to "the eye of mind," the poem's ekphrastic description seems to stress the ideal visuality of the painting only for the purpose of immediately belying it, and this it does by pointing to the one thing in the Homeric story that the painting, precisely because it is an artifact of vision, cannot truly represent. Lucrece now "throws her eyes about the painting round, / . . . [and] At last she sees a wretched image bound, / That piteous looks to Phrygian shepherds lent" (1499–1501). This "wretched image" is the figure of Sinon, the betrayer of Troy, and he is pictured through the same checkered combination of red and white with which from its beginning the poem consistently imagines the chiastic end of what is visually pure:

> In him the painter labor'd with his skill
> To hide deceit, and give the harmless show
> An humble gait, calm looks, eyes wailing still,
> A brow unbent, that seem'd to welcome woe,

> Cheeks neither red nor pale, but mingled so
> That blushing red no guilty instance gave,
> Nor ashy pale the fear that false hearts have.
>
> (1506–12)

Unlike Ulysses and Ajax, whose "face their manners most expressly told," Sinon's face, specifically, the "mingled" colors of his cheeks, disguises what he is, and this is something very different from the way, before, a single part "Stood for the whole to be imagined." "Neither red nor pale," but, rather, "mingled," Sinon's cheeks do not betray the telltale blush of guilty red nor "ashy pale" of fearful white, and so his cheeks become demonstrative icon of the failure of visionary iconography, an image of the clouding of the clarity of vision. Sinon's very appearance, therefore, his "mingled" look, displays a blind spot in "imaginary work," showing forth an image of the way a visual appearance fails to be, or to stand for, the meaning of the way it looks. And the poem, returning to its initial claim that "by our ears our hearts oft tainted be," explains this disruption or distortion of specular transparency by seeing it as illustration of the lying "words" of "perjur'd Sinon":

> The well-skill'd workman this mild image drew
> For perjur'd Sinon, whose enchanting story
> The credulous old Priam after slew;
> Whose words like wildfire burnt the shining glory
> Of rich-built Ilion, that the skies were sorry,
> And little stars shot from their fixed places,
> When their glass fell wherein they view'd their faces.
>
> (1520–26)[30]

There is something momentous, both thematically and tonally, about the way this stanza calls up the loss of everything the English Renaissance self-servingly identifies with the bright light of Troy, something genuinely epic, not mock epic, in the stanza's elegiac retrospection. But the stanza also carefully repeats the terms with which, at its beginning, in the second stanza, the poem accounts for the loss of Collatine's ideal vision, "the clear unmatched red and white." Sinon's "words" spark a "wildfire" that burns "the shining glory of rich-built Ilion" just as Collatine's "praise" inspired Tarquin's "lightless fire." So too, the "little stars shot from their fixed places, / When their glass fell wherein they view'd their faces" fulfill the fall of Collatine's original "delight," which is imagined in the second stanza as a "sky" "Where mortal

stars as bright as heaven's beauties, / With pure aspects did him peculiar duties."
These repetitions work both to memorialize and to generalize the way in which "Collatine unwisely did not let / To praise the clear unmatched red and white"; they make
the burning of "the shining glory of rich-built Ilion" into the mythic precursor of the
loss of Collatine's "delight," but they do so at the cost of identifying the lying "words"
of "perjur'd Sinon" with Collatine's equally catastrophic "praise," as though it were
the very act of speaking, true or false, that spells an end to the ideality of vision.

    What is remarkable about all this—especially if we remember that ekphrasis
is a literary device designed to put the visual into words—is that the poem, now, at
the conclusion of its description of the picture, makes explicit thematic issue of this
displacement of ideal vision by language, so that Lucrece herself, gazing on the picture's portrait of Sinon, will now observe the structural limits of the "skillfull
painting":

> This picture she advisedly perus'd,
> And chid the painter for his wondrous skill,
> Saying, some shape in Sinon's was abus'd:
> So fair a form lodg'd not a mind so ill.
> And still on him she gaz'd, and gazing still,
> > Such signs of truth in his plain face she spied,
> > That she concludes the picture was belied.
>
> > > > (1527–33)

It is as though the long digression of the ekphrasis had been developed only so as
to articulate this paradox: that the picture, not despite but because of its "wondrous
skill," is "belied" by its very honesty, that the "skillful painting," because it is composed of truthful images, "signs of truth," cannot represent the spoken lies of Sinon.
Moreover, having formulated the theme, the poem now strives to put this paradoxical moral yet more literally into words, so that Lucrece's own speaking—remarked
as such, cited as something verbal rather than visual, of the "tongue" and not the
eye—now mimics and performs the way in which the "lurking" "look" of vision is
revealed by a specifically linguistic and, therefore, revisionary "turn."

> "It cannot be," quoth she, "that so much guile"
> She would have said, "can lurk in such a look";
> But Tarquin's shape came in her mind the while,
> And from her tongue "can lurk" from "cannot" took:

"It cannot be," she in that sense forsook,
    And turn'd it thus, "It cannot be, I find,
    But such a face should bear a wicked mind.

                                                    (1534–40)

In the context of the unfolding action of the poem, this ekphrastic movement, from "imaginary work" to "the picture was belied," from the imagination of true vision (the "skillful painting") to the performance of equivocating language (she "turn'd it thus"), defines what goes on in the time, both narrative and thematic, it takes for Lucrece's letter to reach its destination: "Thus ebbs and flows the current of her sorrow, / And time doth weary time with her complaining" (1569–70). Accordingly, since this is what enables the "return" of "post," it seems all the more important that when Lucrece's letter is now finally delivered, i.e., when "the mindful messenger, come back, / Brings home his lord and other company" (1583–84), this same imagery of time, along with everything the poem has heretofore associated with it, is reapplied to Collatine in what are increasingly explicit ways. This is what I want to look at now—the ways in which, in the final section of the poem, time takes place in Collatine—for this is how the poem builds up to and arrives at what is structured as its strong, subjectifying climax.

After the ekphrasis, when Collatine has returned to Collatium, Lucrece begins to tell her story, though she begins and will continue its narration through a process of delay: "Three times with sighs she gives her sorrow fire, / Ere once she can discharge one word of woe" (1604–5). Drawing out the story, through a series of deferments that heighten its suspense, Lucrece first reports the fact of her rape but does not reveal her rapist's name. Collatine's response to this first segment of Lucrece's story is carefully described:

But wretched as he is he strives in vain,
    What he breathes out, his breath drinks up again.

As through an arch the violent roaring tide
Outruns the eye that doth behold his haste,
Yet in the eddy boundeth in his pride
Back to the strait that forc'd him on so fast
(In rage sent out, recall'd in rage, being past),
    Even so his sighs, his sorrows, make a saw,
    To push grief on, and back the same grief draw.

                                                    (1665–73)

It is evident the poem here makes a point of importing into Collatine the imagery of eddying wind and tidal water with which it not only imagines the rape—"'my uncontrolled tide, / Turns not, but swells the higher by this let'"—but so too the promise of the rape's final revelation, as when Lucrece decided "she would not blot the letter / With words till action might become them better": "Deep sounds make lesser noise than shallow fords, / And sorrow ebbs, being blown with the wind of words." Yet more precisely, as though the stanza were describing how it feels to be subjected to chiasmus, this back and forth movement, of wind and water, is imagined as a "saw," made up, we can suppose, of little *x*'s or crosses, that carves a groove in Collatine while with his grieving sighs he draws it back and forth across himself.[31] This imagery, along with the whole thrust of the narrative, serves to focus attention on Collatine; we await his response to the conclusion of Lucrece's story, which should occur, we have been promised, when Lucrece reveals her rapist's name. Once again, however, there is another moment of delay, while Lucrece extracts from the assembled company a promise of revenge:

> "But ere I name him, you fair lords," quoth she
> (Speaking to those that came with Collatine),
> "Shall plight your honorable faiths to me
> With swift pursuit to venge this wrong of mine."
>
> (1688–91)

And then, a few stanzas later, in what would seem to be the climax of the story:

> Here with a sigh as if her heart would break,
> She throws forth Tarquin's name: "He, he," she says,
> But more than "he" her poor tongue could not speak,
> Till after many accents and delays,
> Untimely breathings, sick and short assays,
> >   She utters this, "He, he, fair lords, 'tis he,
> >   That guides this hand to give this wound to me."
>
> Even here she sheathes in her harmless breast
> A harmful knife, that thence her soul unsheathed.
>
> (1716–24)

What is surprising about this, of course, and specifically ante-climactic, is that—despite the traditional version of the Lucrece story, and despite what is announced in the poem's Argument: "She, first taking an oath of them for her revenge, revealed the actor, and the whole manner of his dealing, and withal suddenly stabbed herself"—Lucrece here fails to name her rapist. The poem explicitly insists upon the fact that Lucrece does not "throw forth Tarquin's name," but throws out, instead, as prologue to her suicide, this series of anonymyzing, deictic "'he'"s: "But more than 'he' her poor tongue could not speak." Again, therefore, we are obliged to await the naming of Tarquin, the straightforward and outspoken speaking of his name, which, if ever it occurs, will function as conclusion to the theme of naming introduced at what the poem at its beginning stipulates *as* its beginning: when, again, "Happ'ly that name of 'chaste' unhapp'ly set / This bateless edge on his keen appetite; / When Collatine unwisely did not let / To praise the clear unmatched red and white."

The poem will not let Tarquin's name remain anonymous—Collatine himself will pronounce it in a moment—but before the name is mentioned it is significant that the poem allows itself two further moments of delay. First, there is the matter of Lucrece's death, which is described thus:

> And from the purple fountain Brutus drew
>> The murd'rous knife, and as it left the place,
>> Her blood, in poor revenge, held it in chase.
>
> And bubbling from her breast, it doth divide
>> In two slow rivers, that the crimson blood
>> Circles her body in on every side.
>
>> > > > > > > (1734–39)

As at the end of "Venus and Adonis," where Adonis is transformed into "A purple flow'r, check'red with white," the poem here resolves the red-white color scheme through which its vision has consistently been filtered by imagining a "purple," like the chiastically colored cheeks of "perjur'd Sinon," which is the poem's iconic image of what puts an end to vision. In addition, this "purple" manifests its own material or phenomenal formation, a "divided" flowing of "two slow rivers" that spill out from the inside of Lucrece so as to surround her on the outside with a wrinkled or a folded "circle" in whose circuit Lucrece figures as both source and center. If we try to picture this complicated image of tangential circumscription, it looks something like the way we draw a heart.

Surrounded, therefore, by her liquid inside, encircled by her broken heart, Lucrece becomes, at the moment of her dying, the fixed and permanent objectifi-

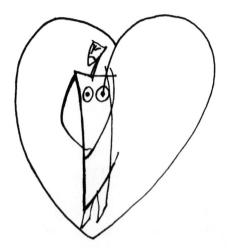

cation of an overflowing spurt, the fleshed out incarnation of the etymological fluidity of the Dedication's "superfluous Moity." In the erotic terms developed by the
poem, she embodies Tarquin's inside-outside movement when he "posts" from
Ardea to Collatium for the purpose of her rape, and she also replicates the "fold" with
which her two lips came together at the moment of her rape: "Entombs her out-cry
in her lips sweet fold." At the same time, as she promised when she folded up her
letter, her "crimson blood," as it "circles her body in on every side," now "stains her
stain'd excuse."

The second moment of delay is equally recapitulatory and equally conclusive.
Seeing his daughter dead upon the ground, Lucrece's father starts to speak his own
memorial lament:

> "Daughter, dear daughter," old Lucretius cries,
> "That life was mine which thou hast here deprived.
> If in the child the father's image lies,
> Where shall I live now Lucrece is unlived?
> Thou wast not to this end from me derived.
>   If children pre-decease progenitors,
>   We are their offspring, and they none of ours.
>
> "Poor broken glass, I often did behold
> In thy sweet semblance my old age new born,
> But now that fair fresh mirror, dim and old

Shows me a bare-bon'd death by time outworn.
O, from thy cheeks my image thou hast torn,
　　And shiver'd all the beauty of my glass,
　　That I no more can see what once I was!

"O Time, cease thou thy course and last no longer,
If they surcease to be that should survive."

(1751–66)

Again the poem foregrounds chiasmus—e.g., "'If children pre-decease progeni-
tors'"—and again the poem unfolds the trope so as to formulate the breaking both
of ideal vision—"'Poor broken glass'"—and of the mimetic logic of successive, imi-
tating repetition: "'I often did behold / In thy sweet semblance my old age new born,
/ But now that fair fresh mirror, dim and old / Shows me a barebon'd death by time
outworn.'" In personal terms, the dead Lucrece, enveloped by her "wat'-ry rigol [i.e.,
a watery 'ring']" (1745), displays to her father his distance from his ideal image of
himself; like father, like daughter, her "'broken glass'" reflects the breaking, or the
having-been-broken, of his specular identity: "'O, from thy cheeks my image thou
hast torn, / And shiver'd all the beauty of my glass, / That I no more can see what once
I was!'" And this in turn determines for Lucrece's father an infinite "old age," since
Time itself, "'by time outworn,'" is now supposed to be chiastically suspended
between the death of life and life of death: "'O Time, cease thou thy course and last
no longer, / If they sur-cease to be that should survive.'"

These two final moments of delay, therefore—Lucrece's death, her father's
lament—together recapitulate the themes, motifs, and movements—the mixed-up
red and white, the loss of ideal vision, the inside-outside in-betweenness—that control the exposition of "The Rape of Lucrece" from its beginning, from "From the
besieged Ardea all in post." Taken together, *as* moments of delay, they now potentiate
the poem's climax, the naming of Tarquin by Collatine. First (and the gesture repeats
the way Venus purples her face by kissing Adonis' castration—"With this she falleth
in the place she stood, / And stains her face with his congealed blood"; 1121–22),
Collatine awakes and "mingles" his own cheeks:

By this starts Collatine, as from a dream,
And bids Lucretius give his sorrow place,
And then in key-cold Lucrece' bleeding stream
He falls, and bathes the pale fear in his face.

(1772–75)

And then, no longer mute, Collatine "at last" pronounces Tarquin's name:

> The deep vexation of his inward soul
> Hath serv'd a dumb arrest upon his tongue,
> Who mad that sorrow should his use control,
> Or keep him from heart-easing words so long,
> Begins to talk, but through his lips do throng
>> Weak words, so thick come in his poor heart's aid,
>> That no man could distinguish what he said.
>
> Yet sometime "Tarquin" was pronounced plain,
> But through his teeth, as if the name he tore.
> This windy tempest, till it blow up rain,
> Held back his sorrow's tide, to make it more.
> At last it rains, and busy winds give o'er.
>
> (1779–90)

This is how the poem conceives the way that Collatine "begins to talk," stressing the at once climactic and inaugural momentum through which speech becomes articulate—"Yet sometime 'Tarquin' was pronounced plain"—as it rises out of babble, "Weak words . . . That no man could distinguish." It is a speaking whose pronouncing is specifically provoked, like the rape, by the logic of the "let," so that what precipitates the "raining" of "the name" is the way the "windy tempest" "Held back his sorrow's tide, to make it more." Accordingly, the swelling force of pent-up sorrow now spills forth as the ejaculation of a name—"At last it rains, and busy winds give o'er"—and thereby introduces into Collatine the liquid temporality of rape: erotic Time (*tempus*) takes place within him when the "windy tempest" (*tempestas*) overflows.[32] Rather systematically, therefore, the end of the poem, focusing on the person of Collatine, returns to its beginning with a climatic but specifically revisionary recapitulation. When he "tears" the name between his teeth, Collatine repeats the way "Happ'ly that name of 'chaste' unhapp'ly set / This bateless edge on his keen appetite," but now "that name of 'chaste'" has been transformed into the name of "'Tarquin.'" This is why I said before that there is something final or conclusive in the way that Collatine receives the letter he initially transmits—Tarquin's "post"—in the inverted form of Lucrece's folded "letter." With the "pale fear" of his face bathed in Lucrece's "bleeding stream," Collatine himself becomes the unintended consequence of the way he "did not let / To praise the clear unmatched red and white," just as he becomes the "post" by means of which "Lust-breath'd Tarquin leaves the

Roman host." And this "let," because it is now finally delivered, is what situates in Collatine the tidal overflow of a tendentious but yet retrospective time whose passing only comes to pass precisely at or as the very moment in which Collatine first speaks.

It is fair to call all this characteristically or typically Shakespearean because, from the beginning to the end of Shakespeare's career, the images, motifs, and themes through which Collatine arrives at speech also control Shakespeare's theatrical imagination of dramatic, characterological destiny. This is the case, for example, in a quite simple way, in an early, reconciliatory comedy like *The Comedy of Errors* where whatever is first "splitted in the midst" (1.1.103) by windy storm—e.g., the father who is "sever'd from my bliss" (1.1.118) or the twins "who could not be distinguish'd but by names" (1.1.52)—is only brought together after registration of a torn paternal "voice": "Not know my voice!—O time's extremity, / Hast thou so crack'd and splitted my poor tongue" (5.1.308–9). And so too is this the case, though far more complicatedly, in a late romance such as *The Tempest,* where windy storm again initiates division—"Blow till thou burst thy wind" (1.1.7); "We split, we split, we split" (1.1.62)—where "time," which is a central theme because it is "sea-swallow'd," "performs an act / Whereof what's past is prologue, what to come" (2.1.251–53), and where concluding union only comes when Prospero delivers to assembled ears his strange but calming story: *Alonso:* "I long / To hear the story of your life, which must / Take the ear strangely"; *Prospero:* "I'll deliver all, / And promise you calm seas, auspicious gales" (5.1.313–15). In the middle tragedies, where Shakespeare develops his most famously and powerfully psychologistic characters, the Collatinian terms of such dramatic personal formation are yet more evidently pronounced, whether we think, for example, of the storm in *Othello*—"The desperate tempest hath so bang'd the Turks, / That their designment halts" (2.1.21–22) and of the play's denominating, self-evacuating climax—"That's he that was Othello; here I am" (5.2.284)—or of the storm in *King Lear* that "germinates" the king's disseminated tragedy—"Blow, winds, and crack your cheeks! blow! / You cataracts and hurricanoes, spout / Till you have drench'd the steeples, drown'd the cocks! . . . And thou, all shaking thunder, / Strike flat the thick rotundity o' the world! / Crack nature's moulds, all germains spill at once / That makes ingrateful man" (3.2.1–9)—or of the mixed-up letters through which *Hamlet's* time and being are subjected to the "leave" of "let": "If it be now, 'tis not to come; if it be not to come, it will be now; if it be not now, yet it will come—the readiness is all. Since no man, of aught he leaves, knows what is't to leave betimes, let be" (5.2.220–24). In all these plays, to which of course I now can only gesture, characters enact the same misogynist erotics as is developed in "The Rape of Lucrece"; they discover the same internal sense of present broken self and retrospective temporality as is summed up in "I no more can see what once I was"; and they all turn into textured subjects when they learn firsthand how "by our ears our hearts oft tainted be."

However, beyond such shorthand references to what is characteristically, in the sense of typically, Shakespearean about the construction of Shakespeare's various *dramatis personae,* I have also suggested, with what I said about *MW,* that for Shakespeare, the person, there is something yet more literally "characteristic" about Collatine's receipt, in inverse form, of the letter he dispatches, for Shakespeare's "*Will*" is also implicated in the writing of two criss-crossed literary letters. The question that remains, therefore, is why, for Collatine or Shakespeare, the writing of a letter is related to the registration of a name.

Our reading of "The Rape of Lucrece" at least allows for a schematic answer, for, as we have seen, the poem associates the act of naming both with writing and with speech. Collatine's "let" puts Tarquin "all in post," but so too does it "praise the clear unmatched red and white." In either case, a name results, first "that name of 'chaste,'" and then the name of "'Tarquin,'" but the latter name, when it is spoken, bespeaks the final mix-up of Lucrece's pristine "red and white." As we have also seen, when Collatine, at the end of the poem, at what I have called its climax, "pronounces 'Tarquin' plain," he exemplifies what happens to a person when he "begins to talk," something the poem amplifies as an inaugural moment of constitutive, subjectifying transition in which the truth and clarity of vision is supplanted and belied by verbal speech. This corruption of ideal vision by spoken language, the reason why "by our ears our hearts oft tainted be," serves to motivate the erotic and temporal movement of the poem, establishing desire as a longing for a visionary origin that the very act of speaking renders lost, introducing successivity into Time by making "now" the aftermath of what has come before. But the speaking of the name with which the poem in this way brings itself full circle is itself provoked by Collatine's originary "let," as though Collatine can only say the name of "Tarquin" and thus become a person, when the epistolic "post" that he himself initially dispatched completes its complicated circuit.

Putting, as the poem does, all these movements and motifs together, we can say that writing in "The Rape of Lucrece" is what leads its subject into speech. The "let" that "posts" a "letter" is the instrumental medium by means of which "that name of 'chaste'" is translated into "'Tarquin.'" In large thematic terms, therefore, writing functions in "The Rape of Lucrece" as that which marks off, but thereby produces by remarking, the difference between what the poem associates with vision and what the poem associates with speech. More precisely, writing is the complication that stands between a language understood as something visual (e.g., the "praise" of red and white), a language that is therefore truthful image of its meaning or its reference (e.g., the semiotics of "imaginary work"), and a language understood, instead, as something spoken (e.g., she "turn'd it thus"), which is a language, therefore, that by virtue of its verbal essence is fundamentally discrepant both to meaning and to reference (e.g., the lies of "perjur'd Sinon"). Poised, however, in between the image and the word, writing does not stand apart as something that is neutral; its complication is no more undecided than was Tarquin when, "with open list'ning ear," he was "crossed" between "foul hope" and "fond despair." As something intermediate, writing introduces difference into what ideally is the same, and in this way makes the movement of the poem, from Collatine's first "let" to "sometime 'Tarquin' was pronounced plain," into a coherent and inexorable progress. As with the implicit quotation marks that indicate, without pronouncing, the way a word becomes a name when use turns into mention (e.g., the remarked repetition whereby "chaste" turned into "'chaste'"), writing thus not only registers but also warrants the unhappy destiny the poem associates with names.

But this returns us to the way the poem theatrically performs its letters, for the typographic gestures to which I have referred make the poem's own textuality—the literal letters that are seen upon the page—into an example of what stands between the image and the word. Accordingly, if Shakespeare's own "*Will*" is graphically inscribed at the criss-cross of *MW*—and four of the examples directly call up images of writing, reading, marking—this reflects the way Shakespeare's own authorial voice is called forth by what belies it. The signature of Shakespeare's name—the letters that chiastically circumscribe his name's beginning and its end—in this way authorizes the subjective content of what, to paraphrase Juliet's famous question, is in and what goes on in a Shakespearean name when it is made such *by* remarking: between the *W* and *M* Shakespeare too can read the provocative difference between an ego of full being and the designated subject of a name, for the very fact that they are written is what proves that Shakespeare's "Will" is different from "I am."

It is, of course, an altogether contingent fact that Shakespeare's name was "William," and I do not mean to argue that if Shakespeare had been called by any other name he could not have written what he wrote. If I insist upon the particular importance of the "*Will*" ←$\mathbb{M}$ formation, it is in part because there are a remarkable number of examples of it in the poem (and also elsewhere in Shakespeare's writings), in part because "The Rape of Lucrece" makes such a vivid issue of the relation between "Will" and "writing" ("What wit sets down is blotted straight with Will"), but most of all it is because this reminds us that the name of Shakespeare is nothing but contingent.[33] It is in this sense, as something that occurs "Happ'ly"-"unhapp'ly," that we should understand how it happens the "superfluous Moity" of the Dedication turns out to materialize the poem's demonstration of the inexorable return of subjectifying letters. On the one hand, we can see this as a personal effort, on Shakespeare's part, to adapt the tradition of the dedicatory epistle to the logic of the "let," as though by writing to his patron Shakespeare means to put himself in "post." On the other hand, to account for the popular success of so personal a gesture, we can see it as a consequence of and a response to the increasingly acute perception and experience in the Renaissance of a specifically textual quality attaching to writing in general, and to letter writing in particular—what Claudio Guillén, speaking of the revival and invention of epistolic genres, has called "the Renaissance awareness of the letter."[34] This explains how the idiosyncratic inflection of Shakespeare's individuated character subsequently becomes the governing model for literary subjectivity as such, for soon enough, when Shakespeare writes for the theater, he will turn this private structure of author-patron epistolic exchange into something public, and his "*Will,*" because its letters are addressed to everyone, will come to seem generic. But this remains a thoroughly contingent fact within our literary history, as contingent as is the accident of Shakespeare's name, and a contingency that will only seem inevitable within a *literary* history of self-remarking, self-performing names. This is why we should read what the editors write to William, Earl of Pembroke, in the Dedicatory epistle to *The First Folio* as a thoughtful caution rather than a boast: "There is a great difference, whether any Booke choose his Patrones, or finde them: This hath done both." At a moment when contemporary theoretical debate about the relation of psychology to literary letters simply repeats, without inverting, the topoi and the story of "The Rape of Lucrece," at a moment when the resignation of Shakespearean designation claims the authority of an extra-literary force, at a moment when moralizing contextualizations of literature illiterately reinscribe the characters of master texts, it is all the more urgent to recognize, by reading, the specifically literary formation of the subjective "appetite" occasioned by "Happ'ly that 'name' of chaste unhapp'ly set."[35] For this is the only way to break the legacy of Shakespeare's "*Will,*" the only way to open up a time outside the temporality of rape. It is now about time to think ourselves outside the Shakespearean constellation of the "let," the "letter," and the "post."

Reprinted from *Representations,* no. 20 (Fall 1987), 25–76.

1.   John Heming and Henry Condell, eds., dedicatory epistle to William, Earl of Pembroke, and Philip, Earl of Montgomery, *The Shakespeare First Folio* (1623).

2.   The Argument, "The Rape of Lucrece"; Shakespeare citations will be to *The Riverside Shakespeare,* ed. G. Blakemore Evans et al. (Boston, 1974); references to the original edition (1594) will be to the facsimile edition published by the Scolar Press (London, 1968). Citations of poems will give line numbers within parentheses in the text.

3.   T. W. Baldwin discusses the influence on The Argument of Ovid's *Fasti* and Livy's *Historia* in *On the Literary Genetics of Shakespeare's Poems and Sonnets* (Urbana, Ill., 1950), 108–12. James M. Tolbert argues The Argument to the poem is not by Shakespeare, "The Argument of Shakespeare's 'Lucrece': Its Sources and Authorship," *Studies in English* 29 (1950):77–90.

4.   There are six attested Shakespeare signatures; "By me *William Shakespeare*" is on page 3 of Shakespeare's will. For discussions, not always persuasive, and reproductions of Shakespeare's handwriting, see Charles Hamilton, *In Search of Shakespeare* (New York, 1985), esp. 38–47.

5.   Joel Fineman, *Shakespeare's Perjured Eye: The Invention of Poetic Subjectivity in the Sonnets* (Berkeley, 1986).

6.   Facsimile edition, "Hap'ly that name of chast, unhap'ly set."

7.   George Puttenham, *The Arte of English Poesie* (1589; facsimile ed., Kent, Ohio, 1970), 216.

8.   "Bi-fold" is from *Troilus and Cressida;* this is Troilus' response to Cressida's duplicity: "O madness of discourse,/That cause sets up with and against itself!/Bi-fold authority, where reason can revolt/Without perdition, and loss assume all reason/Without revolt. This is and is not Cressida!" (5.2.142–46). The passage is relevant to the Troy ekphrasis the poem develops later on, especially Troilus' dumbfounded response to "how these two did co-act": on the one hand, "Shall I not lie in publishing a truth," on the other, the hope "that doth invert th' attest of eyes and ears" (5.2.118–22).

9.   Sigmund Freud, "Certain Neurotic Mechanisms in Jealousy, Paranoia, and Homosexuality" (1922), in *Sexuality and the Psychology of Love,* ed. Philip Rieff (New York, 1970), 162. Freud sees this as the logic of projective jealousy, and footnotes Desdemona's "Willow song" as evidence: "'I called my love false love, but what said he then?/If I court moe women, you'll couch with moe men,'" 161; see note 33, below.

10.   René Girard, *Deceit, Desire, and the Novel* (Baltimore, 1965); *Violence and the Sacred* (Baltimore, 1977).

11.   Claude Lévi-Strauss, *The Elementary Structures of Kinship* (Boston, 1969). Patricia K. Joplin discusses the rape of Philomela in Girardian and Lévi-Straussian terms in "The Voice of the Shuttle Is Ours," *Stanford Literature Review* 1 (1984): 25–53. Nancy Vickers discusses the rhetoric of praise in "The Rape of Lucrece" in much the same terms, "'The blazon of sweet beauty's best': Shakespeare's 'Lucrece,'" in *Shakespeare and the Question of Theory,* ed. Patricia Parker and Geoffrey Hartman (New York, 1985): 95–115.

12.   Eve Kosofsky Sedgwick, *Between Men: English Literature and Male Homosocial Desire* (New York, 1985), esp. 161–79. Pierre Macherey, *Pour une théorie de la production littéraire* (Paris, 1970). Traditional commentary on the story of the rape of Lucrece is usefully reviewed in Ian Donaldson, *The Rapes of Lucretia: A Myth and Its Transformations* (Oxford, 1982). Moralizing discussions of the ethical questions raised by the rape and suicide of Lucrece rapidly become formulaic "themes for disputation." Accordingly, aspects of her story provide convenient topical commonplaces through which to display and to teach rhetorical skills; hence, the purely rhetorical tradition of arguing on both sides of the question, *in utramque partem, Pro Lucrecia* and *Contra Lucreciam,* e.g., Coluccio Salutati, George Rivers, et al.; see Donaldson, *Rapes of Lucretia,* 38. As I argue in connection with Tarquin's "cross," the story of the rape of Lucrece systematically activates essentially, and therefore interminably, contestable questions so as to elicit from readers a suspended investment in the story that, as something suspended, determines the inevitability of rape.

This is why triangulating characterizations of the relation of desire to violence in literature, such as those to which I refer above, regularly promote, whatever their explicit intentions, an erotics that conduces to rape. The tradition behind this literary strategy is an old one, which is why I say above that the desire for violence and the violence of desire are traditional expressions of each other. A paradigm for this, one that is quite important to Shakespeare, comes at the end of Chaucer's *The Knight's Tale,* which seems to resolve and to defuse the opposition between a violent Mars (represented by Arcite, who is nevertheless a lover) and a desiring Venus (represented by Palamon, who is nevertheless a warrior) in the figure of Emeleye, the representative of Diana who, as goddess both of the hunt and of childbearing chastity, is image of the domesticated integration of violence and desire. The terms of this happy reconciliation go back to Homer, from whom derives the medieval tradition according to which the legitimate marriage of Mars and Venus spawns as its issue the child-god Harmonia (spelled "Hermione" in the Middle Ages, a point relevant to *The Winter's Tale*). In *The Knight's Tale* (and elsewhere) the harmonious resolution of the chiastic conjunction of a venereal Mars and a martial Venus is accomplished through the exigently accidental violence that puts an end to the public fight for love conducted by Palamon and Arcite. But this harmonious and triangulated resolution of the two lovers' quarrel is staged for a fourth point of vantage, that of amazon Hippolyta and warrior Theseus, who thus come to occupy, by virtue of their witness to triangularity, the place in which violence and desire come together in chiastic disjunction, the vantage point, therefore, of rape. "Hippolyta, I woo'd thee with my sword," says Theseus at the opening of *A Midsummer Night's Dream,* "And won thy love doing thee injuries" (1.1.16–17):

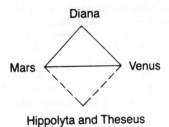

Diana

Mars   **Venus**

Hippolyta and Theseus

Since Chaucer is the most eminent rapist in our literary tradition (thanks to the Cecily Champagne episode in which he was accused of *raptus*), there are anecdotal, biographic grounds with reference to which we can understand why it is so regularly the violent case in Chaucer that *Amor Vincit Omnia*—usually with the help of Cupid's arrows. Chaucer consistently induces from the chiastic concatenation of violence and desire a specific form and substance of literary desire, e.g., the way, at the opening of *The Canterbury Tales,* a male Aphrodite (April) "pierces" a female Mars (March) or the way his/her liquidity spills forth to surround the parched channels through which it is supposed to flow: "Whan that Aprill with his shoures soote,/The Droghte of March hath perced to the roote,/And bathed every veyne is swich licour . . ./Thanne longen folk to goon on pilgrimages." I discuss the way the criss-crossed invaginations informing these lines derive from a general literary logic of erotic yearning in "The Structure of Allegorical Desire," in *Allegory and Representation: Selected Papers from the English Institute, 1979–80,* ed. Stephen Greenblatt (Baltimore, 1981). I discuss the tradition behind the Mars-Venus topos in my forthcoming book on Shakespeare's plays, *Shakespeare's Will* (University of California Press). We can note here, however, that *The Knight's Tale* occupies a central place in Shakespeare's dramatic imagination; e.g., he concludes his career by retelling the story in *The Two Noble Kinsmen.* I mention this because, though this essay on "The Rape of Lucrece" is primarily concerned to establish the poetics of Shakespearean rape, the argument it develops is intended to serve as a basis for a discussion of how the *theatrics* of rape functions in Shakespeare's plays. Again, though Shakespeare's use, in narrative and drama, of the chiastic concatenation of violence and desire is nothing but traditional, there is something novel and historically significant about the way he uses the commonplace to produce powerful literary subjectivity effects, rather than the abstract, allegorical agents through which the commonplace is motivated in pre-Shakespearean literature.

13.   Cited in *Riverside Shakespeare,* 1837.

14.   Compare with *Twelve Night*'s purple "violet," the magic flower of erotic mix-up in *A Midsummer Night's Dream,* which is turned purple by Cupid's erring arrow: "Yet mark'd I where the bolt of Cupid fell./It fell upon a little western flower,/Before milk-white, now purple with love's wound" (2.1.165–67); also "The forward violet" of sonnet 99. Purple is the color, and violets "breathe" the odor, of Shakespearean rape.

15.   A full discussion of the relation of *Twelfth Night* to "The Rape of Lucrece" would require an account of the way the false letter of *Twelfth Night,* written by a woman's hand, leads Malvolio to sport "cross-garter'd" stockings. With regard to what I argue above, it is important that the "signature" of the letter emerges from the literal connection of "cut" and "cunt": "By my life, this is my lady's hand. These be her very c's, her u's, and her t's, and thus makes she her great P's" (2.4.86–88). This is the same signature system as is developed in "The Rape of Lucrece," as Malvolio himself remarks: "And the impressure her Lucrece, with which she uses to seal" (2.4.93–94).

16.   The following four paragraphs are adapted, with some revisions, from *Shakespeare's Perjured Eye,* 39–41, where I used this stanza to example Shakespeare's use of rhetorical chiasmus; I want here to consider how chaismus functions thematically in "The Rape of Lucrece."

17.   Cf. the inside-outside glove in *Twelfth Night:* "A sentence is but a chev'ril glove to a good wit. How quickly the wrong side may be turn'd outward!" (3.1.11–12). Referring to gynecological tradition, Stephen Greenblatt gives a naturalizing account of this love-glove in "Fiction and Friction," in *Reconstructing Individualism: Autonomy, Individuality, and the Self in Western Thought,* ed. Thomas Heller, Morton Sosna, David Wellbury (Stanford, Calif., 1986), 30–63.

18.   The proverb survives through Freud: "Some obstacle is necessary to swell the tide of libido to its height; and at all periods of history, wherever natural barriers in the way of satisfaction have not sufficed, mankind has erected conventional ones in order to be able to enjoy love," "A Special Type of Object Choice Made by Men" (1910), in *Sexuality and the Psychology of Love,* 67.

19.   *Riverside Shakespeare* prints a dash, but the facsimile edition a comma.

20.   The next stanza continues, "For with the nightly linen that she wears/He pens her piteous clamors in her head" (680–81); compare these "folded" "lips" and "pen" with *King Lear:* "If I had thee in Lipsbury pinfold, I would make thee care for me" (2.2.9–10).

21.   The title on the frontispiece is *Lucrece,* but the running title at the head of all the pages of the facsimile edition is *The Rape of Lucrece.*

22.   Cf. Lucrece's "'Let my good name, that senseless reputation,/For Collatine's dear love be kept unspotted:/If that be made a theme for disputation,/The branches of another root are rotted'" (820–24).

23.   The relevant Freudian parallel is the Wolfman's "W-espe," which, on the one hand, at the level of the signifier, spells out the Wolfman's initials, "S.P.," on the other, as "wasp," at the level of the signified, calls up the image of the butterfly that determines the Wolfman's erotic object-choice (*coitus a tergo*) through its associations with castration and the primal scene, *From the History of an Infantile Neurosis* (1918), in *Three Case Histories,* ed. Philip Rieff (New York, 1970), 286–87. As I argue above, it is only within a specific literary tradition that the visualization of letters necessarily entails this kind of subjectifying erotic designation.

24.   Example 1 does not play on "Will," but leads immediately to a thematization of epideictic "name": "He stories to her ears her husband's fame,/Won in the fields of fruitful Italy;/And decks with praises Collatine's high name" (106–8). Two stanzas after example 2: "And in his will his willful eye he tired./With more than admiration he admired" (417–18). A play on "will" occurs within example 3, but this is further amplified in the following stanza, where it is developed in terms of the logic of the "crossed," pricking "let": "'I see what crosses my attempt will bring,/I know what thorns the growing rose defends,/I think the honey guarded with a sting:/All this beforehand counsel com-

prehends./But Will is deaf and hears no heedful friends'" (491–95). A play on "will" occurs within example 4, with "'Myself thy friend *will* kill myself. . . . This brief abridgement of my *will* I make.'" In example 5 redoubled "will" appears in the doubled "wil-dness." Example 6 imports the doubleness of "will" into the ambiguities of "marble will"; see footnote 26.

25.   "*Willm Shakspere*" appears on page 2 of Shakespeare's will; also, "*Willm Shakp*" appears in a document relating to a legal suit. "Wm *Shakspē*" occurs on the mortgage deed of Blackfriars house.

26.   This corresponds to thematic ambiguities raised by the syntax of example 6, which allow the "as" of the couplet to coordinate both male and female "will": with male will "forming"—either molding by encircling or engraving by carving—the waxy minds of women, as it chooses; and with female will, thus doubly "styled," the simulacrum—"as" as the likeness or masquerade—of the marble minds of men. In either case, Lucrece is not the "author" of her "will."

27.   Cf. Tarquin's argument: "Then for thy husband and thy children's sake,/Tender my suit; bequeath not to their lot/The shame that from them no device can take,/The blemish that will never be forgot,/Worse than a slavish wipe, or birth-hour's blot;/For marks descried in men's nativity/Are nature's faults, not their own infamy" (533–39).

28.   Cf. Thersites' judgment in *Troilus and Cressida*: "All the argument is a whore and a cuckold" (2.3.72–73).

29.   The synecdochical procedure that allows a part to stand "for the whole to be imagined" presupposes a figurality that works by visually imaging the trope's signified (e.g., to take the standard example, fifty sails for fifty ships); this is quite different from a figurality based on the linguistic substitution of one signifier for another signifier, which is how Jacques Lacan understands the general operation of metaphor. Lacan explains this, and points up the nominalist folly informing a synecdochical understanding of poetic trope, in "The Agency of the Letter in the Unconscious or Reason since Freud," in *Écrits,* trans. Alan Sheridan (New York, 1977), 146–78.

30.   This blind spot *in* vision is thematically present in the poem from the very beginning; hence the book-reading context for the first *MW* example: "But she that never cop'd with stranger eyes,/Could pick no meaning from their parling looks,/Nor read the subtle shining secrecies/Writ in the glassy margents of such books./She touch'd no unknown baits, nor fear'd no hooks,/Nor could she moralize his wanton sight,/More than his eyes were open to the light" (99–105).

31.   Note that, at the level of the signifier, the "tide" which "outruns the eye" is articulated as "saw" and "draw," the past tenses of "to see" and "to draw."

32.   Though this marks its climax, the poem does not end right here, but continues on for a short while, first, developing a rivalry in grief between Lucrece's father and Collatine—"Then son and father weep with equal strife,/Who should weep most, for daughter or for wife" (1791–92)—then, gesturing, very briefly, toward the promised revenge. The father-in-law versus husband competition is central to Shakespeare's understanding of a structural contradiction energizing patriarchal marriage. When, in marriage, the daughter substitutes her husband for her father, her passage from the one male to the other amounts to a forswearing of the father, e.g., Brabantio in *Othello*: "Look to her, Moor, if thou hast eyes to see;/She has deceiv'd her father, and may thee" (1.3.292–93). For this reason, for Shakespeare, the woman has always already committed adultery by virtue of her having entered into marriage. The way the poem's conclusion scants the political consequences of the story—the expulsion of the Tarquins from Rome and the institution of the republic, events to which the Argument gives more weight—suggests that Shakespeare was more concerned with the personalizing consequences of the rape, i.e., the way the "let" returns to Collatine, than with the rape's historical significance. For this reason, the poem leaves some of its readers wanting more, but more of the *same,* e.g., J. Quarles's extension of the story in *Tarquin Banished; or, the Reward of Lust,* which concerns itself with what happens to Tarquin after the rape; this was published as an appendix to a 1665 edition of Shakespeare's poem; see Donaldson, *Rapes of Lucretia,* 179.

33.   Shakespeare plays, famously, on his own name in the so-called "Will" sonnets, where, since "will" refers to both male and female genitals, his lyric first-person is designated by disjunctive copulation, e.g., sonnet 136: "Make but my name thy love, and love that still,/And then thou lovest me

for my name is *Will*"; see *Shakespeare's Perjured Eye,* chap. 5. There are many "*Will*" ← **M** examples in the plays, e.g., the vocative "will" of William Page in the *Merry Wives of Windsor:* Evans: "What is the focative case, William?"; William: "O—*vocativo,* O" (4.1.50–51), or the "Will" of Desdemona's "Willow song": "'The fresh streams ran by her and *murmur'd* her *moans,/*Sing *will*ow, *will*ow, *will*ow'" (4.3.44–45); "'Sing *will*ow, *will*ow, *will*ow; If I court *moe w*omen, you'll couch *with moe men*'" (4.3.56–57). I discuss the theme of naming in *Othello* and its relation to Shakespeare's name in "The Sound of O in *Othello:* The Real of the Tragedy of Desire" (*October,* Spring 1988; reprinted in this volume).

More generally, it can be shown that Shakespeare regularly finds the same old story in the remarked designation of a name. Consider, as a small example, but one relevant to "The Rape of Lucrece," what Titus says in *Titus Andronicus* when he sees his daughter, the raped Lavinia, making inarticulate gestures because her arms have been cut off and her tongue has been torn out: "Mark, Marcus, mark! I understand her signs" (3.1.143–44). Later, Lavinia will successfully reveal her rapists' names when, after first pointing to a passage about Philomela in "Ovid's Metamorphosis," "She takes the staff in her mouth, and guides it with her stumps, and writes" (4.1.76, stage direction).

34.   Claudio Guillén, "Notes Toward the Study of the Renaissance Letter," in *Renaissance Genres: Essays on Theory, History, and Interpretation,* ed. Barbara Lewalski (Cambridge, Mass., 1986), 70–101. Guillén argues that the diffusion of printing technology, the Humanist revival of classical epistolary modes (neo-Latin and vernacular prose and verse epistles), the incorporation of fictional letters in literary works, the publication of letter manuals, plus an increase in private correspondence, leads to the formation of a specifically literary stylization of voice: a written voice that strives to seem conversational, spontaneous, individuated, intimate. Guillén sees this as an important factor behind the rise of the novel. In a larger historical context, we can say, as Brian Stock implicitly suggests in *The Implications of Literacy: Written Language and Models of Interpretation in the Eleventh and Twelfth Centuries* (Princeton, N.J., 1983), that an oral culture only becomes such after the fact of diffused literacy: a writing culture looks back to an authentic orality that exists only as a function of retrospective nostalgia. This is how the writing "post" of "The Rape of Lucrece" works to establish "The golden splendor of the sun" as "An expir'd date, cancell'd ere well begun"; in the terms proposed by the Dedication, this is why "this Pamphlet without beginning is but a superfluous Moity."

35.   I refer here, of course, to some of the consequences arising, directly and indirectly, from the by now well-known debate between Lacan and Jacques Derrida, which centers around this claim at the end of Lacan's seminar on Poe's "The Purloined Letter": "The sender, we tell you, receives from the receiver his own message in reverse form [*une forme inversée*]. Thus it is that what the 'purloined letter,' nay, the 'letter in sufferance' means is that a letter always arrives at its destination"; Jacques Lacan, "Seminar on 'The Purloined Letter,'" trans. Jeffrey Mehlman, *Yale French Studies* 48 (1972): 72 (a full version of the seminar appears in Lacan's original *Ecrits* [Paris, 1966]); in French, the message is inverted, not reversed (41). For Lacan, this is a shorthand way of summarizing his understanding of how it happens a subject comes to be a desiring subject when he accedes to speech, passing (though Lacan means to describe a structural, not a chronological, staging process) from an "Imaginary" register of visual identification and idealization to a different register that Lacan calls "Symbolic," which he associates with a necessary slippage of meaning inherent in subjective speech, and by reference to which he accounts for the subject's insertion into the cultural order. Derrida objects to this Lacanian claim on the grounds that it universalizes a "logocentric" determinism; he summarizes his objection by pointing out that a letter does not always arrive at its destination since it sometimes goes astray. On these grounds, Derrida proposes to oppose, deconstructively, "writing," "*écriture,*" to Lacan's sexist, spoken "logos"; a short version of Derrida's argument appears in "The Purveyor of Truth," trans. Willis Domingo et al., *Yale French Studies* 52 (1975), but the argument is considerably amplified in *La Carte Postale* (Paris, 1980).

What I have tried to suggest through the above reading of "The Rape of Lucrece"—with its account of a subjectifying progress from true vision to false language, via the intermediating circle of Collatine's "let"—is that this debate gains its charge because it repeats a familiar literary story;

this is why "The Rape of Lucrece" seems so precisely to predicate the topoi and argumentative terms of the debate. As we know from *Romeo and Juliet,* where a "purloined" (i.e., post-poned) letter is what causes the lovers' tragedy, literary letters *always* arrive at their destination precisely because they *always* go astray. Derrida's powerful critique of Lacan, therefore, is readily assimilable to Lacan's general claim (as is apparent in Lacan's late introduction of a third term, the "Real," to function as disjunctive supplement to the Imaginary-Symbolic dialectic). This is why it is so dangerous to rewrite literary stories in an extra-literary register, for, when one does so, one ends up acting out a Shakespearean tragedy. The point is especially important when erotic intentionality is at issue. One contemporary example will have to stand for many. In a translation of a portion of Luce Irigaray's "When Our Lips Speak Together," we read "I love you: body shared, undivided. Neither you nor I severed. There is no need for blood spilt between us. No need for a wound to remind us that blood exists. It flows within us, from us. It is familiar, close. You are quite red, and still so white. . . . The whiteness of this red appropriates nothing. It gives back as much as it receives, in luminous mutuality"; trans. Carolyn Burke, *Signs* 6, no. 1 (1980): 70. Commenting on this portion of the text, the translator adds an approving footnote: "Irigaray's use of 'red' and 'white' differs consciously from the traditional Western opposition of these terms as symbols of passion and purity. In general, she tries to locate a locus in writing where such 'opposites' may coexist, in a new way" (70). As we have seen, however, the Western tradition does not "oppose" red and white; quite the inverse: "when our lips speak together" in Irigaray's text, therefore, they may call out in a thematic way for "luminous mutuality," but their literary effect is to replicate the inside-outside in-betweenness of "her lips sweet fold," a replication that opens up "a locus in writing" that invites the intrusive interjection of the footnote. This is a model of "reader-response," and the example suggests why it is very dangerous to underestimate the seductive subtlety of Western literariness.

In my book on Shakespeare's sonnets I argued, on more or less formal, even formalist, grounds that in his sonnets Shakespeare invented what is an altogether novel but subsequently governing model of subjectivity in our literary history—recognizing, I will say in passing, that the word *literary* in the phrase *literary history* has a particular historical formation, just as the word *history,* in the same phrase, is a function of a particular literary form. This argument about the invention of Shakespearean subjectivity, whether right or wrong, is a strong one because it straightforwardly asserts that, at a specific level of generality, and within the context of a specific, notably self-conscious, literary tradition, there is something exigent, necessary, predetermined, about the construction and reception of Shakespeare's lyric subject. Putting the point as bluntly as possible—and intending the erotic connotations—I argued in my book that in his sonnets Shakespeare comes upon, i.e., he "invents," the *only* ways in which or through which subjectivity, understood as a particular literary phenomenon, can be coherently thought and effectively produced in the literature of the West. Putting the point somewhat less bluntly, I argued that Shakespeare's sonnets, locating themselves within a literary tradition whose contents and contours they both revise and supplant, produce a generic phenomenology of subjective consciousness in which the intentionality of the literary subject, i.e., his desire, is motivated by strictly psychological, rather than by biological or by theological, motives.

Summarizing, very briefly, the main lines of that argument, I began by saying that Shakespeare writes at the end of a tradition—one quite central to the development of the Renaissance sonnet—that identifies the literary, and therefore literary language, with idealizing, visionary praise, a tradition in which there obtains, at least figuratively speaking, an ideal Cratylitic correspondence, usually figured through motifs of visual or visionary language, between that which is spoken and that which is spoken about. However, because Shakespeare, when he sits to sonnets, registers the conclusion of this tradition of the poetics and poetry of praise—a tradition that reaches back to the invention of the "literary" as an intelligible theoretical category— he is obliged, in order to be literary, to recharacterize language as something duplic- itously and equivocally verbal rather than as something truthfully and univocally visual. It was my argument that this linguistic revision of a traditional language of vision both enables and constrains Shakespeare to develop novel literary subjects of verbal representation for whom the very speaking of language is what serves and works to cut them off from their ideal and visionary presence to themselves. Citing Shakespeare's sonnet 152, I called this generic Shakespearean subject the subject of a "perjured eye," and I further maintained that the reader of Shakespeare's sonnets, precisely because Shakespeare's sonnets remark themselves as something verbal, not visual, of the tongue and not the eye, will therefore find, though in a paradoxical way, that the language of the sonnets performs, and thereby stands as warrant for, what the sonnets speak about. Putting this point in familiar theoretical terms, I was saying no more than that the performative dimension of Shakespeare's sonnets served recursively to secure their constative dimension, but that this collation of the performative and the constative, because a limit case of such a correspondence— with the sonnets effectively performing, as in a Liar's Paradox, their own belying— yields a determinate poetic persona.

According to this argument, a variety of literary features—at the level of theme, motif, and trope—contribute to and follow from what I take to be an historically sig- nificant entropic evacuation of the poetics of idealization. Further, according to this argument, these literary features, taken together, in turn determine, in quite specific ways, the psychologistic profile of the literary subject who opens his mouth to speak in the aftermath of praise. For example, guided by the way Shakespeare's sonnets move from the young man subsequence to the dark lady subsequence, and distin- guishing between a bliss that is always virtually achieved and, in contrast, a desire that is always, by virtue of its constitution, structurally unsatisfiable, I argued that Shakespeare's sonnets, because they displace ideal vision by corrupt language, thereby confront the traditionally homogeneous speaker of epideictic lyric with an essential, and theretofore unspeakable, heterogeneity, with the result that the speaker of Shakespeare's sonnets, fleshing out this difference, becomes the subject of an altogether unprecedented verbal desire for what is not admired. In the book, putting this point very grandly, I said that Shakespeare's sonnets, because they explicitly put the difference *of* language into words, thereby invent and motivate the poetics of heterosexuality, by which I meant to specify a necessarily misogynist desire, on the part of a necessarily male subject, whom the sonnets call "Will," for the true-false Woman who exists as a peculiar and paradoxical but still necessary "hetero-," or other, to the essential sameness of a familiar and profoundly orthodox "homo-." In this way, paradoxing the orthodox, Shakespeare's sonnets manage to activate at a psychologistic level what are of course, in the literary tradition Shakespeare inherits, conventional, but not characterologically textured, erotic topoi. One local virtue of such an account, I thought, is that it allows one to speak to the gender determinations of Shakespeare's sonnets—and, beyond the sonnets, to the gender determinations that operate in Shakespeare's other writings—in a way that does not import into the discussion unspoken assumptions about agency and motivation that stand at conceptual odds with—indeed, usually undercut from the start—the ethical and political concerns of reductively psychologistic criticism of Shakespearean characterology—for example, criticism that strives to speak up for the putatively free "will" of some of Shakespeare's characters. In passing, I will say, parenthetically, that this atavistic and sentimental allegiance to the idea and the idealization of the autonomous human and humanist subject, male or female, precisely because it begs the question of the subject, amounts to a chracteristic failure of Shakespearean criticism—characteristic and Shakespearean because such criticism, whatever its explicit ideological intentions, not only responds to but also capitulates to the historical hegemony of Shakespearean characterology: this is surely the greatest weakness of much contemporary criticism of Shakespeare—criticism that wants to be, but in my opinion fails to be, either feminist or New Historicist. I will add, because I think the issue is increasingly important, that much contemporary Shakespeare criticism knows this very well and is therefore conducted in an extreme intellectual bad faith for which the discipline of Shakespeare studies will eventually pay a very heavy price.

It will be recognized that the subjectivizing consequences, within the domain of literature, that my argument about Shakespeare's sonnets wants to derive from the disjunctive conjunction of, on the one hand, a general thematics of vision and, on the other, a general thematics of voice, bear striking similarities to Jacques Lacan's account of the constitution of the subject through the capture of what he calls an Imaginary register—which Lacan figures through visionary motifs—by what he calls a Symbolic register—which Lacan figures through motifs of spoken speech. I briefly remarked this affinity in my book and argued that the similarity derived from the fact that the Lacanian subject in particular, and the psychoanalytic subject in general, were epiphenomenal consequences of the Renaissance invention of the literary subject. Some people have disagreed with this claim, preferring to put things the other way around. In either case, however, whether we see Lacan as Shakespearean or Shakespeare as Lacanian, the argument I developed, depending as it it did on exigent determinations arising out of the relation of visionary presence to verbal representation, lays itself open to the kind of criticism Jacques Derrida has directed against what he understands to be Lacan's logocentric, phallogocentric, sexist account of the construction of the linguistic subject. For Derrida, and for poststructuralism in general, there is a difference constitutive of, yet different from and extrinsic to, the structuralist difference of language, a difference—more precisely an activity of *différance*— that Derrida figures in terms of writing and textuality, the peculiar phenomenality of which serves to break the totalizing structurations of Lacan's broken subject. Even though the argument of my book restricts itself to a discussion of the domain of literature, it is open to the same kind of critique, for in establishing its large opposition between, on the one hand, the thematics and ontology of literary vision and, on the other, the thematics and ontology of literary voice, the book assimilates the activity of writing to speech, thereby leaving to the side the fact that Shakespeare's sonnets are necessarily written and not necessarily spoken, just as their words on the page are necessarily visualized as typographic letters and not necessarily heard as vocalized words. I acknowledged this possible objection in the introduction to my book but argued that Derrida's criticisms of Lacan, especially as these are formulated in the name of writing and textualty, are themselves a part, and a systematic part, of the system of the perjured eye, rather than a critique thereof. For reasons that will become apparent, I quote a portion of the relevant paragraphs from the introduction:

> In this context . . . it is significant that Derrida's subsequent attempt to rupture Lacan's rupture, Derrida's putatively postsubjective account of supplemental *différance,* seems, from the point of view of Shakespeare's sonnets, nothing but another "increase" that "from fairest creatures we desire" [I was here referring to the first line of Shakespeare's first sonnet, "From fairest creatures we desire increase"], a subjective indeterminacy, that is to say, which is already predetermined . . . by the exigencies of literary life [here assuming, in advance, the wrinkle, literally the "crease," that Shakespeare introduces into the poetics of copious "increase"]. More

generally, I argue that what Derrida calls "writing," the thematics of the deconstructive "trace" that Derrida associates with *écriture,* is not beyond Shakespeare's sonnets but is instead anticipated and assimilated by them to the theme of language, with the two of these together being opposed to the theme of vision.[1]

I would still say much the same—in fact, precisely the same—but I am nevertheless now more interested in how it happens that this wrinkle or crease of textuality—what Derrida calls *écriture,* what Lacan calls the Real, a Real that can be neither specularized nor represented, but the marks of which are the condition and consequence of both specularity and representation—precipitates and is precipitated by the disjunctive copulation of the specular and the spoken. I am interested in this because, having formulated, I believe, in the book on Shakespeare's sonnets—though, again, only at a specific level of generality, and, again, I could be wrong—the formal constraints governing the formation of literary subjectivity in our literary tradition, I am now concerned, in the book I am writing called *Shakespeare's Will,* to understand how and why it happens that these formalist constraints are realized at a particular moment, by a particular individual, and with particular consequences. Thus, where the book on Shakespeare's sonnets was concerned with the formal invention of a generic Shakespearean persona, I am now concerned to understand how it happens that a particular and idiosyncratic person, Shakespeare, informs and is informed by that formal persona; and this is an interesting question, I think, because it helps to explain how it happens that a single individual, Shakespeare, the person, speaks to and founds an institution, the Shakespearean. To answer this question, however, it is necessary to understand why in our literary tradition it is necessarily writing, as such, that exists as that which constitutively intermediates between voice and vision.

In the context of this question, i.e., the question of the text and its relation to vision and speech, I turn now to the famous, so-called Rainbow Portrait of Queen Elizabeth, which is the picture I selected for the cover of my book on Shakespeare's sonnets, on the grounds that, to my mind, it illustrates the book's argument. The meaning of this picture, tentatively attributed to Isaac Oliver, has always been somewhat enigmatic, but what interests me in particular about the picture, and is the reason I chose it for the cover of my book, is the somewhat bizarre design of ornamental, isolated eyes and mouths and ears with which the painting decorates the queen's elaborate dress. This iconography, of eyes and mouths and ears, derives, one assumes, from Virgil's famous description of Rumor or *Fama* in Book IV of *The*

The Rainbow Portrait of Queen Elizabeth I, attributed to Isaac Oliver, c. 1600. Reproduced by permission of the Marquess of Salisbury, Hatfield House. Photo: Courtauld Institute.

Aeneid—"as many tongues, so many sounding mouths, so many pricked ears"—a conflation transmitted to the Renaissance through such authors as Boethius and Chaucer—though just why a celebratory portrait of the queen should so directly associate her with the negatively charged figure of Rumor—e.g., Spenser's House of Fame—is something of a mystery, though by no means an irresolvable one.[2] The topos is of course known to and favored by Shakespeare, e.g., *Titus Andronicus*: "Like the house of fame, the palace full of tongues, and eyes, and ears" (2.1.126–27); *2 Henry IV*: "Open your ears, for which you will stop the vent of hearing when loud Rumour speaks" (Ind.1); or *2 Henry VI*, "Where fame, late entering at his heedful ears, hath placed thy beauty's image" (3.3.62–63). That Shakespeare characteristically concatenates ears-eyes-and-voice is also well known, e.g., Bottom in *A Midsummer Night's Dream*: "The eye of man hath not heard, the ear of man hath not seen" (4.1.211–12), or when Troilus "invert(s) the attest of eyes and ears" (*Troilus and Cressida*, 5.2.122), just as this concatenation is something Shakespeare tends to associate with the specifically rhetorical, e.g., *The Merry Wives of Windsor,* Pistol: "He hears with ears." Evans: "What phrase is this, he hears with ears, why it is affectatious" (1.1.148–50). Given all this, what is genuinely mysterious and surprising about the Rainbow Portrait, especially if we assume this large picture was originally displayed at court, is the way the painting places an exceptionally pornographic ear over Queen Elizabeth's genitals, in the crease formed where the two folds of her dress fold over on each other, at the wrinkled conclusion of the arc projected by the dildo-like rainbow clasped so imperially by the Virgin Queen. I think of this ear as one version of the "increase" that "from fairest creatures we desire" to which I earlier referred. In reproduction, the vulva-like quality of the ear is perhaps not so readily apparent, but, enlarged and in florid color, the erotic quality of the image is really quite striking, as is the oddly colorless quality of the rainbow, a kind of dead rainbow.

For reasons that I think are relatively obvious, I took this picture as a straight-forward illustration of two central arguments in my book on Shakespeare's sonnets, first, that the difference between language and vision, i.e., the difference between eyes and mouths, is what precipitates a specific fetishistic erotics, the vulva-like ear, an erotics that is correlative to an equally fetishistic principle of sovereign power that is imaged by the picture's depiction of the queen as a whole. This kind of erotics calls forth this kind of sovereignty, and vice versa. So too, I took the painting's caption, on the left, in the odd, dimensionless space that writing tends to occupy in pictures, as a summary statement of the way in which certain deconstructive thematics, whatever their intentions, necessarily participate within the system they intend to rebuke, a point I consider important, given a variety of recent, more or less abortive, attempts to deconstruct the Renaissance text. *"Non sine sole Iris,"* as the picture puts it, i.e., "No rainbow without the Sun," is for me a very eloquent and true description of the way the iridescent fragmentation of a photo-logocentric light works, and always has been seen to work, to resecure the ruling order of the sun. This reading of the picture could be amplified by discussion of the queen's Medusa-like hair and headpiece, also the pearl necklace wrapped around her neck and dangling down her torso, also the winding, labyrinthine snake embroidered on her right arm, from whose mouth there hangs what seems a ruby heart.

What I want to mention here, or really what I will be obliged simply to assert, is that there are reasons to associate this salacious ear that both covers and discovers the genitals of Queen Elizabeth with a specific and historically determinate Renaissance sense of textuality; and this is a point worth following out, I think, first, because this suggests an identifiable complicity that links, by means of an unspoken necessity, Renaissance textuality, sexuality, and ideology one to each of the two others, in a link or collation the historical stability and specificity of which at least raise the possibility that it is Renaissance textuality, as such, that predicates a particular system of sexuality and ideology. Second, I think this point would be worth following out because, if demonstrated, then it would again follow that various contemporary, deconstructive conceptualizations of reading once again recapitulate—or rather, effect a repetition that capitulates to—the movements and motifs of the Renaissance text, and this not simply at the level of topoi, but in a more general registration of the phenomenality of the textual.

As I say, I cannot here develop this argument in any detailed, textured way— if it happens that anyone wants to see a preliminary version of this argument, he or she can take a look at my essay on "The Rape of Lucrece," "Shakespeare's *Will*: The Temporality of Rape." I can, however gesture toward that argument by means of two quotations. The first is from a poem on hearing by John Davies, which comes from his *Nosce Teipsum,* i.e., "know thyself," a collection of poems on the immortality of the soul. (Davies's poetry is relevant because, as Roy Strong notes in his book on *The Cult of Elizabeth,* the Rainbow Portrait "was painted during those vital two or three years when Davies was employed by Cecil as court pageant poet," and is thus a direct source for the painting's iconography.) The poem on "Hearing" follows a corresponding poem on "Sight," one that articulates various Renaissance commonplaces about "the quick power of sight," and it is in contrast to this immediacy of vision that Davies in the succeeding poem identifies the ear as organ of delay:

These wickets of the Soule area plac't on hie
Because all sounds doe lightly mount aloft;
And that they may not pierce too violently,
They are delaied with turnes and windings oft.

For should the voice directly strike the braine,
It would astonish and confuse it much;
Therefore these plaits and folds the sound restraine,
That it the organ may more gently touch.

As streames, which with their winding banks doe play,
Stopt by their creeks, run softly through the plaine,
So in th' Eares' labyrinth the voice doth stray,
And doth with easie motion touch the braine.

It is the slowest yet the daintiest sense.[3]

As that which slows the logos, leading it astray within its labyrinthine folds and plaits, the ear for Davies functions as the intermediating maze that saves the brain from a too quick arrival of the sense or voicing of speech, a speech that would otherwise strike the brain like an astonishing flash of light. It is for this reason, taking Davies' poem as index of something larger than itself, that we can understand the ear, a specifically Renaissance ear, as instrument of delay and deferral—what Derrida calls the *différance,* both spatial and temporal, that is prior to any difference whatsoever, and what Shakespeare, I have tried to argue—as in my essay on "The Rape of Lucrece"—also comprehends in terms of temporal distension and dilation when he writes his metaphor of "post." I believe this helps to explain why for Shakespeare the ear is so often figure of momentous suspense, as in *Hamlet,* when the fall of Ilium "takes prisoner Pyrrhus' ear," and I believe also that this Shakespearean ear eventually determines Derrida's account of the reader's, any reader's, relation to a text, any text. Compare, for example, Davies's poem on "Hearing" with the passage from Derrida's essay on Nietzsche, "Otobiographies":

You must pay heed to the fact that the *omphalos* that Nietzsche compels you to envision resembles both an ear and a mouth. It has the invaginated folds and the involuted orificiality of both. Its center preserves itself at the bottom of an invisible, restless cavity that is sensitive to all waves which, whether or not they come from the outside, whether they are emitted or received, are always transmitted by this trajectory of obscure circumvolutions. The person emitting the discourse you are in the process of teleprinting in this situation does not himself produce it: he barely emits it. He reads it. Just as you are ears that transcribe, the master is a mouth that reads, so that what you transcribe is, in sum, what he deciphers of a text that precedes him.[4]

The metaphoremes, and the erotics that informs them, that appear in Derrida's text do not come from nowhere; quite the contrary, I propose that they come from the Renaissance in general, and from Shakespeare in particular. To show that, however, it would be necessary to show that for Shakespeare it is specifically the ear that is the organ of the text, of the specifically typographic text, and that is something, given the constraints of time, as well as the nature of things, that must, for now, be postponed, though Shakespeare's sonnet 46 would be one place to begin.[5]

Notes

Paper read to the Shakespeare Association, Boston, Massachusetts, April 30, 1988; published posthumously in *Representations,* no. 28 (Fall 1989), 6–13.

1.   Joel Fineman, *Shakespeare's Perjured Eye* (Berkeley and Los Angeles, 1986), 46.

2.   *Aeneid,* IV, 183: *"Tot linguae, tot idem ora sonant, tot subrigit auris"* (*subrigit,* from *surgo* or *surrigo,* rise, raise). The number is infinite because there are as many mouths as men. An obvious Foucaultian reading, i.e., the Queen's total surveillance: surveyed and supervised subject of power.

3.   John Davies, *The Complete Poems,* ed. Alexander B. Grosart, 3 vols. (Blackburn, England, 1869), 1:106.

4.   Jacques Derrida, "Otobiographies," trans. Avital Ronell, in *The Ear of the Other* (New York, 1985), 36.

5.   —remember the "question" of the text, cf. Dora, Lacan, the moon and the semicolon; the rhetorical question

—people don't want to read nowadays, substituting thematic reaction for reading

—force of the story is to show that textuality predicates a specific sexuality and ideology, and if people aren't willing to read, they will be caught up in this fetishistic project.